SPRAY THE BEAR

REMINISCENCES FROM THE GOLDEN AGE OF ADVERTISING

By

Walter W. Bregman

ISBN: 1-4033-0657-5

Library of Congress Control Number: 2002102483

This book is printed on acid free paper.

Printed in the United States of America
Bloomington, IN

1st Books - rev. 6/13/02

DEDICATION

This book is dedicated to all the admen living and dead who unwittingly contributed to my reminiscences of the golden age and especially to Art Hohmann, Bob Hanslip, Jay Levinson, Jim Hill, Dan Solomon, Bill Eldridge, Pete Conway, and Hal Tulchin.

"Those were the days, my friend..."

And to Robbie, my wife of forty-five years, who has patiently listened to me tell these stories so many times that she finally persuaded me to write them down.

She not only knows the stories, she knows the songs, too.

Wally Bregman
Del Mar, 2002

Author's Note

As I write these words some forty years after my first advertising adventure and fifteen years after my last, I look back and try to understand just why the 1950's through the 1980's were the Golden Years of Advertising. Why did we have so much fun, do so many crazy things, produce such great work, and make so much money? Why were account men and copywriters the then Masters of the Universe? Why was advertising and marketing the "chosen" profession for most every MBA?

I think the answer is the confluence of several independent factors, which, upon merging, produced the fertile environment out of which grew the "Golden Years."

1. **The advertising agencies in the mid-twentieth century were largely eponymous organizations founded, controlled, and directed by the man whose "name was on the door."** Ted Bates ran Ted Bates; Fairfax Cone ran Foote, Cone and Belding; David Ogilvy ran Ogilvy and Mather; Bill Bernbach ran Doyle, Dane, Bernbach; Norman B. Norman ran Norman, Craig & Kummel; and, of course, Leo Burnett ran the Leo Burnett Company. These men were giants in their field. Almost all were creative men at heart and none were "bean counters." Leo used to say, "Just do great work and the money will follow." Their agencies reflected their personal philosophy of advertising: Bates' "Unique Selling Proposition," Norman's "Empathy," and Burnett's "Inherent Drama of the Product." With the founder, owner, boss firmly in charge of day-to-day operations, it was *de rigueur* for an agency to resign an account rather than run advertising of which the principal was not proud. This tough guy, "gunslinger" attitude percolated down through the organizations, and from the lowliest employee on up, agency people developed swagger and hubris not unlike that of the venture capitalists and "deal makers" of the 1990's. And, while J. Walter Thompson, McCann-Ericson, and Young and Rubicam expanded into branch offices, most agencies operated out of a single home office, giving subordinates almost daily exposure to the "Masters of the Universe."

2. **There were no public agencies until McCann's Marion Harper sold the stock of Interpublic.** By and large there was no external scrutiny of just how much money the agencies made and how they spent it. It was nobody's business and the owners liked it that way. This meant, of course, that agency principals were not subject to "analysts' forecasts," Wall Street rumors, or quarterly projections. If and when an account was lost or resigned those who had been working on it merely went into the "repo-depot" until a new account was obtained. There were no massive layoffs to "reduce overhead" and "make the quarter" because the owner's philosophy was to grow the agency, not shrink it. This "security blanket" forged a bond among employees and, while such a "cradle to grave" atmosphere can sometimes create stagnation and torpor, it seemed to have the opposite effect on "the agency guys." Our *esprit de corps* was of the highest as we worked impossible hours under difficult and demanding conditions.

3. **The agency profits in the fifties, sixties, and seventies were enormous.** There was so much money flowing that the lowliest of the low regularly flew first class and stayed at the Plaza and the Bel Air. The reason was television. In the middle to late fifties TV took the country by storm. For the agencies, the growth of TV was a bonanza. The time honored fifteen- percent commission system remained in place while the base against which the fifteen percent was applied increased exponentially. Suddenly an agency could produce a single commercial and run it for months, even years, as in the case of the famous (infamous) Ted Bates Anacin spot. As a result, there was more money flowing in than anyone knew what to do with. Oddly enough the existence of such a huge cash flow had little impact on the salaries of the average working stiff. Its true impact manifested itself in the expense accounts and "on the road" lifestyle we all lived.

4. **The logical result of the above was that being an "adman" was the dream of every newly minted MBA and college graduate.** Gregory Peck had created the model in *The Man in the Grey Flannel Suit* and William Whyte's *The Organization Man* added fuel to the fire. It was so easy to recruit outstanding candidates that salaries were kept artificially low ("The agency business is a great place to work if your folks can afford to send you there" – Anonymous). Wherever one looked the ad agencies had the best and the brightest. There was another reason that bright young people were attracted to the advertising world. Age was no barrier to success. It sounds odd today in the age of Bill Gates, Steve Jobs, Scott McNealy, and the dot-comers, but back then the road to the top in the corporate world required years of trudging up the organizational ladder one short rung at a time. In the agency world winning a new account could mean instant "battlefield commissions" and promotions galore, regardless of age.

5. **With one exception all the elements were there: charismatic leadership, corporate independence, fierce loyalty, enormous profits, and bright, hard-charging young employees.** Without apology and without regret, I must add that the final contributing factor to the craziness, *joie de vie,* and outlandish behavior that took place in the Golden Age was alcohol. It was everywhere. As a young timebuyer it was not unusual for me to have several two-martini lunches a week, each followed by a couple of drinks before going home. As an account man, entertaining the client was a required exercise. Drinking was not discouraged by management; to the contrary it was encouraged. A lot of what we did and said flowed from a long-stemmed martini glass.

And so as you travel my road and read my recollections and fables of those bygone years, try not to be judgmental. Just enjoy the ride. It was the way it was and will never come our way again. Was it Camelot? No, but it came damn close.

One last note. The stories you are about to read are for the most part ones in which I was an active participant. I can attest to their veracity. There are others that I learned about secondhand but knew all the principals extremely well. A small number are industry folklore and have been so indicated.

I hope you enjoy this book and its wonderful cast of characters from the "Golden Age of Advertising."

Walter W. Bregman
Del Mar, California

PART I: THE BURNETT YEARS

I joined the Leo Burnett Advertising Agency in Chicago on February 3, 1958, at the lowest possible entry level training position: media research analyst. Until December 1, 1965, when I left Chicago for England, I progressed through the ranks of spacebuyer, timebuyer, assistant account executive, account executive, brand supervisor, account supervisor, and vice president, and account supervisor.[1]

In the media department it was my privilege to work on practically all the accounts Burnett had at the time from Pfizer to Chrysler, and Philip Morris to Kellogg, and Pillsbury to Hoover, and all the rest in between.

After I joined the Client Service Department, however, I spent almost all of my years on the Procter & Gamble business.

The following stories emanate from those wonderful seven and a half years.

---

[1] I am proud to have been, at 30, the youngest vice president in the agency's history.

Spray the Bear

Joy liquid detergent was one of the oldest and most important brands that Leo Burnett handled for Procter & Gamble. It was also a brand upon which I served as assistant account executive for a year and a half. In the course of handling any P&G brand, the agency and the brand group were constantly challenged to come up with new product ideas that could expand sales. One of the standard techniques was to develop what was called a "flanker brand."

In Joy's case, we decided to remove the yellow color and produce a clear product. The idea was that the clear product would somehow convey mildness. The name we came up with was "Crystal Clear Joy." Simultaneous with the development of the product and the name, of course, was the development of advertising copy. In this instance, the creative people decided that the way to convey crystal clarity and mildness was through the use of winter ice and snow references; specifically, they decided that a polar bear would be a very memorable device.

In due time, a storyboard was created, the advertising was presented to the client, and the commercial was approved for production. The basic storyline took place in a winter setting with the presenter sitting in the front seat of an antique open car next to a polar bear. The polar bear was to hold a bottle of "Crystal Clear Joy," which the bear would hand to the presenter at the appropriate moment. (I know this sounds silly today, but at the time it seemed to make maximum use of the visual elements of television.)

By way of background, the reader must remember that this was taking place in the early 1960's before fax machines, the Internet, and even conference calls. We used the old-fashioned telex machine to communicate back and forth between offices.

The pre-production meeting was held in the Hollywood office of the Leo Burnett Co. while the account group and brand group were in Chicago and Cincinnati taking care of our daily work. The first hint of a problem occurred when we received the following telex from the West Coast office.

"Impossible to use polar bear—stop—they are much too vicious and untrainable—stop—tell us what you want us to do—end."

After considerable discussion between the account group and the brand group we sent the following: *"Can you use a man in a polar bear suit?—end."*

"It will look stupid, ridiculous and phony—stop—no way will this idea work—end," they quickly replied.

"How about taking a brown bear and painting it white so he looks like a polar bear —end," we helpfully suggested.

After two or three hours they responded. *"We tried your suggestions—stop—we took a trained brown bear and painted it white—stop—unfortunately the paint matted up and it looked like a huge brown rat—stop—what is your next suggestion?—end."*

To us it seemed extremely simple and the West Coast people seemed unbelievably stupid but that's the way it is between the account group, the brand group, and the production people.

We quickly fired off the obvious answer: *"All you have to do is spray the bear and your problem will be solved—end."*

Unfortunately at this time fate intervened and the secretary who was transcribing the telex made a fatal error. Instead of sending the word "spray" she left out a key letter and mistakenly typed the word "spay."

The response from the West Coast was incredulous and immediate. *"Suggest you reconsider your last recommendation—stop—we hardly see how this will solve our problem—stop—besides we are using a male bear—end."*

In the end, everything was sorted out, the bear was returned to its trainer, the commercial was scratched, and Crystal Clear Joy had to be supported by a totally different commercial.

Christmas Windows

In December of 1958 1 was a junior timebuyer at the Leo Burnett Company. Our offices were located in the Prudential Building, at that time, the largest and most prominent skyscraper in Chicago. Over the years, a Christmas tradition had developed wherein the building maintenance staff visited each office on the Randolph Street side, that is, all those that faced south, and left a note on the desk. The note said either, "When you leave your office, please turn your lights on and raise your blinds," or "When you leave your office, please close your blinds and turn your lights off."

The purpose of this exercise was to illuminate the entire south side of the building with a gigantic "XMAS" viewed vertically from the top of the building to the bottom.

With the above as background, imagine four aggressive, intelligent, semi-inebriated agency types sitting in the Bomb Shelter having "just one more to let the traffic subside." The Bomb Shelter was the bar located in the IC station underneath the Prudential Building. It was usually the last stop before we went home to our wives and children.

This particular night there were four of us—Bill Eldridge, Art Hohmann, David Smith, and me. Suddenly, Don Wells, a brilliant account supervisor, came into the bar. He was clutching a piece of paper and was obviously excited.

"I've finally figured it out," he said breathlessly. "This is going to be the greatest night of our lives."

He then opened up the paper he had been holding. It was a large piece of graph paper on which he had depicted the entire south side of the Prudential Building. Every window was covered with some kind of code marking.

"I've spent all day on this project and now it's completed."

"What the hell are you talking about?" Dave Smith slurred.

"What I'm talking about is the greatest practical joke in history, that's what. It's going to be fantastic."

We gathered around as he waved his hand over the paper. He had somehow figured out how to change "XMAS" to the "F" word with a minimum of window and light changes. Remember, this was in the days before the digital scoreboard or computers. Nonetheless, Don was a clever fellow and he had worked out every detail—which windows to turn on, which to turn off, and which to leave alone. After a few more "white ones," he gave us our assignments and we took the escalators up to the lobby, boarded the elevators, and soon started changing windows on the top floors.

I believe it was halfway between "FMAS" and "FUAS" when they caught us.

Surely, had we succeeded it would have been one of the most memorable Christmases in the history of Chicago.

Goldie's New York

Sometime in 1960 while I was timebuyer on the Philip Morris account, I was sent to New York to make a presentation to the client. More importantly, I had finally saved up enough money to take my wife with me. Traveling to New York was always exciting and I knew that the Burnett crowd stayed at the Plaza so, we did, too. I also knew that all of the agency movers and shakers went to a bar on 52nd Street called "Goldie's New York."

The reason for this watering place's popularity was that Goldie, the proprietor and piano player, had been one of the original "Marlboro men" and thus had become a favorite of the Marlboro account group. (They were the darlings of Burnett at the time because of the success of the Marlboro resurrection.)

Everyone knew that if you were alone in New York and wanted to meet somebody from Burnett, all you had to do was go to Goldie's and sure enough, you'd run into someone.

Our first night in town, my wife and I went to the theater, and then I casually suggested we go to Goldie's for dinner afterwards. Like many midtown saloons, Goldie's was basically built like a tunnel. It had a long mirrored mahogany bar running down one side, a piano at the end where Goldie himself held forth, tables for two opposite the bar, and larger ones at the end of the room behind the piano.

The maitre d' greeted us at the door and escorted us to a small table on the side, not too far from Goldie and his piano. As we sat down, I looked across the room and saw another fellow from Burnett named John Ianeri. He was in an intimate and obviously romantic conversation with a very attractive brunette. Assuming he was with a girlfriend I quickly looked away, but not before I saw him recognize me and also turn away. This action clearly indicated that, in fact, he was with a girlfriend.

We both averted our eyes for the entire evening. Then as luck and work schedules would have it, I didn't see John for four or five weeks.

Finally, we found ourselves alone in an elevator one day. After an uncomfortable minute or so I finally said, "John, for God's sake, how the hell could you take some girlfriend to Goldie's when you know

6

everyone from Burnett who was in town was going to show up there?"

He looked at me in astonishment and said, "Girlfriend! You moron, that was my wife! Who the hell was the broad you were with?"

Sheepishly I replied, "That was my wife!"

And so it was that suspicion got the better of both of us.

Honi soit qui mal y pense.

My Toughest Boss

There are those who would say that their boss is the toughest—anyone, for instance, who worked for Norman B. Norman, Ernest Gallo, or Joel Smilow (as president of International Playtex he made *Fortune Magazine's* list of Ten Toughest Bosses in 1973).

The fact is my toughest boss was a man named Hal Tillson, who was a media supervisor at Leo Burnett with responsibilities for Pillsbury, Chrysler, Pfizer, and several other accounts. All the media reps knew him as a tough guy to bargain with and a man who suffered fools badly.

One day a particularly obnoxious rep came to call (Hal referred to him as "The Wizard of Ooze"). As he entered Hal's spacious office the secretary escorting him asked, "Would you like some coffee?"

"Don't bother," Hal interrupted. "He won't be here that long."

In those days before cable or satellite TV reception a station's coverage was "line of sight" and thus a function of its power and transmitter location. Every station claimed superior coverage numbers and every major agency developed its own proprietary county penetration numbers in order to calculate the cost per thousand numbers for any individual media buy.

At Burnett, a wonderful middle-aged lady named Esther Boyle produced our detailed coverage maps. Esther was a wizard with an Exacto knife and Zippatone. The latter was a colored transparent film that Esther carefully cut into tiny county-size shapes and delicately applied to a standard Rand McNally map to indicate relative coverage (red=100%, green=75%, etc.).

One day, Hal and I were preparing for our first TV coverage presentation to the newly acquired Chrysler Motors account when his secretary burst into the room.

"Esther Boyle slipped on the ice coming into the building and broke her arm," the excited young girl exclaimed.

"Which arm?" Hal fired back without looking up.

That's tough!

The Fountain of Joy

One of my early assignments in account work was as an assistant account executive on Procter & Gamble's light duty liquid detergent, Joy. I was fortunate enough to work for a wonderful man named Bob Williams. Unlike many who shared his hair coloration, "Easygoing Red," as he was known, was slow to anger, generous to a fault, and a wonderful teacher. (Upon retirement he actually moved to Durham, North Carolina, and became a college teacher.)

On one particular occasion, we had a shoot scheduled in New York for our "Dawson Family" series of slice of life commercials. As assistant account executive, I was in charge of supplying the "color corrected" Joy bottles for the shoot. Back then, we were, of course, shooting 60-second commercials in black and white. The "beauty bottles" had photostatted labels attached to them that had been hand retouched to exclude "mouse type" and to be readable by the then embryonic television cameras.

Bob made it clear that it was my job to get the bottles to New York as quickly as possible and to do it as cheaply as possible. I took the case of product and was about to take it down to the mailroom when I realized that there was no real need for the liquid product itself to go to New York. After all, the bottles were only going to be used as props in the final close-ups.

With this in mind, I went to the maintenance closet near the elevators and poured the detergent down the drain. I then proudly took the empty case of bottles down to the mailroom, secure in the knowledge that I'd saved the Leo Burnett Company at least three or four dollars in shipping costs.

Little did I know that I had just poured over two gallons of active detergent into the building's wastewater system and that in approximately fifteen minutes the fountain in front of the Prudential Building, along with every drinking fountain drain in the building, would be blowing bubbles and would continue doing so for the next twenty-four hours.

It is a tribute to Bob Williams' forbearance and forgiveness that I continued to work for the company for eight more years.

The Evil Twin

The Leo Burnett Company required that a CRC (Creative Review Committee) examine all creative work before it went to the client. This obviously put a huge strain on the members of the committee in general and Leo in particular. To facilitate all these meetings the fourteenth floor (the creative floor) had two identical conference rooms built side by side (14-A and 14-B) with a "hidden door" set into the adjoining wall so that the committee members could move seamlessly between meetings without going out into the corridor. The way it worked was that one group would conduct their meeting while the next scheduled group was setting up, and so it went throughout the day.

On one occasion after a young account man's first CRC with Leo ended and he had walked out of the meeting, he, for some reason, walked into the adjoining conference room. To his astonishment he saw Leo conducting a meeting. As he had not seen Leo leave the first conference room and was not privy to the connecting door, he was dumbfounded.

A little while later he told his supervisor, Jim Hill, of his amazing experience. (Hill, as will become apparent in later stories, was a consummate practical joker, raconteur, and all around humorist.)

"Oh God," Jim said, "I wish you hadn't seen that."

"What do you mean?" asked the worried young man.

"Well, it's a pretty well-kept secret around here, but as long as you saw them…"

"What do you mean 'them'?" asked the now totally confused AE.

"I'll tell you, but you must promise not to mention this conversation to a soul," Jim said very seriously.

"I promise."

"OK. You see, Leo has an identical twin brother named Leonard. When things get hectic, Leo secretly stays in town for the night and Leonard takes the train in from Lake Geneva where they both live. No one is the wiser 'cause they think it's Leo on the train. Then one goes into 14-A and the other into 14-B and the CRC's commence. No one is the wiser. It usually works like a dream unless someone stumbles on the deception like you did."

"My God, that's incredible," said the naive youngster. "Can anyone tell them apart?"

This was going better than Jim expected, so he set the hook. "Yes, there is a secret way. You see, Leonard lost the tip of his left little finger in a lawn mower accident many years ago. That's the only difference between them."

Two weeks later when the young AE had his next CRC, he was observed staring at Leo/Leonard's left hand but could never get close enough to make a positive identification.

Another victory for Hill's fertile mind.

Senor Wenses

At the Leo Burnett Company it was no secret that Leo didn't really like or enjoy the P&G account. He would frequently chide the supervisors on the account with remarks like, "Are your brand managers still carrying slide rules in holsters to the copy meetings?" (Some actually did!) Nonetheless, his name was on the door and Leo felt personally responsible for the quality of all the advertising that was produced by his company even if he didn't much enjoy working on it.

After a series of frustrating meetings, we finally came to an accommodation with Leo. We would not bother him with the creative review process utilized on all other accounts, but we would show him all interlocks and answer prints before they went to the client.

With this background, one of the accounts we handled was the small but extremely profitable heavy-duty hand soap, Lava. While we had the highly successful "These are the hands of..." campaign running, in true Procter fashion, we were asked to come up with a back-up campaign in case the current ads began to lose traction on "Burke" (a television recall measuring technique held holier than the grail by the client in Cincinnati).

The "creatives" went to work and in due time developed a wonderful new campaign using the then famous Senor Wenses—the idea being that he would talk with his hand fully made up—"Ahright! Ahright!"—and then, using Lava, wash the lipstick, mascara, and eye makeup off his hands— "Ahright! Ahright!"—demonstrating before the viewers' eyes how clean they could, in fact, be with Lava.

We presented this idea to our clients in Cincinnati and they liked it, but with true Procter & Gamble frugality, some junior birdman (probably wearing a slide rule in a holster) said, "Why do we have to pay Senor Wenses a thousand bucks to do the test commercial? Anybody can put lipstick on his hand and do it."

And so we produced the commercial as it was storyboarded but naturally without the talent and finesse of Senor Wenses. The test film was made, as suggested by the client, with "anybody putting makeup on his hand."

Per standard procedure, we scheduled a CRC (creative review committee) in one of the fourteenth floor conference rooms (14-A or

14-B). The Lava meeting started more or less on time. The account executive, Hall "Cap" Adams (who would go on to become chairman and president of Leo Burnett years later), presented the strategy to which Leo paid scant attention; he presented the selling proposition in which Leo showed even less interest. Finally with nothing left to say he "rolled the film."

Faithful to the storyboard, a hand appeared with makeup on it; the voice-over talked as the fingers moved and then washed the hand off with Lava. At the end of the 60-second commercial, the lights came up; all eyes turned to Leo, who sat slouched in his chair, a Marlboro hanging from mouth, his lower lip drooping, the usual ashes on his lapel.

The tension was palpable. Here was the master! He turned, hooded eyes gazing forth, and said, "Looks like a talking asshole." He then got up and left for the meeting being held next door.

The commercial was never presented to Cincinnati.

The Fashion Plate

Bill Eldridge (aka William T.) was by all accounts a marketing genius, an unguided missile, and a bona fide character. He came by his marketing expertise naturally as he was the son of Clarence Eldridge, called by many the "Father of American Marketing" as a result of his years shaping General Motors' advertising. Bill came by the rest of his reputation via Williams College, Cornell, and two terms of service in WWII and Korea.

He was a smart, tough guy with a loud raucous wit, a hair-trigger temper, and deeply held opinions on everything and everybody.

I personally saw him place his head against the propeller (yes, the propeller) of an Air Canada plane that refused to board him because of an oversold ticket situation. He roared at them, "Board me or kill me." They boarded him!

On another occasion he and his wife hosted a post-Northwestern football game party for which she had made gallons of pasta. When the conversation got around to politics and veered left of his position (not hard to do), he stood on a table and said, "That's it, everybody out, I'm not sharing my food with a bunch of goddamn Commies."

Despite his wife's protests, he would brook no interference. The guests filed out into the snow while the Eldridges were stuck with enough pasta for a month.

He also had a long-standing feud with the creative department in general, and their leader, Draper Daniels, in particular. No advertising developed by them ever met his exacting standards and he let them know it.

Bill was not a snappy dresser; in the summer he favored half-open knit ties and crumpled seersucker suits with pipestem pants that ended somewhat around the middle of his ankle.

On one particular summer morning, our car pool, including Bill, entered the lobby of the Prudential Building at the same time Daniels also appeared. He was nattily attired in a smart summer gabardine suit and snap-brim Panama hat while Bill wore his usual high-water pants and crumpled suit.

As we crossed the threshold of the jammed elevator for our ride up, Draper looked Bill up and down, did a brilliant "stage wait," and said, "Ah, good morning Bill...I see you're still making your own clothes."

For the first time in the memory of man, W.T. Eldridge was speechless and we rode up to the fourteenth floor (the creative department) in absolute silence.

The Secret New Product

In the early 1960's, one of the most important package goods accounts in the Midwest was the family owned and operated Johnson Wax Company of Racine, Wisconsin. Because it was literally "up the road" from the headquarters of the Leo Burnett Company, it was a major new business target. It didn't hurt that Foote, Cone and Belding, our cross-town rivals, handled the account.

After many attempts, it finally happened that Burnett was invited to Racine for an interview and potential briefing on a new product.

Then as now, it was standard operating procedure for a client to evaluate a potential new agency on the basis of their work on a new product. In this way the incumbent agency was put on notice, and the new agency could be given the once-over without disrupting existing working relationships. The new agency was expected to put in a disproportionate amount of work if it was to have any hope of establishing a long-term relationship with the client.

Burnett didn't have a "new business" team per se, as it was the agency's policy to present the actual "team" who would work on the business if it was successful in winning it. Further, a senior member represented the various staff groups.

For the initial visit to Racine, the agency put forth a complete group of account executives, creatives, media supervisors, research people, and the head of media research, Dr. Seymour Banks. (Until I joined the agency in February of 1958, Seymour had the unique distinction of being the only Jewish employee of the Leo Burnett Company. While certainly not anti-Semitic, our company, with the exception of Philip Morris, basically served "WASPy" clients: Pillsbury, Kellogg, Green Giant, Swift & Company, Santa Fe Railway, P&G, Brown Shoe, etc. Similarly, S.C. Johnson, at the time, was not only totally populated by gentiles, but also somewhat shielded from non-mainstream America.)

Thus the stage was set for the briefing on our new product assignment. Our team was introduced to their counterparts at the client's and everyone settled in for the extensive explanation of the product for which we were to develop marketing and advertising.

The V.P. Marketing began the meeting by explaining that at S.C. Johnson all new products must have a hard-hitting, evocative name and, to this end, they had hired a major name developing company. He then proceeded to introduce their representative, who would take us through their development work and recommendation.

An earnest young man stood and carried a series of charts to the podium at the end of the room.

"As you know, the process of name development is extremely complex and difficult," he began. "All names and words evoke a reaction in human beings; these reactions take place at both the conscious and subconscious level.

"It is also true that in English, certain sounds are also capable of evoking a reaction. At our company we have conducted an extremely comprehensive and expensive series of research studies to ascertain which sounds produce which emotional responses.

"Without going into the entire study, let me explain the background of our work on this particular assignment from Johnson Wax. As you know," (we didn't) "the product under study is a heavy duty wax remover for wooden floors. Naturally such a product requires a name that connotes a heavy duty, no nonsense, effective end result. We concluded that to avoid conflicts and legal problems, and to start with a 'clean slate,' we should develop a name that in and of itself means nothing, but whose combination of letters would evoke the proper reaction."

This was not particularly sensational but for the time was somewhat unusual.

"Here is where we started," he said and produced some charts with a series of letters on them. "For example, names that begin with 'sh, sl, mo, bl, and pl' connote softness and are totally inappropriate for this product. Similarly, names that end in 'le, ly, ge, ies' are similarly unacceptable."

"On the other hand, there are some great sounds to connote heavy duty." He was clearly getting warmed up. "We found that a name beginning with the combination of 'c, d, t, k,' or 'g' along with the letter 'r' really sounds tough. Combining the beginning letters with hard-hitting concluding letters such as 'rt, dt, nt, or ck' results in a perfect name for a no-nonsense, heavy duty wax remover."

He built up to his big finish by removing the other charts and leaving a single one with "your new name" emblazoned on it. A piece of cardboard covered the magic name.

"And here it is, the absolutely perfect name for your new product," he said as he whipped off the covering. There it was:

DRECK

Seymour Banks burst into laughter, thinking that this was some sort of elaborate practical joke, and blurted out, "That's very funny, what's the real name?" He was the only one laughing. Dreck is, of course, Yiddish for "shit."

We didn't get the assignment.

Military Careers

When I joined the Leo Burnett advertising agency in 1958, the management consisted of a triumvirate at the top: Leo Burnett, the creative engine that pulled the train; R. N. "Dick" Heath, the business man who handled all the administrative and personnel issues; and General W. T. "Bill" Young (US Air Corps – Ret) who was the new business rainmaker, and an extremely suave and sophisticated gentleman.

It is said of Bill, perhaps apocryphally, that when he and his wife had their first child somewhat late in life, he moved out of the Ambassador East Hotel because he didn't want his child to be raised over a saloon (The Pump Room).

Bill's career in the Air Corps during WWII was entirely served in Washington, D.C., and, in fact, he never flew then or thereafter. When he had to travel to either coast it was via the New York Central or the Santa Fe Railways.

All Burnett employees, whatever their position, had black plaques with their name on it in white letters and this sign would follow you to whatever desk or office you occupied. Most simply said "Wally Bregman" or whatever, but Bill Young's said "W.T. Young, Gen. Ret."

This infuriated my neighbor, Warren Michael, who had served four years in the Army and had not only been in the first wave at Normandy, but had been wounded twice and heavily decorated.

Finally, it got the best of him and after a run-in with "the General" over some business issue, he had the art department make up a new sign for his office that read:

Warren B. Michael – Corp. Ret.

Flowers on the Train

At the Leo Burnett Company in the early 1960's, one of the premier account groups was the Campbell Soup team, populated by the account supervisor Bob Everett, account executives Bill Eldridge and John Ianeri, and assistant Frank Simpson. Two of the usual practices of this group were to take the overnight train to Camden and to "put on" Frank Simpson (see River Rat Club). Frank was eager, intelligent, and desperate to make a name for himself in the agency business. At the same time, he also wanted to be "one of the boys."

This particular incident took place on the train in the bar car. The four were having a few drinks as they rocketed through Indiana on their way to Camden. Via a prearranged signal Eldridge plucked a petal from a daisy in the glass vase on the table and, smacking his lips, devoured it along with his martini. A few minutes later John Ianeri took a sip of his drink and plucked another petal from the daisy and ate it. In a few minutes so too did Bob Everett.

Simpson, not wanting to seem out of step or *déclassé*, similarly took his drink in his hand, took a swallow, and plucked a petal from the daisy. As it touched his lips, the three others broke into uproarious laughter, pointed at the hapless butt of their joke, and, addressing the other guests in the bar car, said in unison, "Look at that dumb shit eating a daisy!"

Simpson was mortified, not for the first time or for the last.

The River Rat Club

Referring once more to the famous, or better said infamous, Campbell account group, the story goes that, yet again, they were traveling to Camden on the same train, in the same bar car, through the same part of Indiana. Seemingly spontaneously, Bob Everett began talking to Bill Eldridge about the famous River Rat Club. Frank Simpson was spellbound.

"And on the first floor, of course, they are all topless," said Everett.

"Oh, yes," said Eldridge, "but, of course, that's not as great as the second floor, that's where they're bottomless and completely nude."

"But," John Ianeri chimed in, "on the third floor it's unreal, they have the rubber sheets, the warm oil, the whips, branding irons, and all those wonderfully naked women."

"Yes," said Bob, "it's a shame we can't go tomorrow night but we do have those Franco-American boards to go over, the ones they're sending in for the presentation. But, Frank, what the hell, you don't have to worry about that. Why don't you go on over?"

"No, no," said Frank, a little too quickly. "I've got some work to do myself."

The next day after dinner, during which the River Rat Club was again thoroughly and lasciviously described and discussed, Everett suggested that the Franco-American people meet in his room. He bid goodnight to Simpson and arranged to meet him the next morning for breakfast. They all then boarded the elevators and went off in their separate directions. Naturally, the three conspirators quickly returned to a back table in the bar and waited to see naive Frank sneak out the front door and grab a taxi.

They were not disappointed. He jumped into the cab and said, "Hey, buddy, do you know where the River Rat Club is?"

As everyone acknowledges, no cab driver in the world has ever admitted to not knowing where anything is, so naturally the cab driver replied, "Absolutely, boss!" and pulled out.

What followed was one of the all time great comedies of errors as the baffled cab driver drove frantically back and forth around Camden and then Philadelphia looking for the nonexistent River Rat Club. On several occasions, he stopped other cab drivers and asked them. They,

21

of course, being members of the brotherhood, gave him equally conflicting directions that led to additional long and fruitless searches from the docks to the Main Line.

Some three hours later and seventy-five dollars poorer, gullible Frank arrived back at the hotel, unable to find the exotic, erotic, and nonexistent River Rat Club.

The Camel

It seems Bob Everett fathered a child at what his contemporaries considered to be late in life. Bill Eldridge was not only shocked but also amused by this event. As the story goes, when the child was brought home sometime in late December or early January, Bill either hired or dressed three people up as wise men, somehow rented a camel, and stationed them all on the lawn of Everett's house in suburban Kenilworth, pointing towards the east and looking for a star.

Eldridge never gave up his relentless attacks on Bob Everett. Putting him on and putting him down was a way of life for Bill.

At Burnett the United Way was taken very seriously (it was called the United Fund then). Each floor was divided up geographically and group captains were assigned; the idea was that they were the solicitors in charge of getting the donations. While most of us looked at the job as a chore, Eldridge took the position very seriously and decided that his group was not only going to obtain 100 percent contributions but also contribute the most money in total.

He solicited his boss, Everett, by first leaving the donation card on his desk. He then chatted with him about the charity. Finally, when he got the card back, Bill was absolutely livid. Everett, in Eldridge's opinion, had not given enough.

For the next week, every morning Eldridge would come in early and put a sign on Everett's door saying, "Old Baldy's a Cheapskate," until Everett finally capitulated and gave the amount that Eldridge thought was correct.

For Bill Eldridge, the end always justified the means.

Leo's Wheelchair

While Leo Burnett was one of the great icons of advertising and certainly a giant in his field, he was also human; as a human, he liked his martinis (in those days straight up and made out of gin with a splash of vermouth and a pimiento olive).

On one occasion, Leo was in New York and attended one of the less successful Philip Morris meetings. Joe Cullman, the chairman of the board and CEO, hadn't liked the commercials that were presented. Apparently, Joe refused to look at storyboards or interlocks and would only look at answer prints. Procedurally, the morning was spent presenting answer prints to Joe, and the afternoon, fighting over the "unbillables" as the agency tried to recoup the money spent on the commercials Cullman had rejected.

On this particular day Joe rejected everything and the client refused to pay for any of the production. Leo was thoroughly shaken. The entire entourage, Leo, the account group (Otis Smith, Marty Snitzer, and Cap Adams), and Draper Daniels, the creative director, stalked out of 100 Park Avenue and climbed into cabs for LaGuardia.

Unfortunately, the United flight to Chicago was delayed and Leo was able to imbibe a few more martinis than usual in the Red Carpet Club. On the flight to Chicago, he managed several more.

Upon arriving in Chicago, the account group was unable to convince the semi-comatose Leo that they were, in fact, in Chicago. Finally they succeeded, but then realized that their leader was absolutely, totally inebriated and unable to walk.

Necessity being the mother of invention, Owen Smith called for a wheelchair, which appeared at the ramp. Leo was helped into it, a blanket folded around his legs, and one of the junior account men detailed to push him through the cavernous tunnel of O'Hare. Leo, by this time, while not truly sure of exactly where he was, was nevertheless having a wonderful time. He laughed and joked throughout the journey.

Overhearing him, one of the tourists walking along the ramp was heard to say, "Isn't it wonderful that that poor old cripple has such a great sense of humor?"

Client Loyalty

One of the things that Leo Burnett held near and dear, and passed on to his employees, was his unshakeable loyalty to his clients. He smoked Marlboros, wore Brown shoes, drove a Chrysler, flew United, ate Green Giant peas, and would have worn RealSilk Hosiery if he could have.

Frequently when an employee had the temerity to say, "Well, I really don't like the taste of Kellogg's Corn Flakes," Leo would fix them with a withering stare and say, "Tastes like bread and butter to me."

He firmly believed his clients could do no wrong.

One day we were sitting in a creative review committee meeting in the famous conference room 14-A. Leo walked in and looked toward the end of the table where a new, young account man sat with a package of the hated Winstons in front of him. Leo stopped the meeting, turned to the offender, and growled, "I assume, young man, you have an outside source of income."

That man never appeared in a meeting again without Big Red—the good old Marlboro brand.

Leo Burnett at Seagram's

From its founding, the Leo Burnett Company had never handled a liquor account. The reason was that one of the three founders of the agency, R. N. "Dick" Heath, was a devout Christian Scientist. As such he avoided all alcoholic beverages. In fact, when Schlitz came to us in the early 1960's Dick wanted to turn them down but things weren't going very well and we needed the business. Dick is reported to have said, "OK, but don't expect me to have anything to do with that account." We took it and he didn't.

Some time later, Leo was contacted by Sam Bromfman of Seagram's and asked whether we would be interested in handling an important portion of their business. What followed was a major series of discussions between Leo and Dick as well as other agency principals. Dick Heath was basically the "money man" in the agency and Leo was, of course, its creative heart and soul. Clearly, one could not function without the other. To date both had done a splendid job, but as always in the agency business, future success depended on growth and at the time, there weren't many major advertising categories where Burnett wasn't blocked by competitive assignments. Liquor was one where we were open. Finally Dick capitulated and the two of them were scheduled to make a presentation to "Mr. Sam" at his New York office after a Philip Morris meeting.

When they arrived Dick discovered that he had "accidentally" left the presentation at 100 Park Avenue, the Philip Morris offices, and it was too late to go back for it.

"No problem," Leo said. "Just find a copy of *Life* magazine."

At that time the Burnett Agency bought more pages and spreads in *Life* magazine than any other advertising company. Ads for Pillsbury, Green Giant, Kellogg, Santa Fe Railroad, Marlboro, Swift Premium Meats, RealSilk Hosiery, The Tea Council, Chrysler, Maytag, Hoover, and several others truly dominated the magazine week in and week out.

Dick picked up the latest issue of the magazine and when called, they took it into the conference room where the top Seagram executives had assembled. Initially the audience was shocked by the simplicity of the presentation materials, but as Leo took them through each ad first describing the product's objectives and then how Burnett advertising solved it, they were first captivated and then sold. Simultaneously, Dick Heath became increasingly more depressed.

At the end, Mr. Sam asked them to step out while they deliberated.

In the lobby Leo said, "You know, I think they are going to give us the business."

"I know," Dick responded morosely.

"It'll be great for the agency."

"Yes, it will."

"And we can do a great job for them," Leo continued.

"I'm sure we can."

"And if we don't take it, it will go to some New York agency like Doyle, Dane, Bernbach." (There was a bitter rivalry between New York and Chicago agencies.)

"Yep."

"So," Leo went on, "here's what I propose…when they call us back we thank them politely and turn them down." There was no way Leo was going against the wishes and beliefs of his longtime partner.

And that's exactly what happened. The reason Leo and Dick were kept waiting so long was that the Seagram's people were trying to decide whether or not to give Burnett the whole business or just a major portion.

We never found out their decision because before Sam could say anything Leo said, "Before you tell us your decision, we want to thank you for allowing us to present, but we have just decided that we cannot take the business."

In the end, Leo Burnett did accept a liquor account (Schenley) but not until after Dick Heath retired.

I like to think that these bonds of loyalty and friendship exist today, but I very much doubt it.

Leo Visits Campbell

Again, making reference to the Campbell account group, the story goes that on the good nights they would frequent a particular bar in Camden. Somehow the story drifted back to Chicago as to what a wonderful place it was and how much fun they had there. On one particular night Leo himself was in Camden for a meeting with Bev Murphy, the Campbell Soup president, on the next day. Having heard the rumors about the famous bar, he pressed the account group to take him there.

Duly ordered to do so, the entire group went over to the bar, seated themselves at a large round table, and proceeded to have a few drinks. One of the previously introduced practical jokers decided to have some fun. He talked to one of the waitresses wearing a low-cut blouse and high black stockings and slipped her five dollars.

In a few minutes, she walked up to the table and said to Bob Everett, "Hey, it's wonderful you Burnett guys are back in town, I see you're still spending Leo's money."

She continued every time they ordered a round of drinks, "Hey, here comes more of Leo's money."

"Boy, Leo's really got a lot of money!"

"Good old Leo! He sure pays for the big tips!"

The great man sat there and took this for about three rounds. As those who knew him can visualize, with each round his lower lip sunk deeper and deeper, his chin curled further down into his chest. When he could stand it no longer, he called the girl over, took a $100 bill out of his pocket, put it on his balding head, and said, "That's nothing, honey, I'm Leo!"

The Elevator

During the early days of my media research career at the Leo Burnett Company, I, like all of my counterparts, realized that the only way we could make ends meet was by getting in before 8:00 A.M. and staying past 7:00 P.M. For these long hours, the company would give one $1.50 for breakfast and $3.00 for dinner. It was, therefore, *de rigueur* for all of us to work at least past seven o'clock to get the extra three bucks. (My starting salary in February of 1958 was $4,200 dollars per year. I was a married college graduate, veteran with one son and a pregnant wife.)

I remember one particular night quite well. I had worked even later than seven o'clock finishing the assignment I was doing for Dr. Seymour Banks and Francis Keyes. I put on my coat, turned off my Frieden calculator (no computers in those days), and rang the bell on the eleventh floor (the media floor) for the elevator.

To my astonishment, when the elevator doors opened, there was Leo Burnett and his secretary, Mary Keating, chatting away. I was totally taken aback as this was the first time I had ever come face-to-face with the great man. I quickly recovered and hustled into the elevator as the door closed.

Leo and Mary were discussing some subject of great importance having to do with new business, agency management, or departmental reorganization.

I tried to look away and act like I was not paying attention. After a few minutes, however, I realized the elevator was wandering aimlessly up and down the shaft. Apparently when Leo had gotten in he never pushed the button for the first floor. I hadn't either, assuming when I picked up the elevator that it was on a downward journey to the lobby from the fifteenth floor where Leo's office was.

The Lord only knows how long the two of them had been in there chatting when I got in, and Lord only knows how long they would have stayed there if I hadn't, with great trepidation, pushed the button for the lobby, knowing that I had to catch the 8:04 out of the Northwestern Station for my home in Highland Park.

Jif Strategy

My close friend and fellow account executive, Art Hohmann, worked on P&G's Jif Peanut Butter account. Since its introduction the brand had been troublesome from a strategic standpoint. The problem was that there had existed two warring camps.

On one side were the advocates of the "fun" strategy: "There's a great new peanut butter, Jif, terif..." embodied by a cartoon kangaroo. On the other side were those advocating the serious nutritional approach: "Hey Mom, here's a great new way to give your kids a healthy lunch..."

Unfortunately for the brand group and the agency, Jif had not attained its share and shipment goals and had not taken business from Skippy and the myriad of off-price and private label brands.

It was with this background that Bob Sheterley, the P&G food division general manager, called for a "brand review." A "brand review" is serious business and can mean that the assignment of the account to another agency is imminent. On the other hand, the brand group is not considered blameless and budding careers are considered to be in the balance. In net, when a "brand review" was called, sphincters tightened from Cincinnati to Chicago.

To assure the client that the agency was as concerned as they were, Art invited the top agency brass, including Leo himself, to sit in on the meeting. (Leo's disdain for P&G was well-known and was exemplified by his comment to Gordon Rothrock one day after he had seen him shepherding some of his clients around the agency: "Ah, Gordon, I see your clients are wearing long pants now.")

In anticipation of the big day Art, his assistants, and the brand group worked diligently to prepare hundreds of charts and exhibits explaining in excruciating detail the history of the Jif brand and analyzing the results from every possible angle. Both parties also agreed that, because there was no clear-cut answer, no one would bring up the strategic question of "fun versus nutrition." Even Bob Sheterley knew that this was not a productive area for discussion at this time.

The day of the big meeting arrived. Its importance was underlined by the fact that it was booked into the agency boardroom on the fifteenth floor, a room few if any of the "working stiffs" had ever seen. It began promptly at nine o'clock and for the first two hours everything went perfectly. The agency and brand personnel flawlessly went through their scripts describing the BD (brand development) for each of the thirty-nine sales districts and the remedial steps being taken in each. Needless to say Leo was bored to tears.

Finally, as the presentation was about to successfully conclude, Sheterley turned to the assembled throng and asked the rhetorical question, "OK, does anyone have any further questions of the agency?"

There was supposed to be total silence for ten seconds after which the senior client would conclude the meeting and leave. Instead, one of the "junior bird men" on the client side decided to make a name for himself.

"Mr. Burnett," he said, addressing the barely awake Leo, "I am quite confused by your agency's advertising for Jif which seems on a 'fun' strategy and the brand's labeling and product development which seems directed toward a 'nutrition' strategy. Would you care to comment on this apparent dichotomy?"

The room went totally silent. The unthinkable had happened. Someone had opened the Pandora's box that was supposed to remain firmly shut and locked. Everyone was stunned, all except Leo.

"I've been waiting for someone to bring this up and I'm delighted that you had the intelligence to ask this question," he began. "It is certainly the pivotal issue upon which the entire future of the brand is balanced. The agency has done a tremendous amount of thinking about this complex subject and has extensively evaluated both points of view. We have, in the end, come to a single, clear conclusion."

At this point Hohmann had recovered from shock and was entranced. He was about to see the essence of Leo Burnett, the consummate advertising genius and salesman at work. He was going to witness, in person, the qualities that had not only made this man a legend in his time but had also built his agency to its preeminent position. Leo was weaving the entire response out of whole cloth and was about to provide the answer they had all been seeking but failed to find.

Everyone watched and waited in breathless anticipation as the great man prepared to cut the strategic Gordian knot.

"And so," Leo paused for dramatic emphasis, "here's Art with our recommendation."

Total silence.

Hohmann did the only thing a good account man could do. He slowly looked at his watch which read eleven o'clock and said, "Hey, look at this, it's time for lunch."

The room erupted in laughter and the meeting ended.

The Meet Me in St. Louis Flight

One memorable night after a P&G meeting, in the midst of a huge Midwestern snowstorm, the account group, the creative team, and I arrived at the airport only to find that all incoming flights had been canceled, even though Cincinnati was open at that time. (I believe the group consisted of myself, the account supervisor; Jim Cone and Peter Husting, the account executives; and Jack Hirshboeck and Tom Laughlin, copywriters.) As we stood around in desperation and confusion, believing that it was going to be yet another lost night, I happened to see a United Airlines flight crew going by.

As they passed by, the captain said something to the crew like, "Well, I guess we'll have to deadhead this plane back to Chicago."

I stopped him and asked him what they were doing at this airport. I knew that United didn't fly to Cincinnati. He explained that they had had a scheduled roundtrip DC-8 flight from Chicago to Akron-Canton, but had been diverted into Cincinnati. All of their passengers had been bused to Akron-Canton, but the Akron-Canton to Chicago segment had been canceled. Due to the snowstorm the airline had decided not to bus the passengers down to Cincinnati. Thus, he had to fly his plane empty back to Chicago.

I immediately asked him if it would be possible to take the five of us to Chicago on his plane. (Remember, this was 1963 before there was any concern about hijacking and terrorism, and long before the current rigid restrictions on in-flight security.) The pilot thought a minute and then said, "Sure, fine, I think we can pull your tickets. Come on along."

Delighted, we boarded the waiting DC-8, along with pilot, co-pilot and flight engineer, and six stewardesses who were also part of the crew of this enormous aircraft. It was normally configured to hold approximately two hundred people.

Off we flew in great luxury. As there was at least one stewardess for each of the five of us seated in first class, drinks flowed like water. The pilot had left the door to the cockpit wide open and we roamed freely back and forth—a real party atmosphere.

As we approached Chicago, the captain announced that a new cell of the snowstorm that had hit them earlier was now over Chicago and that O'Hare was completely snowed in. There was no chance we could land there. At this point, fueled by our high cocktail intake, we passengers tried to help out by suggesting alternative destinations such as Tahiti, Honolulu, Rio de Janeiro, or Paris.

The captain quickly brought us down to earth and explained that the alternates at this point were limited to Minneapolis, Milwaukee, and St. Louis. Unbelievably, he said he didn't much care which one we went to, so we were free to take our choice. A vote was taken and St. Louis won. The drinks continued to flow, and in an hour or so we landed. It was about nine-thirty in the evening.

Once on the ground with the engines stopped, the captain said that we would be leaving the next morning at eight o'clock sharp. All of us, including his crew, were free to do as we wished as long as we were back at the plane by eight. Because of United's "eighteen hours from bottle to throttle" rule, the pilot, co-pilot, and engineer said good night and went to their hotel. The rest of us checked into the stewardesses' motel and then took off for the then famous Gaslight District in downtown St. Louis.

The evening progressed famously as the eleven of us all became very close friends. We wandered from watering hole to watering hole singing old songs with banjo players, and listening to Dixieland and jazz. Needless to say we all consumed prodigious amounts of alcohol.

Miraculously the next morning, true to our captain's orders, we arrived at the airport ready to fly back to Chicago. We boarded the plane somewhat shakily. All, including the stewardesses, had titanic hangovers. Fortunately, the short trip over to Chicago was flown in absolutely smooth air and clear, brilliant sunshine. The storm had passed through during the night.

As we prepared for our arrival into Chicago, the captain suddenly keyed the intercom. "You're not going to believe this folks, but an Eastern Connie (Constellation) has just this minute collapsed a nose wheel on the only runway that had been plowed out. O'Hare is closed. We have been ordered to over fly Chicago and go on to our alternate destination, which is ... you guessed it ... Cincinnati."

We were in shock. Upon arrival in Cincinnati, I and all of my people had to call our wives and explain how it happened that we had flown over Chicago twice, spent a night in St. Louis with six stewardesses, and ended up back in Cincinnati at noon on Saturday.

It wasn't easy and as I write this, forty years later, I'm not even sure my wife believes me now.

Milton Biow's P&G Sales Meeting

History reveals that Milton Biow, one of the great advertising men of our time, had the following experience at the year-end sales meeting of Procter & Gamble.

One must understand that the Annual Sales Meeting was a big, big deal in Cincinnati. All the agency principals were invited and their speeches sanitized by the executive staff. What they said, how they said it, and how long they said it was subject to constant scrutiny, review, and revision.

At Milton Biow's first performance he refused to show his talk to anyone. He told the staff that he didn't need any audiovisual aids and he certainly didn't need any help with his talk. The P&G underlings were in a total state of disarray but there was little they could do. Milton Biow was a major force to be dealt with.

After a short introduction Biow strode on to the bare stage of the downtown theater where the meeting was being held. He looked out at the hundreds of Procter executives and said, "My agency has been trying to get Procter & Gamble business for many, many years; finally we found out that we were on the short list. Then at last the phone call came from Havvie (A. N. Halberstadt, then V.P. of advertising).

"He said, 'Milton, come to Cincinnati.' I knew that this was the moment I had been waiting for. This was it; this was our big break. We must be getting Tide or Oxydol or Crisco or Camay. I didn't want to be late, so I chartered a plane and put my whole team on it." (This, by the way, was in the late forties or early fifties, and chartering a plane at that time was quite a big deal.)

"We flew out of LaGuardia into Cincinnati on our chartered DC-3. We landed. We had a limo take us to Sixth and Sycamore (P&G's headquarters). With trepidation we went to the sixth floor and met Havvie. As we had coffee, the big moment came, he said, 'Milton, we're giving you Lava.'"

Milton looked out into the audience executed a marvelous Jack Benny-like "stage wait" and said, "We took the train home."

The staff was apoplectic, the top management was speechless, and the audience was in stitches.

Milton went on, "So we had a small budget brand, so what, we had to make good and do it on a shoestring. We had a problem. The world was changing. The original consumers of Lava were diminishing as factories were automated. What to do? How do you keep the trade enthused about a 'workingman's brand' when there are fewer and fewer 'workingmen'?"

He reached into his jacket pocket and took out three little objects. "Here's how! In my hand I have the answer:

1. Here is a nut and bolt—it stands for our traditional franchise, blue-collar workers. We never can forget them
2. Here is a child's jack—it stands for the millions of children that come home dirty from playing and have to use Lava to get cleaned up. And,
3. Here is a piece of screening—it represents the millions of men doing chores on the weekend. Only Lava can get their hands clean.

My staff will now pass out your own surefire Lava sales kits."

And sure enough, from the back of the hall Biow agency personnel appeared. They walked down the aisles of the theater and passed out little bags with the three miracle selling tools inside. It was an incident unprecedented in P&G Sales Meeting history.

Milton Biow walked off the stage to thunderous applause. Within the next few weeks Lava sales took off and in a few short months the Biow Agency was rewarded with the advertising assignment for several large brands.

Biow was truly a genius!

Chicken Kiev

In the middle 1960's, competition between American Airlines and United Airlines on the lucrative Chicago to New York route was intense. United's answer, in those days before political correctness, was to offer daily "executive flights" from JFK to LaGuardia. These flights were "men only" (the presumption being that there were no female executives) and offered special meals, drinks, favors (traveling clocks, dopp kits, etc.), and the luxury of being able to take off one's shoes and jacket and work.

On one such flight, I was seated at the window next to a young man who seemed rather nervous but, as I had a great deal of work to do, I paid little attention to him until after cocktails and the meal service began.

A very pretty stewardess came by and asked us if we wanted the chicken or steak. (I always thought that they assigned their most attractive stewardesses to the "executive" flights but could never prove it.)

The fellow on the aisle ordered the chicken and I took the steak. In a few minutes the flight attendant brought our meals and said to my seatmate, "Here is your dinner, sir. It is one of our specialties, Chicken Kiev. Let me prepare it for you."

"Oh, don't bother, I'll do it myself," the young man replied.

"No, I insist. I'm very good at it and if you don't do it right, the butter flows out on the plate and you lose all the flavor."

"But," he said, "if you do it wrong the butter will go all over."

"Don't worry," she said and proceeded to cut into the chicken breast, which disgorged a stream of hot butter that hit the passenger in the chin and then ran straight down his front drenching his tie and shirt in the oily, yellow fluid.

The shocked young man said not a word but appeared transfixed in horror.

"I'm so sorry, let me get some towels to wipe you off," the chastened flight attendant said and ran off to the safety of the galley.

The young man next to me seemed to be on the verge of tears. "I've had it," he exclaimed. "I'm on my way to New York for the most important job interview of my life. The headhunter and his client are meeting my plane and we're supposed to spend two or three hours

37

together in the Red Carpet Room. Now look at me, I look like a bum. What kind of an impression am I going to make? I don't have a spare shirt or tie because I was planning on catching a plane back to Chicago after the interview."

Unfortunately, I couldn't help him as I was only going to be in New York one night and didn't have a shirt or tie to spare. But after a few seconds, I had a brainstorm.

"What size shirt do you wear?" I asked.

"Why, what difference does it make?" my despondent new friend asked.

"Humor me, I think I have an idea," I replied.

"Well," he said "I wear a 16 ½, 34, for all the good it does."

At this point the "helpful" stewardess reappeared with dry and wet towels, which only made the butter stains worse.

"Stop wiping and listen to me," I said. "I think I have an idea." I proceeded to tell her about the job interview and the circumstances surrounding it. She got the drift and soon an announcement emanated from the forward bulkhead microphone.

"Good afternoon, gentlemen, we seem to have a little problem and need your help. I have just spilt butter all over the front of one of your fellow passengers who has a very important meeting at the airport. He must get a clean shirt size 16 ½, 34 and a tie that goes with a blue suit before we land. Please ring your call button if you can help."

How many people responded is unknown, but call bells and lights went off all over the plane. Soon my seatmate was newly attired in a white button-down shirt and an attractive repp tie. He looked like he had just stepped off the cover of GQ.

I don't know whether he got the job or not, I hope he did. I'm pretty sure he returned the shirt and tie. I do know that the hapless stewardess thought twice before she stuck a knife or fork into her next Chicken Kiev.

The Key Case

One night I flew to New York on a trip to visit our Marlboro client on the United Air Lines (another client) "executive flight"—translation "men only." We landed, and, as always, everybody lined up at the door waiting to get off. Suddenly one of the stewardesses keyed the loudspeaker and said, "Excuse me, gentlemen—before anyone gets off, we seem to have found a key case somebody left on his seat. Let me try to describe it so perhaps whoever lost it will be able to identify it. It's made of black leather, it has five keys on it; there is a key to a Yale lock, and what appear to be two General Motors car keys—and, oh, what's this? There seems to be a wedding ring on one of the key holders."

To the best of my knowledge, nobody claimed it, at least while we were standing in the aisle.

I'm sure someone did later on!

Walter W. Bregman

The Christmas Flight

Flying home from Cincinnati late on a Friday night was nothing special for those of us on the "regular run" but doing so the day before Christmas was a little unusual. On this particular night, Art Hohmann and I were booked on Eastern Flight 121, a Constellation that flew from Cincinnati to Midway (or was it O'Hare by then?). Having fortified myself with the gargantuan airport bar martinis, I walked through the lightly falling snowflakes, climbed up the air stair door into the cabin, slumped into my seat, and stared at the bulkhead on which a sad, plastic Christmas wreath hung.

Once the plane was in flight, Art turned to me and said, "Look back there." As we were sitting in the front row of seats the entire cabin was arrayed behind us. I did as he asked. Row upon row consisted of bored businessmen, jaded travelers, and parents with children. All were either leafing through magazines or closing their eyes; all enduring the incessant bouncing, vibration, and creaking anyone who has flown in a Constellation will remember; all hoping that the flight would end safely and soon.

Art turned to me and said, "Come on, let's cheer them up."

Whereupon he jumped out of his seat and reached up on the bulkhead for the microphone on which the crew made their safety announcements. He mashed down the "push to talk" button and said, "Come on, folks, it's Christmas Eve. Let's sing some carols!"

And so it was that for the next hour and a half of that turbulent flight to Chicago, the world's greatest practicing agnostic led the entire cabin and crew in singing Christmas carols.

One of my more memorable Christmas Eves!

A Class Act

During the Procter years, when those of us who worked on the account spent seemingly endless days and nights at the Terrace Hilton Hotel in Cincinnati, one of the Burnett practices was that anybody who needed material brought over from Chicago would have it given to another account executive who was traveling to the client and he would turn it over to the fellow who was waiting, thus avoiding the use of couriers. (There was no Federal Express in those days. As a matter of fact, it was just slightly after the Pony Express.)

Art Hohmann and I, who were on the Joy brand at that time, were leaving the office to go to Cincinnati on our usual Delta Airlines flight when one of the young creatives ran breathlessly up to us and said, "Would you please take these new Salvo storyboards to Jim Rice?" He proceeded to give us one of the "Schlepper bags" we used to carry the large presentation size storyboards.

"No problem," we said, and took the bag, went down to the Gibraltar Room for a few fast drinks and then took off for the perilous trip to Midway and the even more perilous flight to Cincinnati.

Upon arrival in Cincinnati, we thought that perhaps it would be worth our while to stop by the Beverly Hills Club in Covington, Kentucky (across the river from Cincinnati), for a few tilts at "Lady Luck." (The BH was an elegant but illegal gambling joint that operated with full knowledge of the local authorities and always had the top cabaret acts in the country, Jimmy Durante, Sophie Tucker, Tony Martin, etc.) We had a few free drinks, a few laughs, saw a great show, lost a little money at the tables, and took the usual complimentary cab back to the hotel.

After checking in, we realized that we had almost forgotten to give the storyboards we had been entrusted with to Jim Rice. We got his room number from the desk clerk, took the elevator to his floor, and knocked on the door. Jim, as it turned out, had been out with Bob Hanslip, his client, and had a few more drinks than even we had had. Being a Navy veteran, he slept in his "skivvies" so when we knocked on the door, he opened it and stood in his underwear, half asleep and half drunk.

Art, quick-witted to the end, said, "You grab his hands and pull him into the hall, hand him the storyboards, and I'll slam the door."

Dutiful assistant that I was, I grabbed Jim, led him out into the corridor and put the handle of the big bag in his hands while Art reached behind him and slammed the door.

We then both ran into the elevator and were whisked away before his eyes even opened. Secure in the knowledge that we had pulled one of the great practical jokes of all time, we slept the sleep of the good.

The next morning we went down to the eighth floor for breakfast. (Yes, the eighth floor. At the Terrace Hilton the lobby was on the eighth floor; offices and parking were below, and rooms were above.) We sat down at the usual table where the Burnett group gathered, surrounded by other tables where the Tathum-Laird, Benton & Bowles, Compton, Y&R, and Grey people sat. We smugly waited for Rice to appear and regale us with the woes of his previous night's experience. We were sadly disappointed. The world's greatest practical joke was a flop.

In a few minutes Jim Rice appeared shaved, sparkling, bright-eyed and bushy-tailed. He greeted us warmly and proceeded to order breakfast. Never to this day has he ever admitted that the incident described above took place. He also failed to explain how he got back into his room at three o'clock in the morning wearing only his undershorts and carrying a bag of storyboards. That's class!

The Carport

The P&G Annual Sales Meeting in Cincinnati (described previously) was the one event that all of the young brand managers and account executives eagerly looked forward to. First of all, they had absolutely no hand in the preparation or delivery of the speeches. This was handled way above their pay grade. Secondly, after the meeting, there was always a chance to meet with the top executives of both your agency and P&G in a state of semi-bon ami.

One year, Burnett had its usual cocktail party and, as all the agencies did, rented one of the suites in the Terrace Hilton. My Salvo Tablet Detergent brand manager at the time was my great good friend and partner in many misadventures, Bob Hanslip. That night he and I outdid ourselves in the imbibing department. Nonetheless, despite my pleadings to the contrary, he decided to drive home to his house in suburban Terrace Park.[1] The house was a typical three-bedroom ranch with a carport on the side. Because Bob and his wife had four kids, he had decided six months earlier to convert the carport into a bedroom for two of his children. For decorative reasons he had put a raised brick flowerbed under the windows and astride what had been the access to the carport.

This night in his advanced state of inebriation, he drove home, turned into the driveway, forgot about the remodeling and put the front wheels of his 1959 Chevy smack in the middle of the raised flower bed; the car's radiator penetrated the jalousie bedroom windows and came to rest near where his two children slept.

An unconfirmed rumor has it that upon hearing the crash and seeing the car hood in their bedroom, the two Hanslip boys cried in unison, "Mommy—Daddy's home."

Fortunately no one was hurt, and the car was removed the next morning before the neighbors could see it.

---

[1] Terrace Park was a development in which at least twenty mid-level P&G executives lived. I had so many friends there and was in town so often that I became a semi-regular on their softball team.

Our First Client Dinner

One of the duties and responsibilities of a young and upwardly mobile account executive on the Procter & Gamble business was what was called "the obligatory client dinner in your house." In my case, my wife, Robbie, and I had our first client dinner with the Salvo brand group. I invited Bob Hanslip, the brand manager, and Bill Wickman, his boss, the associate advertising manager on the business and my boss, Bob Williams, and his wife, Joan.

Hanslip and I arrived at my house in suburban Highland Park around six o'clock on the Northwestern train from Chicago and proceeded to drink martinis. My wife, meanwhile, was terribly nervous about this "important client dinner" and was busy preparing a very expensive Chateaubriand, which she had purchased for the occasion. (It was proper to put all dinner costs on one's expense account, and, therefore, she was splurging.)

After Bob and I had our two or three martinis we received a disturbing phone call saying that Bill Wickman was delayed at Midway. Because he was the "big client," we all agreed to wait—or, at least, I agreed to wait without telling my wife. She practically burst into tears and told me the dinner would be ruined.

Moments later, the Williamses showed up, and we drank more martinis with them. Soon we were all plastered and still no Wickman. Finally at Robbie's urging we sat down at the table to a hard, shrunken, blackened Chateau. I asked my wife to pass the potatoes, whereupon she picked one off the serving plate, reared back and threw it at me. It hit me square in the chest and bounced on to the floor.

Bob Hanslip was basically unintelligible and could hardly stay seated in his chair. Joan Williams told the same story four times; each time she was interrupted, she would go back and begin to tell it all over again. Her husband Bob was no better; he demonstrated how someone he knew was once so drunk that he poured his drink down the front of his shirt instead of into his mouth and, in fact, Bob did it three times, pouring the drink down the front of his own shirt each time.

Finally, Wickman showed up and was so pleased to find his subordinate in the condition he was in that nothing would do but he had to go out to the car and get his camera and take a picture of Bob Hanslip in his inebriated state. At this point, Bob was feeling poorly and said he felt he had to go outside and get some air. We didn't think anything of it until some forty minutes later when he failed to show up.

At that time, we lived in Highland Park Highlands where, typical of such developments, each house was chockablock with the one next door. Our driveways were virtually abutting. When we finally went outside to look for Hanslip, we found him sprawled on the ground in our neighbor's driveway with his head in their planter. Apparently he had been sick several times.

Robbie and Joan Williams were the first to find him, and they attempted to pick him up and bring him back into the house. This proved to be impossible, so Bob Williams and I helped, while Wickman took more pictures. With great effort we put him to bed in our den.

The next morning, more than a little hungover, I came downstairs and, much to my chagrin, found my neighbor, Howard Caine, an account executive at the Ed Weiss Agency, standing in his driveway washing off his planter with a garden hose. He seemed puzzled as to how his planter had gotten so fouled. I told him the story and thanked him very much for being so nice about it.

He turned to me and said, "Hell, he was a client. You'd do it for me, wouldn't you?"

When we got to the agency, I went to the art department before our meeting and had a sign made with a rope on it for Bob to wear around his neck.

It simply stated:

> **If you find me in your driveway, please do not hurt me. Call my account executive, and he will have me removed.**

Salvo Sales Meeting

One of the unsuccessful products that it was my privilege to introduce for Procter & Gamble was Salvo Tablet Detergent. Bob Hanslip and I traveled around the country and did twenty-nine sales meetings in about forty-five days as we spread the word about this miraculous product far and wide across the United States. The only problem was, as we found out and as millions of consumers across the United States found out, we had a slight technical problem: the little "hockey pucks" didn't dissolve very well.

Nevertheless, we were assured by R&D back at Ivorydale that by the time the national sampling began, they would have solved the problem. The difficulty was that we had scheduled the meetings before we discovered the flaw. Management decided, however, against the agency's advice, to go ahead with the meetings in the hope that R&D would save us. (They didn't.)

The theme of the meeting was quite complex. All the salesmen had to put on field jackets, helmet liners, and pistol belts while the agency and the brand group showed war movies with black light and exploding gunfire. It was typical of the sort of early sixties show business that characterized Procter & Gamble sales meetings.

The way the Salvo meeting was structured, after the "fun and games" were over, we moved to the product demonstration in which we produced three full-size washing machines and proceeded to demonstrate the effectiveness of Salvo versus Vim and Quick Solv, our two competitors from Lever Brothers and Colgate-Palmolive. We had been given all the help we could get from R&D. They had toiled mightily and produced the so-called "special dirt" specifically designed to provide a cleaning win for our product versus the competition. Unfortunately, after the first few sales meetings it became clear that in a free and open encounter, Salvo could not beat the other two, and of equal importance, they dissolved and we didn't.

At that time, we had an assistant brand manager by the name of Craig Busey, who was a very creative fellow and was charged with the responsibility of giving the product demonstration. The plan was that everybody on the team had a part. Mine was doing the advertising and media plan; Bob Hanslip's was doing the background and strategic positioning, and Busey's was doing the product demonstration.

After the third meeting, Craig realized that normal hot water wasn't hot enough to dissolve Salvo but worked for the competition. To solve this problem, he bought some little immersion coils frequently used to heat up coffee in a cup and dangled them in the Salvo machine for an hour before the product demonstration. Thus the water in our machine was always a good ten or fifteen degrees hotter than the competition.

But even this didn't work all the time, so he perfected a technique that did work. He would start the demo with our machine, and say, "Now in this machine I will put the miraculous new Salvo product along with these soiled garments," which he proceeded to do. He would start the machine.

Then he would go to the Vim machine and begin talking about the Vim product, and all the while, of course, our machine was running.

The trick was to see how long he could talk before he put Vim in its machine and started it. And then, how long he could talk before he put Quick Solv in its machine. With the advantage of three or four minutes ahead of Vim and sometimes seven or eight minutes ahead of Quick Solv, the Salvo tablets always dissolved. After fifteen minutes or so, Busey would say, "Well, that's the end of the washing cycle," and turn off all the machines. As one would suspect, Salvo had cleaned all the clothes and dissolved while the others had failed dismally. Of course, the Salvo machine had run the full cycle; the Vim machine eleven minutes, and the Quick Solv machine seven minutes.

And that was the way we demonstrated the product's superiority to the sales force.

Unfortunately, Mrs. Consumer didn't have three machines, nor did she have the advantage of allowing Salvo to run longer in the washing cycle and at a hotter water temperature.

Despite the wonderful Wally Cox advertising Burnett produced, Salvo died a horrible death.

As the saying goes, "Nothing is worse for a bad product than good advertising." What is even worse is good advertising and sampling!

Wally Cox

One of the wonderful experiences of my advertising life was working with a truly saintlike person whose troubled life ended all too soon, Wally Cox.

The story begins when we were in very serious trouble on Salvo copy. We had been struggling for over a year without the top talent of the agency applying itself. Finally in desperation and frustration, I appealed to Leo Burnett himself. I pleaded that he put the "first team" on the business and finally provide my client with the copy they deserved, not only because it was the "Burnett way," but also because it represented a potential four million dollars in billing.

For one or both of the above reasons, Leo responded to the brash twenty-nine-year-old account man and put the agency's copy chief and star creative man, Draper Daniels, on the business. Draper went back to his office, and in about thirty-five minutes knocked out a wonderful commercial utilizing a thin, wimpy little man in a white suit who, by reverse imagery, presented the strength and cleaning power of Salvo.

Accompanied by Daniels, Bob Edens, and Jack Hirshboeck, I took the new campaign down to Cincinnati to present it to the copy section. Edens did a masterful job of selling and concluded by saying, as he described the little thin fellow in the white suit, that "he would be somebody like Wally Cox."

At that point, Murray Howe of the copy section said, "What about Wally Cox?"

Ever fast on his feet, Daniels replied, "Yes, exactly. That's precisely who we want to use."

I was immediately dispatched to the conference room telephone in the corridor to call our New York office and find out if Wally Cox was available. They called back shortly and said, "Well, he might be, but it would probably cost at least $25,000."

Having worked with P&G for five years by this time I knew what to do. I went back into the meeting and said, "Well, he's probably available, but it may cost us as much as $50,000."

The client responded predictably and said, "That's ridiculous! We won't pay any more than $25,000."

Whereupon I said, "Well, we'll go back and try, but it's unlikely that he's available at that price."

Of course, we got him. The white suit "presenter" never materialized because once we met with Wally, we started to write "slice of life" copy tailored to his marvelous understated and inventive personality.

As mentioned elsewhere, the campaign was a smash hit and established new records on the Burke recall "meter" which was great for the advertising but bad for Salvo (the good advertising for a bad product syndrome).

One night after dinner, Wally Cox told the following story.

It seems that years ago Wally, Marlon Brando, and Marilyn Monroe, among others, had all been members of Actors Studio in New York and had, in fact, roomed together for a short period of time. In later years Wally more or less lost contact with Marilyn as he went on to create the TV sitcom role of Mr. Peepers and live quietly in Westport, Connecticut, while she, of course, took Hollywood by storm as the sex symbol of the fifties and sixties.

But Marilyn never forgot Wally. After the demise of Mr. Peepers, like many long running sitcom stars, Cox was typecast and unable to obtain other roles. He, with other has-beens and never was's, resorted to serving as a panelist on "Hollywood Squares."

Marilyn found out and wanted to help him out. It was 1962 and she was shooting what turned out to be her last picture.[2] She went to the producer and, unbeknownst to Wally, demanded that he be given a cameo part in the film. Motion picture lore indicates that what Marilyn wanted, Marilyn got. The producer readily agreed and Marilyn went off to deliver the happy news to Wally.

According to Wally, he was in his Connecticut house one night when the phone rang. A studio operator came on the line and said, "Is this Mr. Wally Cox?"

Wally answered, in his inimitable diffident way, "Yes, this is Wally Cox."

"Please hold, we have a call from Miss Marilyn Monroe," the operator said.

---

[2] *Something's Got to Give* – Monroe died on August 4, 1962, while the film was still in production.

Marilyn was put through immediately, and the trademarked breathless voice at the other end said, "Wally, it's me, Marilyn. Remember me...from school?"

One of Wally's great regrets was that he never got to work with Marilyn and repay her random act of kindness.

Another night after a shoot, Wally Cox, Joel Smilow,[3] Joan Smilow and I had had dinner at the Four Seasons. We were walking out of the Seagram's Building past the fountain and down the steps. An old scruffy panhandler was sitting on the stone curb. Like most New Yorkers, the Smilows and I ignored the disreputable beggar and briskly walked by. All of a sudden Wally stopped, turned, went back, and put a five-dollar bill in the fellow's hand.

He then rejoined us and said, almost apologetically, "You know, I've been poor, too, and I just can't resist those guys."

God bless you, Wally. You deserved a lot better than you got.

---

[3] Joel Smilow subsequently became my boss when he hired me, in 1979, to replace him as President of International Playtex, Inc.

Lionel Stander

The idea of the advertising for Salvo that was brilliantly conceived by Draper Daniels, the copy chief at Leo Burnett, and executed by the enormously talented Wally Cox, was to contrast Wally's meek, mild, Mr. Peepers persona with the strength of Salvo. (In fact Wally was extremely strong and well developed. He fostered his "Mr. Peepers" reputation by buying clothes two sizes too big.) At the end of the commercial Wally always put a box of Salvo on his "nonexistent" bicep and said, "Nothing can beat the strength of Salvo."

The Cox campaign broke all the Burke records at P&G. The Burke research company measured recall of commercials by randomly dialing homes and determining the percent of viewers who recalled seeing a commercial. A Burke number in the teens was considered good and anything over twenty was great. The first Wally Cox commercial got a staggering forty-one on the Burke scale and set a modern day record.

Naturally, we ran the hell out of the first pool of commercials as we rolled the product out from west to east. With the amount of exposure we were giving the commercials they rapidly approached wear-out. Procter & Gamble considered a commercial worn out when it had been exposed ten times to the heaviest viewing quintile. Don't ask me how they figured this out; I just know we had to abide by the rules and produce a second pool of commercials.

While Wally Cox was the star in each commercial, they were basically "slice of life" stories. Wally always saved the day for someone by introducing him or her to Salvo. In one of the new spots we decided to go a little bit afield and utilize a bewildered "tough guy" in the laundry room of an apartment building. I am sure you can fill in the blanks and come up with the story line.

As the "foil" to Wally the agency/client production team cast the perfect actor; an old time "tough guy" along the lines of Wallace Beery; tall, craggy faced with a distinctive voice—Lionel Stander. Today he is best remembered as the tough but oh so sensitive chauffeur/butler Max in the hit series "Hart to Hart." At the time, however, he had been all but forgotten. But as you will see, not *totally* forgotten.

The commercials were shot and tested and "Tough Guy" broke our previous record. Not only did people remember the commercial but the internals were fantastic (recall of the name of the product and individual copy points). For the time being, the Leo Burnett Agency and the Salvo team were heroes of the universe; but not for long.

A week after the new commercials went on the air I got a call from my counterpart, the Salvo brand manager, Bob Hanslip.

"We've got to pull "Tough Guy" off the air," he said.

"What the hell are you talking about? It's the best spot we've ever done," I replied in shock.

"Yeah, that may be true but I got my orders from the top."

"Why?"

"'Cause he's a Communist, that's why," Bob answered.

"Who is?"

"Your buddy Stander, that's who," he replied. Suddenly Lionel was my buddy.

For once I was speechless but finally sputtered, "Who the hell says so?"

"Somebody wrote a letter to McElroy (the chairman of the board) and it got bucked down to me through about a dozen people. It says we 'should be ashamed employing a known Communist at a time like this.' (This was 1963 just after the Cuban missile crisis and at the height of the cold war.) They said they would start a boycott if we didn't pull the spot. The powers that be say to take the path of least resistance and pull it."

The leaning tower of Jell-O had spoken!

Not knowing what else to do, I said, "Look, leave it with me for a couple days. I'll take it out of rotation for a while but let's let things cool off before we completely pull it."

He agreed. Now I had to figure out what to do and I had absolutely no idea. The whole thing seemed nutty and besides by now I knew and liked Lionel. I called the agency's lawyer and told him my problem. He told me the one thing I already knew. If we pulled the commercial for the reason P&G wanted to we all could be sued for economic discrimination. It was not against the law to have been a Communist even if he had been. Once we cast him and shot and aired the commercial we were stuck.

Fortunately, the company lawyer had an idea. He had a friend in Washington, a law school classmate who was with the FBI. He agreed to call him and ask him to "pull the file" and informally let us know the details of Lionel's communist affiliation. The results were revealed a few days later.

The FBI agent called me and said, "What I'm about to tell you is totally off the record and I will deny any attribution. Further, I can't put anything in writing. I'd be fired if anyone found I'm even talking to you. The only reason I am is that it looks like a good guy is getting screwed, so here goes.

"In 1947 the House Un-American Activities Committee (HUAC) under Senator Joseph McCarthy of Wisconsin turned its attention to Hollywood. In a series of sensational hearings many people were denounced as Communists and "fellow travelers." The end result of the hearings was the famous "Hollywood Ten" who were publicly blacklisted by the industry. But underneath, at least another 400 were quietly put on the "don't hire" list. Your friend Stander was one of the latter group. The funny thing, not so funny really, is that he never was even accused of being a Communist.

"Here's what happened. Lionel was a Yale graduate, a member of an old Greenwich, Connecticut, family and a former Air Corps pilot with a distinguished war record. Except for the war years, he had been acting in Hollywood films continuously since 1931 and was a well-known and respected member of the movie world.

"The hearings were being held in Washington and many stars such as Humphrey Bogart, Lauren Bacall, Groucho Marx, Danny Kaye, and Ira Gershwin agreed to testify. Others like your friend Stander were subpoenaed and were presumably expected to expose their friends and coworkers.

"Well, when it finally came time for him to testify, the hearing room was packed with spectators and the press. Down the aisle he traipses with, on each arm, a gorgeous blond in a low-cut dress and mink, and the three of them take their seats right in front of the presiding congressmen.

"As you can imagine, the place goes crazy. Flash bulbs went off like popcorn and the audience went out of control. When the chairman finally restored order he asked Stander if he was represented by counsel and Stander rises to his full six foot four, looks all around the courtroom, and says in his unmistakable Brooklyn tough guy voice, 'Yeah, I'm represented by these two broads!'

"More pandemonium. By the time it is over he is cited for contempt of Congress and is added to the unofficial blacklist. Since that time he first worked in the family securities business in New York and then moved to Italy where he made a fortune in spaghetti Westerns (*Five Easy Pieces*, etc.). Because he spoke fluent Italian they didn't have to dub him. He could shoot it both ways himself.

"Recently, he moved back to Hollywood where he was married for the fifth time and decided to go back to work. I guess he figured all the HUAC bullshit had blown over but obviously it hasn't."

The agent concluded, "That's the whole story. We have no evidence that he was anything but a smart aleck to the HUAC and that pissed them off. They made him pay the price."

"Wow, what a story," I thought. "What a great guy, I can't let him get screwed."

I decided that the only way this was going to get resolved was by going to the top, or close to it, at P&G. I had my secretary call up Jack Hanley's office, the VP in charge of the soap division, and ask for a private meeting. This was unheard of because I was a lowly account executive and there were at least four levels at P&G and Burnett between Mr. Hanley and me.

The ending was really anticlimactic. I flew to Cincinnati, taxied to Sixth and Sycamore, and took the elevator to the executive floor, where I told my story to a fascinated senior executive.

All he said was, "OK, let's keep this between us. You go ahead and put the commercial back on the air and I'll take care of things at this end."

Little did he know that by doing so he was hastening the demise of Salvo and contributing to the biggest P&G new product disaster in history.

Many years later I ran into Lionel at the Principe Di Savoy in Milan and told him the story. He looked me up and down, tipped his glass of scotch in my direction and said in that wonderful voice of gravel, "Thanks, kid."

Alice Faye

During the 1960's one of my brand responsibilities for P&G was Lilt Home Permanents. Lilt alone among all the Procter brands had a unique media and copy strategy; all of its money was spent on "specials" and all of its commercials were done "live." Our media vehicles were restricted to the Oscars, the Emmys, Miss USA, and Miss Universe. The idea was to identify the brand with glamour and beauty. It worked and we rapidly overtook the "gold standard" of the industry—Toni. A by-product of this effort was that all of us involved (brand and agency) sort of ended up in "show business," an anathema in Cincinnati.

For the Academy Awards of 1963, the company elected to introduce a new Lilt product called Foam-in Lilt (instead of the waving lotion being applied to the rolled-up hair as a liquid, it was applied as a foam. This made for both a neater job and greater control of the quantity applied). In conjunction with R&D, we found that this product could produce both a "soft wave" as well as a "tight curl" depending on the mandrels used and the amount of lotion applied. Creatively, we decided to utilize a movie star with two grown daughters upon whom we could demonstrate the new product's unique flexibility.

Upon contacting our Hollywood office we found to our surprise that three recognizable stars did, in fact, have the requisite daughters: Betty Grable, Jeanne Crain, and Alice Faye. After being contacted by our West Coast people, only Alice Faye was willing to meet with me.

At the meeting, she showed me pictures of her two daughters; the oldest was Phyllis (named after her father Phil Harris), and the youngest, "little" Alice. They looked great! The problem was that Alice (the mother) didn't want to do the commercial. (In those days for a Hollywood star to "do commercials" wasn't considered proper.) She said she didn't need the $40,000 dollars we offered and didn't want to go back into show biz.

She had been the biggest female box office draw in the late forties but had been ostracized when she refused to make a picture she hated. She was the first "contract" star to challenge the studio system and they had to make an example of her. When they said, "You'll never work in this town again," they meant it.

I was desperate, so from somewhere I hit upon an idea.

"You may not need the money, but how about the girls?" I asked.

Pay dirt! Those great big blue eyes got even bigger.

"You mean we could pay them the money?" she asked with great interest. "Phil and I have been trying to help them out for years but they're so proud and stubborn, just like their father."

"Sure," I said. "We don't care how you split it up and we won't tell if you don't. Here's what we could do. We'll give each girl $19,000 and you can work for double scale (a union requirement).

And so I found myself visiting "little" Alice in Metairie, Louisiana, and Phyllis in Tucson, Arizona, to "negotiate" a deal, which had already been sealed by their mother.

A month or so later we all ended up in Hollywood to tape those sections of the commercial that would form the "B roll" (footage that would be inserted into the live sections the night of the Oscars).

The idea was that "big" Alice (not really, she was trim, slim, and gorgeous) would sweep down a circular staircase to the accompaniment of a voice-over announcer: "Ladies and gentleman it is my great pleasure to introduce the world famous star of stage, screen and radio, Miss Alice Faye." Her theme song, "You'll Never Know" (all stars of the forties had a theme song) would swell up in the background. She would then sweep up to the camera and say something like, "Hello, welcome to the Academy Awards of 1963. Tonight we are introducing a wonderful new product from Lilt..."

All was in readiness. Our director, Hal Tulchin, was a genius working with star talent. The set was fabulous and both the daughters had shown up. Alice was resplendent in her baby-blue gossamer gown. The only problem was that after she swept down the staircase, she looked into the camera with the Dan Quayle, startled deer in the headlights look, and went completely blank. Stage fright!

As blocked, the opening shot was the "master" and our intention was to do it all in one continuous take. For the next hour, over and over again, Alice would be introduced: "Ladies and gentleman, it is my great pleasure to introduce the world famous star of stage, screen, and radio, Miss Alice Faye"; the music would swell; she would "sweep" and then freeze without saying a word.

Tulchin and the client were going nuts. It was 11:00 and we had nothing "in the can." We had no idea what to do. Finally we took a break and Alice fled to her "leaning board." (I'd never seen one before. It is a slanted vertical board with arms so that she could lean against it and rest without wrinkling her gown.) The rest of us huddled trying to figure out a way out of this terrible, expensive predicament. Finally, Jay Levinson, the creative supervisor on the job, had an idea.

"When we go back to shoot, let me replace the voice-over announcer for the first take."

"What are you going to do?" I asked.

"Just leave it to me."

As we had little choice, we agreed.

Again, we lit up the staircase; Alice was positioned at the top, looking beautiful but nervous. The assistant director called for silence and "slated" the take (number 12 –UGH!!!), sound said "speed," and the video man said, "rolling."

Levinson took the mike and said, "Ladies and gentleman, it is my great pleasure to introduce the mother of "little" Alice and Phyllis, the wife of Phil Harris, famous bandleader, the "has-been" actress, Alice Faye."

Everyone on the set was horrified except Alice, who again swept up to the camera but this time delivered her lines flawlessly with great charm and warmth. Even though she did several more perfect takes with the "real" announcer, we ended up using the first one and dubbed in the correct audio. Alice was back; Jay had broken through and for the rest of the shoot, she never missed a "mark" or a line.

One night my wife and I, the client, Maurie Kelley, his wife, and several of the creative people decided to take Alice and her daughters out for dinner. We selected a Hollywood landmark and Alice's favorite, the Cave de Roi, a restaurant/supper club actually built underground with a large staircase leading down to the maitre d' station.

Our limo drove up and we all alighted, led by Alice. As we walked down the staircase (she swept) an unbelievable coincidence took place. The orchestra (yes, in those long ago days, restaurants actually had orchestras) began playing "You'll Never Know." The problem was that Alice thought it was in her honor and began regally waving to her nonexistent fans, who were busy dancing, talking, and eating. I don't think she noticed but the rest of us were mortified.

Later in the evening, we all took turns dancing with Alice. I was thrilled. Finally one of the young creative guys took a turn. He took

Alice in his arms and took the floor. After a few minutes my wife, Robbie, and I were horrified to hear him say, "Miss Faye, you'll never know what a thrill this is for me. My mother took me to see all your movies."

The final event of the shoot was the most critical—the live portion into which we would integrate the taped beginning and end. It was the famous Lilt "contemporaneous demonstration" wherein a home permanent would be given to each of the daughters, one soft and one tight. Throughout the show we would "check on them" and finally reveal the "fantastic" end results at the end of the show. The only problem was that no one really knew how the permanents would come out until they were rolled out. We were in the capable hands of our "world-famous hair stylist," Julius Caruso, who was a great hairdresser with one tragic flaw. He couldn't be counted on to pronounce "permanent" correctly. Half the time he would say "pernament." It was a TV version of Russian roulette.

The night of the Oscars was upon us and just as we were to go on air, Phyllis announced to her delighted mother that she was pregnant. Alice was thrilled; we were distraught. For physiological reasons beyond my skill level, home permanents do not take on pregnant women.

The only answer was to go on the air and take our chances. And so it happened that "little" Alice's end result shot was a gorgeous ECU (extreme close-up) and Phyllis' was from as far away as we could get the camera and still be on the set. I'm not sure anyone but the agency and the client ever knew the difference, but as usual it was the agency's fault. By the way, we got lucky with Julius and he pronounced "permanent" perfectly!

When the show was over and we all prepared to go our separate ways, Alice announced to one and all that she was hosting a "wrap party" at a restaurant across the street from the NBC Burbank studio we were using. She invited everyone, every grip, juicer, prop person, script girl, and editor, from top to bottom; a considerable number because of the complexity of this shoot.

It was a great party complete with champagne and wonderful food. Alice had put the whole thing together as a total surprise.

During the course of the party, I found myself standing next to a grizzled grip who had been everywhere and seen everything in his thirty years in Hollywood. He looked at Alice with tears in his eyes and said to me, "Son, believe me, these kid stars nowadays are real jerks. Miss Faye is a real star and they just don't make 'em like that anymore. She's a real class act."

And he was right. We lost Alice a few years ago, but I, and a lot of other people, will never forget her.

Miss Universe

One of the dubious advantages of being on the Lilt account was that every July 10th or so we would troop down to Miami Beach, take over the Jackie Gleason Theater, and supervise the production of live commercials for the Miss Universe Contest. These "epics" featured such "celebrities" as John Daly, Arlene Francis, Art Linkletter, Julius Caruso, self-described world-famous hairstylist, and others, including former Miss Universe contestants and winners.

Many wonderful stories came out of this particular event, but one that comes to mind took place after the telecast. One of the shady characters that hung around the Miss Universe show gave a party on his houseboat. Even in those days owners of fabulous "partyboats" moored them along Collins Avenue across from the "Gold Coast" hotels like the Fontainebleau where we were headquartered. The boat owner invited all of the local hangers-on, the members of the cast, and those of us in the account group and brand group.

I particularly remember standing next to Maurie Kelley (a highly respected member of the brand group and one of the "squarest" and nicest clients I'd ever had), as he was looking off at the lights of Miami Beach from the rail of the unbelievably expensive and well-outfitted houseboat. Next to him was an absolutely gorgeous woman in a gold lame bikini who appeared to me to be equally unbelievably expensive and well outfitted. She had certainly never made it in the Miss Universe competition but obviously was making money from her physical talents in Miami anyway.

Maurie, the straight arrow, was of course, immune to her obvious charms and, trying to be a nice fellow, struck up a conversation.

"What's your name?" he asked.

"Wanda," she said.

"Mine's Maurie."

"Oh," she replied turning to him.

"What do you do, Wanda?" asked Maurie.

The gorgeous scantily clad young woman put her arm around his neck and whispered, "Just about anything you want to do, Maurie."

The astonished P&G executive stammered, blushed pink, and beat a hasty retreat back to the relative safety of the Fontainebleau.

In the account group was a tall, dark, and handsome young account man named Jim Cone. As he both looked and carried himself like a movie star, we nicknamed him "Slick." Jim Hill, our boss and V.P. of client service frequently said he was too good-looking to be smart and that's why the client didn't trust him. To solve the perceived problem, Hill threatened to buy some plastic pimples and a saltshaker full of dandruff that we would apply to Cone before each meeting, thus assuring his credibility.

One year, after the Miss Universe contest telecast, CBS decided to throw a party for the cast, the talent, the agency, the producers, and all of the hangers-on. The show ended around eleven o'clock and after everyone removed their makeup and went back into the party, it was about midnight. The party ended around one-thirty.

As we walked into the lobby of the Fontainebleau after the celebration, there were fifteen or twenty LOL's (little old ladies), literally in tennis shoes, clutching pieces of paper and seeking autographs. First they clustered around Arlene Francis and got hers, then John Daly, then Jack Linkletter, even Julius Caruso. And then came Jim Cone.

I'll never forget the look on the face of the most aggressive of the LOL's when she turned to the tall, suntanned, attractive young man and said, "Excuse me, sir, are you somebody?"

Jim smiled wanly, looked a little bit sad, and said in his deep baritone, "No, I'm sorry, I'm not."

"I'm sorry too," she said and turned and walked away.

Slide Rules

This may be apocryphal, but it is a wonderful story.

So the story goes, it was the Christmas season and while P&G discourages any presents being given to their brand people, an enterprising young account executive at the Compton Agency found a special sale on slide rules, the wonderful Japanese-type with sixteen different indexes that came in a morocco-leather bound holster. (These were the days before calculators when anyone who was anyone had a monstrous slide rule, and those who were really serious carried the case on their belts. Today they carry pagers, cell phones, and Palm Pilots.)

At any rate, having bought these miraculous slide rules at a ridiculously low price, the generous agency man sent them to all of his friends in the brand groups. As the story goes, the P&G'ers received the presents warmly and proceeded to use them daily for the following month or so.

From January to March was the period of the most intense effort throughout the year. It was budget time; when no stone is left unturned. Reams of paper are generated and thousands of calculations are required. Obviously the owners of the newly gifted slide rules gave them a thorough workout.

Unfortunately, what they didn't know until it was too late was that the reason the gift provider got them so cheaply was that the super slide rules were "seconds." The Japanese had dumped them on the U.S. market because the index lines had been printed slightly out of scale. Had anyone bothered to check, they would have found that 2 times 2 equaled 4.136. Thus, all of the calculations for the budget presentations for the year 1961 by all of the brand groups that were given the slide rules were totally incorrect.

The question of the Compton man that never will be answered is, "What did he know, and when did he know it?"

Mr. McElroy in the Elevator

The headquarters of Procter & Gamble was in a large office building on the corner of Sixth and Sycamore. In the back was a fenced-in yard where the top executives parked their cars. In keeping with the tradition of the company, none of the major executives ever drove a car younger than three years to work, although we suspected that they all had brand-new Cadillacs at home that they drove on the weekend. The idea being that at heart they all were regular fellows.

The offices of the senior executives were on the sixth floor. Occasionally we would get glimpses of these captains of industry either coming or going from the office, although few agency executives ever visited this sanctum sanctorum.

One evening, I was leaving the building alone around 4:30 P.M. Despite the strong work ethic engendered by the company no one was allowed to work in the office past 5:00 P.M. Everyone took home huge bulging briefcases—called Procter bags—to show that they actually worked very hard at home. Maybe some of them really did.

As I entered the elevator on the fourth floor I found myself in the company of Mr. McElroy and several other young executives.

He looked around and said, "How about those Reds? What a game they had on Sunday. That new young rookie really knocked one out of the ballpark. Great game!"

Everyone agreed.

A few minutes later I was standing in the lobby waiting for the rain to let up with my dinner companion, the brand manager on Secret deodorant.

Mr. McElroy was obviously waiting out the rain too and stood several yards away. Suddenly, he was surrounded by another group of young executives of the same mind.

He turned to them and said, "How about those Reds? What a game they had on Sunday. That new young rookie really knocked one out of the ballpark. Great game!"

I suppose I shouldn't have been surprised that a company that issues "film breaking jokes" to be used when the projector in a sales meeting breaks down (as in "Gee, the film broke and while they're fixing it let me tell you a little joke") is certainly not going to leave their CEO speechless. Some secretary was clearly charged with the responsibility of developing and issuing him his daily dose of trivia.

Net, net leave nothing to chance.

The Goldfish Near-Pack

One of the promotion devices used by the Procter & Gamble Company for many of their products was what was commonly called a "near-pack." Instead of taping a premium on the package (a paring knife on a Joy liquid detergent bottle or a sachet on a bar of Camay) a near-pack allowed the company to offer much bigger and elaborate premiums. The way it worked was that the premiums were boxed separately and shipped along with specially labeled product. When a consumer picked up the product he or she could also take a free premium from the promotional display.

At Leo Burnett, we handled Jif Peanut Spread (not peanut butter, but that is another story). We found the near-pack to be a wonderful device because children who shopped with their mothers were always attracted by our displays. We had previously promoted Jif with kites, world maps, and beach balls. All had been smash hits. Now we were ready for our greatest promotion ever:

THE JIF FREE GOLDFISH PROMOTION

The promotion development department at Burnett along with their counterparts at P&G had arranged to purchase millions of goldfish in the Orient and have them bagged in plastic with sufficient food to last till they were purchased in the store. The display featured a huge blow-up plastic goldfish and slots for the bags of goldfish. As with all P&G efforts the goldfish near-pack had been thoroughly tested with wonderful results.

Clearly, the success of the promotion depended on exquisite timing. The sales force had to handle the sell-in. The company had to ship the specially labeled jars of Jif and the premium supplier had to ship the goldfish; they all had to arrive at the store at the same time. Next the promotion advertising had to hit the air and we were off to the races.

Unfortunately, Mother Nature interfered with our delicate timing. While the product and goldfish for the West Coast arrived on time, all the goldfish for the Midwest and East Coast were concentrated on several rail cars. These rail cars became stranded in the worst autumn snowstorm to hit the prairie states. Packed in the unheated cars the millions of goldfish were frozen solid and P&G became the proud owners of untold numbers of glacial, dead fish.

Back at the agency, we received a frantic phone call from the brand group. Whenever anything went horribly wrong, the agency was always called in the hope that somehow we could be found culpable or at least share the blame.

After the initial shock of picturing railroad cars filled to overflowing with frozen, dead goldfish we naturally went in to a damage control mode.

I called the creative director on the business, Jay Levinson (now famous for his twenty-nine books on Guerrilla Marketing and Guerrilla everything else).

"What the hell do you think we can do? We've already produced the commercial and sold in the product," I said.

Without missing a beat, he replied, "I've got it. It's quite simple; we'll just re-shoot the commercial and call it "THE JIF FREE FROZEN PAPERWEIGHT PROMOTION."

I didn't bother to share this inspiration with the client. We later learned that the millions of goldfish were shoveled into a landfill before they thawed out and began to smell.

I don't remember P&G using any near-packs after that.

Lava Jet Mechanic

One of the most successful campaigns for a low-budget product was produced by Leo Burnett for P&G's Lava soap. The product was a hardmilled handsoap containing pumice. It was designed to do the really hard jobs of handwashing and was extremely popular in the "smokestack" states and rural areas.

The basic premise of the commercial series was to open on an exciting shot of a rugged, hardworking blue-collar man working at his job (among others, workers in steel mills, construction sites and farms had been used); dissolve to him just finishing as the off-camera voice says, "These are the hands of Sam Smith, steel mill foreman" (cut to a tight shot of really dirty hands). Off-camera voice: "How do you get those hands clean?" Cut to Sam Smith washing with Lava and getting hands really clean. "There's only one way, mister, Lava Soap." Smith holds up clean hands and Lava bar (go to black).

Over the life of this campaign it became increasingly difficult to continue to come up with attractive real people who had exciting and photogenic jobs. We were really up against it to come up with a new idea.

Finally, the production and casting people told us that they had a real winner, a great-looking guy who was a jet mechanic. Wow! This was great. The opening shot would be of him working in a hangar on a huge jet engine with all the accompanying whining noises and great video. Then he would climb down the ladder from the engine as the announcer said, "These are the hands of Joe Charles, jet mechanic, etc."

The commercial was written, storyboarded, approved by the client, and produced. It was the best ever and set a new standard for Lava on the Burke test (the noting and awareness technique used by P&G at that time).

As with all commercials, this one had to be submitted to network "standards and practices" in order to ensure that we were abiding by the standards of truth in advertising. It cleared without any problem.

Only later did I discover that the whole commercial was a fake!

In fact, Joe was a mechanic all right but he worked on bicycles. It happened his full name was Joe Charles Jet. Thus the actual script submitted to S&P at the networks read,

"These are the hands of Joe Charles Jet, mechanic" but nobody noticed the literally true punctuation and the commercial ran a full cycle.

I'm quite sure P&G didn't know either.

The Conference Room Floorstand

Procter & Gamble, as everyone knows, is a highly proceduralized, highly stratified company that goes by the book. Frankly, it makes the U.S. Navy look like a Chinese fire drill.

One day we were sitting in one of the client's conference rooms waiting, as we always did, for the brand group or the copy section to show up. In the corner of the room stood an old life-size Miss Universe floorstand featuring the reigning queen in her jeweled tiara. For some reason she was holding her hand in the air like the statue of liberty and overlooked a large bin in front of her where the Lilt bottles or packages would be displayed. The floorstand had obviously been left over from a promotion meeting and was soon to be thrown out.

The presentation we were to make was for some long forgotten copy in which a fake canary was used as a prop. After the meeting, as we were packing up, someone had the brainstorm to wire the fake canary to the upraised hand of the soon to be discarded Miss Universe floorstand and append a note that said, "Do not remove."

The *piece de resistance* was to invoke the potential wrath of the Gods by signing the note "MPL" which stood for M. Peter Link,[4] then one of the three group product managers responsible for all of the P&G soap division brands. Few ranked higher in the P&G pantheon.

To my certain knowledge, that floorstand and its fake canary remained untouched in that conference room for at least three months.

---

[4] Tragically, Pete and his wife Liz were killed a year later in a Lockheed Electra crash at the Cincinnati Airport.

P&G Urinals

During the 1960's and 1970's P&G was consistently number one on the *Fortune Magazine* list of "most admired companies." The company came in first in every category from working environment to financial results. To those of us who either worked directly for the company or, in my case, dealt with them on a daily basis, the reason for their outstanding success was obvious.

They had a tried and tested procedure for every function within the company. The sales manual covered every possible exigency. The marketing documentation was no less complete. Nothing was ever left to chance. The expression "maximum flexibility within firmly fixed boundaries" was never truer than when applied to P&G's modus operandi.

One illustration, of course, was the previously mentioned "approved" jokes to be told when the film broke during a sales meeting. The sales V.P. literally had to approve the humor to which his sales people could conceivably be exposed.

Another example of how the "Procter way" manifested itself was in corporate maintenance. Whenever one light blew out in any office or on a factory floor, all the bulbs were changed. Efficiency studies had revealed that it was cheaper to change all the bulbs at once rather than wait until they blew out one at a time.

The most egregious instance of corporate oversight occurred one day when I visited the men's room on the fifth floor of the headquarters building at Sixth and Sycamore. Hanging across the first urinal in the row was a chain with an attached sign stating "Out of Order." I remarked to Bob Hanslip that it seemed odd that a company so detail oriented wouldn't have fixed this particular toilet. After all, it had been out of order for the last few days.

"Oh, it's not really out of order," he said.

"Well, then why the hell do they have a sign saying it is?" I asked.

"Here's how it works," he said. "Every urinal has a little counter attached to the back of the flush handle. Some guy from building maintenance checks the counters every month or so. Because this particular urinal is first in the row it gets the most usage. When it gets way ahead of the others in flushes, he shuts it down till the others catch up. That way they all get even wear."

To this day I'm not sure Bob wasn't, pardon the expression, "pulling my chain."

G. Gordon Rothrock

G. Gordon Rothrock defined the expression "contradiction in terms." He was born and raised on a farm outside of Bismarck, North Dakota. After service in WWII as an enlisted man, he attended Northwestern University on a baseball scholarship and played minor league baseball during the summer. Subsequently, he joined the Leo Burnett Company and rose rapidly through the ranks to become Vice President of Client Service for the P&G group.

The contradiction was that to all intents and purposes Gordon appeared to be either a scion of an old Eastern, Ivy League family or a member of the English nobility. His dress, carriage, and deportment all marked him as someone of the landed gentry.

One time we were having an extremely contentious meeting in Cincinnati. Neither side was willing to budge from their strongly held positions. As noon approached the senior "Procter" looked at his watch and in keeping with the hallowed tradition of P&G said, "Well, it's about that time. Why don't we all go to lunch at Pigalle." Pigalle was the finest and most expensive French restaurant in town. Lunch there was reserved for the most difficult meetings. "And, we'll pick up where we left off afterwards."

At this point, Gordon rose from his chair, dramatically looked from one end of the conference room table to the other, and said in his deep, stentorian voice, "Thank you so much, but the agency chooses to dine alone." I didn't know whether to laugh or not, but he was serious and we ended up in the company "mess hall."

On another occasion (this story is from my friend Art Hohmann), Gordon, who had just been promoted to his position, having replaced the much loved Don Wells, called an "all hands" meeting in his office. It was just after all the client service personnel had returned from the annual P&G Sales Meeting.

"It has come to my attention," Gordon intoned, "that some of the P&G brand people were taken out and supplied with young ladies of the evening." (Yes, he really called them that instead of hookers.) "Let me make it quite clear that Burnett does not condone such actions. The first person that does this gets fired. Have I made myself understood?"

At this point, Art got up to leave the room and as he reached the door, said over his shoulder, "This meeting doesn't concern me. I was the *second* guy to buy them broads!"

A few years later, Gordon received the dream assignment. He was sent to London to open the U.K. branch of Leo Burnett. For him, he was returning to his homeland and birthright. He immediately became more British than the Queen. He bought a bowler and several black wool suits, carried a furled umbrella, and read the *Guardian*.

In addition within weeks his speech was peppered with "bloody," "the loo," "the lift," "Bob's your uncle," "old love," etc. He even joined an exclusive English club, the Oriental. It was located just down the street from our office and he could be found there every day lunching at the Club table and after work drinking Sun Downers, bemoaning the loss of the "Empire."

Upon his return to Chicago three years later, Gordon stayed in the mold. Each morning he stood wistfully on the Northwestern Railway platform in Winnetka clad in his black suit, bowler hat, and furled umbrella with his airmail copy of the *Manchester Guardian* under his arm.

The old ways died hard.

Dear Mom

The copy presentation system at P&G in the sixties and seventies and, for all I know to this day, was repetitive, tedious, and boring.

In each and every instance, the agency presented to increasingly smaller groups that had increasingly greater responsibility and authority (see Jim Hill—Bluebird, Swimming Pool, and Sports Equipment) until at last, if you were lucky, you got to the grand high poobah himself. He, while not exactly having the power of life and death, came close to it. He could kill a campaign with a comment. Down the drain went months' worth of time, money and effort on both the agency and client side. Young "Procters'" careers could be immeasurably damaged if he or she sponsored too many ads or campaigns that were subsequently found wanting.

Thus whenever an agency's copy worked itself up to the final approval stage the tension was palpable. Someone would say, "Well, I think we're ready to call in Mr. Artzt." His nickname among the brand and agency types was "The Prince of Darkness." Palms sweated, throats dried, knees weakened.

Not only was he enigmatic, mercurial, and unpredictable, but he had some rather odd meeting room habits as well.

In the first place, regardless of how much advance warning he had of the meeting, he was invariably at least a half hour late (shades of our ex-president).

Secondly, he always entered the room carrying four or five huge ring binders, which must have contained the history of the brand back to Harley Procter.

Lastly, after the agency presentation, he would silently sit at his place at the end of the table, take out his "Procter pad" (a brown five-by-seven leather binder emblazoned with the P&G emblem of the moon and stars, and the owner's name) and write, pause, think, write, pause, think for what seemed an eternity. No one was allowed to speak during this aggravating and demeaning ritual.

At one such meeting, we were again sitting quietly while the great man wrote a line, stared into space, made another note, and stared into space. This time it seemed to go on even longer than usual.

Finally, Jim Hill could take it no longer and said, "Dear Mom, I'm sitting here in a copy meeting. All the other people think I'm writing comments about the advertising, but I thought I'd drop you a line."

The room erupted in stifled laughter and repressed giggles. I don't remember if we sold the copy or not—I suspect not.

It didn't change Ed Artzt's habits one bit.

Cleo Hovel

One of the delights of being in the agency business was the wonderful collection of characters with whom I was fortunate enough to work. One of these was the multi-talented writer, art director, and raconteur, Cleo Hovel.

Cleo was one of those people who thought with his hands. As he developed an idea he constantly doodled with a ballpoint pen on any paper that happened to be available. It is rumored that he created the now famous Charlie the Tuna advertising campaign on the back of a cocktail napkin while sitting at the bar in the United Air Lines Red Carpet Room at Kennedy Airport.

His office was filled with sketches and half completed storyboards. His industrial size wastebasket always overflowed with discarded ideas and partially competed drawings and notes.

Like many of the Burnett personnel who were somewhat senior to me, Cleo had served in the Armed Forces during World War II. As a result he was required to wear hearing aids in both ears. It was his practice to turn them off when set upon by eager account executives who, in their zeal, "had helped [him] quite enough."

One day we were riding in to work on the Northwestern when I asked him if he had seen the current epic movie "*D-Day, the Sixth of June.*"

"No," he said, "I saw it live."

And so he had. He had been a teenaged coxswain on an LCI (landing craft infantry) and had helped put the first wave of invading troops ashore on Omaha Beach. He had made hundreds of trips to and from that beach carrying fresh troops in and the wounded back to the ships sitting off shore. His reward, aside from his medals, was the hearing aids necessitated by eardrums burst by the incessant bombardment.

Cleo was also the consummate presenter. His sketch style was not only captivating but incredibly effective as well. Typically he would stand up in front of the client with a blank 20 by 30 inch sketchpad on an easel. He would then proceed to take the assembled throng though the "thought process" that led to the finished commercial, all the while drawing out the idea on the pad with magic markers. We

76

viewed the process as a cross between a football coach's chalk talk and a nightclub hypnotist's act.

The fact was, of course, that most of the time he reverse engineered the whole thing. In other words he and his people would somehow develop a commercial and then he would figure out how to best use his unusual technique to sell it to the client.

One time I was in a desperate situation with one of my P&G brands, Ice Blue Secret Deodorant. We had been using the same campaign for several years and it was working well. It was a continuing "slice of life" approach featuring our heroine, Katy Winters.

Various people would approach her with their problems:

A librarian – "Oh, Katy I'm so worried about, you know, offending. What should I do?"

A Nurse – "Oh, Katy I'm so worried about, you know, offending. What should I do"?

Katy naturally saved the day by suggesting Ice Blue Secret. In fact, by the third year she had saved from "offending" most of the female population of the fictitious city in which she lived

That was our problem. While Katy was still selling product, the client was worried about the "wear-out" factor and was beating us about the head and ears to come up with a "back-up" campaign. We had been struggling mightily with this problem but to date had been unable to develop anything acceptable. The pressure was becoming unbearable. I appealed to Draper Daniels, the copy chief, for temporary help from one of his other creative groups on the basis that the regularly assigned people were burned out.

He responded by giving me Cleo for a couple weeks. Cleo immediately came up with a couple of commercials. I thought they were at best mediocre but I was desperate and decided to let him try them out on the client.

The presentation was unlike anything they had ever seen. Cleo set up his easel, took out his multi-colored magic markers and said, "Let's talk about armpits." He then proceeded to weave his web and draw his pictures. When he had finished forty-five minutes later he had sold them on producing three commercials, which I thought were not only sort of dumb and but also totally unlikely to score on the Burke scale.

My worst fears were realized. We produced the commercials and they dropped without a ripple through the Burke process. Hardly anyone remembered seeing them, let alone what they said.

The next day I received a phone call from John Smale, then toilet goods division manager and eventual CEO and Chairman of P&G, and later Non-executive Chairman of General Motors.

"Wally, John Smale." This was a rather rare occurrence. John usually left agency calls to the associate promotion manager, in this case Maurie Kelley. "You didn't do very well on those Secret back-ups did you?"

Why was it always "you" when they bombed and "we" when they succeeded? I thought, and then I remembered, hey, this is the agency business, that's the way it is.

"Yes, they didn't do very well, did they?" I responded. "But we've got Cleo and his people working on some new ones and we should be back to the brand group in less than a week." That should handle things, I thought.

"I see," Smale said. "That's really the reason I'm calling you. We don't think Cleo should work on our business anymore and I wanted to tell you personally."

I was shocked. Short of statutory rape or drunkenness in the conference room, I didn't think anyone had ever been "asked off the business." I couldn't imagine what he had done.

"Gee, John, that's pretty severe. What did he do?" I asked.

"Well," Smale replied, "it's not exactly what he did and yet in some ways it is."

Now I was really confused so for once I shut up and listened.

"The problem is that Cleo is such a great presenter that the son of a bitch could present the Cincinnati Yellow Pages and our people would buy it and shoot it. He can sell anything and we can't tell the difference between the good and the bad. We just can't have him coming down here and presenting, it will cost us a fortune. You keep him in Chicago."

And so Cleo Hovel was forever banned from the dubious pleasure of presenting advertising to P&G.

Believe me, many of his associates wished they had his gift and subsequent punishment.

Traveling with David

One of the most unforgettable characters from my P&G days was a wonderful sales and promotion development executive named David Murphy (the real name has been changed to protect the not so innocent). David had the gift of gab as well as dark brooding good looks. He was also a fine athlete, a moderately good piano player and an indefatigable companion who could stay up all night "shooting out the lights" and still be the first in the dining room for breakfast.

One of his most famous escapades occurred on a store check in Phoenix. David decided that we should stay at the Camelback Inn in Scottsdale. (With my relatively unlimited expense account and his restricted one we made ends meet.) I thought his selection was rather odd in that we were only going to be in town for one night and one day. Why stay at such a fancy resort when we had to "hit the bricks" as soon as the stores opened?

After a long night of drinking and bar crawling, we nonetheless met for breakfast at eight o'clock. As usual, Murphy was waiting for me.

"Let's split up so we can cover more stores and still get back here for a quick swim before we go on to L.A.," he said. "You go ahead and take the car. I'll have the hotel get one for me after breakfast. I have a few calls to make anyway."

Dutifully, I acquiesced. The client/agency relationship is, after all, best characterized as that of master and slave. I got out my map of Phoenix on which I had previously marked the major supermarkets and said, "OK. I'll take the northern and western stores and you take the southern and eastern ones." He quickly agreed.

For the next six hours I drove to and fro in the hundred plus degree weather. I'd park my car, walk through the baked parking lots into the freezing stores, count displays, record prices and "deals," and try to get some disinterested cretin of a stock boy to talk to me about shelf movement.

When I returned to the hotel I was soaking wet, exhausted, and convinced I had incipient pneumonia. I stopped at the front desk and asked if Mr. Murphy had returned his car yet.

"Mr. Murphy didn't take a car, Mr. Bregman. He's been out at the pool all day. We plugged in a phone for him in his cabana and except for his lunch, he's been either in the water or on the phone."

In his cabana! I'm picking melted asphalt off my shoes and spending my day talking to the Clearasil poster boys and he's on the phone in his cabana!

Without even taking off my jacket, I rushed out to the pool. There was Murphy sitting under an umbrella with some girl in a bathing suit sipping an "umbrella" drink.

He was on the phone but generously waved me to a seat next to him under the umbrella. He covered the mouthpiece and said, sotto voce, "Want a drink?"

Then he continued his conversation. "OK, that's fine, now go back to the shelf and write down the pricing for all the SKU's (stock keeping units) of Lilt and Toni, and don't forget to check for any shelf or end-aisle displays. When you come back on the phone bring the movement book with you so you can give me the sales for each of the brands."

The son of a bitch was conducting a store check from the goddamned pool! I didn't know whether to be awed or pissed.

When he finished he said, "How many stores did you hit, I got twenty-four." I had "hit" eighteen and it was a struggle.

"How the hell did you do that?" I asked.

"Well, after you left I got the Yellow Pages from my room, had a phone plugged in out here, and started calling. I'd get the store manager on the line and tell him I was calling from Cincinnati on an emergency assignment and desperately needed his help. Naturally it didn't work every time but it did about half the time. So I called about fifty stores. Sheila here has been helping me keep track of the results."

The "umbrella" girl smiled sweetly.

What a guy!

David Murphy also fancied himself to be quite a lady's man and used every bit of his skill to make his conquests easier. For example, when he left Cincinnati for the "Coast" he was always attired in the standard P&G uniform: dark suit, small pattern tie, white button-down shirt, and black wing-tip shoes.

However, as soon as the plane was airborne he would repair to the lavatory with his overnight bag and shortly emerge as a new man.

From the dark sunglasses to the unbuttoned silk shirt and gold chains, to the bellbottom trousers (after all this was the 1960's) and sockless loafers he had shed the role of mild-mannered David Murphy and become the fabulous "Hollywood Man."

On one such trip, I was his seatmate and saw him eagerly peering under the seat in front of us at the American Airlines employee I.D. tag on a cosmetic bag that was stored there.

"Watch this," he said as he slipped by me and leaned forward to talk to the attractive off-duty stewardess occupying the aisle seat.

"Let me guess," he said, "I'll bet your name is Noel and that you were born on Christmas Day."

The pretty woman looked up at Mr. Hollywood, smiled sweetly, and said, "Well, you're half right, sporty. My name *is* Noel, but I wasn't born on Christmas Day. My father's name was Leon and he wanted a boy named after him. Now please sit down and leave me alone, I've heard your dumb pick-up line at least fifty times."

I'd like to say that this exchange made a lasting impression on Murphy, but it didn't!

The Swimming Pool

My boss at Burnett for five years was James R. "Jim" Hill. He was in my opinion the funniest man I have ever met. Not only could he tell any type of joke perfectly, but, more importantly, he had the fastest, natural wit I have ever encountered. And, like all of us at that time, he was probably slightly mad.

One of his great gifts was to see humor in the most difficult situations. When we were in our most depressed state, Jim could always be counted on to come up with the perfect *bon mot,* simile, analogy, or metaphor.

One of the most frequent causes of our mutual frustration was the endless and debilitating process of presenting advertising to P&G. In each situation, we would have to explain an ad or campaign to an increasingly larger group almost always consisting of functionaries who could say "no" but, until top man concurred, could not definitely say "yes."

After one particularly difficult day, we were all sitting around a table at the bar in the Cincinnati airport bemoaning our fate to the accompaniment of several straight ups.

Jim finally looked around and said, "You know what today was like?" We knew what was coming so we waited.

"It's as if they had this great big swimming pool surrounded with seats. The copy section guys sit in the seats and bring with them bags filled with little rocks. The agency guys get in a canoe and slowly start to paddle from one end of the pool to the other.

"As we paddle they throw the rocks into the canoe and we try to throw them out. If we throw enough rocks out and don't sink before we get to the end of the pool we get to compete again. Then the brand group comes in.

"There are fewer of them but the rocks are bigger. We go through the same process, paddling and throwing rocks over the sides. If we succeed again the managers of the copy section and the brand group come in. They only have one rock each but it is really huge. It is so big that they don't even have to make a direct hit to sink the canoe. A near miss will still swamp you. If you get to the end this time without drowning you win.

"Today we just took on too many rocks!"

We all nodded agreement and signaled for another round.

The Bluebird

One night we were again ensconced in the Cincinnati airport bar, again licking our wounds, and again bemoaning our fate.

In our thoughts, our counterparts on the Marlboro business were probably sitting in Goldie's laughing and scratching after a wonderful day at 100 Park Avenue (Philip Morris headquarters) being told for the hundredth time how great the Marlboro Man was and how smart the agency was.

Instead, we had a big black presentation bag full of rejected storyboards and one ad that had been changed so many times by the client as to be unrecognizable from the original submission.

Jim Hill saved the day with a metaphor.

"It's as if we walked in today with this beautiful little bluebird and showed it to them. 'How do you like our bluebird?' we'd ask.

"'Boy, that is some great-looking bluebird,' they'd respond. 'And the agency is to be complimented for bringing it to us.' (The P&G formbook required that any criticism be preceded by a compliment. Jim said it reminded him of his great-aunt who always warmed the water before drowning her kittens.)

"The client would continue, 'We have only one little thought, perhaps if the tail was a little longer it would work better.'

"'OK,' we'd say, figuring that wasn't much of a problem.

"'And maybe the wings could be a little shorter.'

"'OK. No big deal,' we'd reply, desperate to make a sale.

"'And the beak sharper and longer...and the feet bigger...and the head smaller and rounder...'

"'OK,' we'd agree, figuring it can't go on forever, but it does.

"Finally it does end and they say, 'That was really a productive meeting, I think we've accomplished a great deal. Now let's see it fly.'

"I take the bluebird in my hand, launch him into the air and it proceeds to drop to the floor like a stone, roll over once, and die.

"The last comment from the brand manager is, 'Hey, your bird's no good, it can't fly. And you know something, I never really liked that shade of blue in the first place but the agency was so set on it, I just went along.'"

Again, another round of drinks was forthcoming.

The Sports Equipment

As mentioned earlier, the bane of our existence at P&G was the head of the copy section, Ed Artzt. He was an extremely bright man who would go on to become the president and CEO of P&G in later years. But he was also extremely difficult to deal with as he had a capricious personality and would frequently throw us a curve.

On one occasion, after a particularly difficult meeting with him, Jim Hill came up with another of his wonderful metaphors.

What actually happened was that we were prepared to discuss a particular piece of copy on a particular strategy when Mr. Artzt decided, on his own, to go off in an entirely different direction.

We were again sitting in the bar at the airport when Jim came up with a new analogy.

"Imagine that we are sitting back in Chicago and we received a phone call from Mr. Artzt. He says, 'How would you guys like to come down to Cincinnati and have a nice game of baseball with us?'

"We say, 'Fine, we'll get our bats, balls, bases, and uniforms and be on the next plane down.'

"Well, we show up at the field all dressed up in our uniforms. We take fielding practice. We take batting practice. And we're all set for the big game.

"All of a sudden their team shows up but they're dressed in football uniforms and Mr. Artzt says, 'It's such a nice fall day, I thought it would be better if we played football!'

"Well, that's what happened to us today. We showed up ready to play baseball but he decided to play football, and as you know "a fact is an opinion held by the client."

Another lesson learned.

The Little Dog

One evening, Jim Hill had consumed several of the "white ones" at the Gibraltar Room in the Prudential Building and then a few more on the train to Hubbard Woods. As his wife and children were at their summer place in Michigan, he was "batching it." He poured himself one more martini before dinner and sat down to read the paper.

His house was a lovely wooden colonial on a shaded street close to the sidewalk. It had a large porch, which overlooked the street and led to the front door. The houses in this suburb of Chicago, while large and sumptuous, were placed on rather small lots; thus the neighbors' houses were quite close on both sides.

On one side was a neighbor who had a small, yappy dog. This particular dog aggravated Jim mightily and he had a continuing discussion with his neighbor about the dog's nocturnal yapping. The dog also had a habit of pushing open the screen door, standing in the Hills' entrance hall, and continuing his yapping. Jim's wife and children thought it was sort of cute but it made Jim furious.

This evening, the dog was out in front of Jim's porch yapping away as usual. As he continued Jim became more and more disturbed. Then the dog walked up the steps and across the porch all the while continuing his yapping. Jim decided to do something about it and in his inebriated condition prepared to settle with the dog once and for all.

In the living room, in front of the fireplace, the Hills had a bearskin rug, which Jim had inherited from one of his relatives. As the dog approached the screen door, Jim crawled under the rug and snuck up to the door between the entrance hall and the living room. As the dog pushed open the screen door and walked into the entrance hall, Jim reared up in the bearskin rug and let out a mighty roar.

The dog was terrified. It jumped up in the air, started to whirlwind its tiny feet to escape, and collapsed into a small bundle of fur on the entrance hall floor; dead of a massive heart attack.

Instantly sober, Jim quickly shed the bearskin rug and faced a dismal prospect. He had to go next door to his neighbor and explain that he had just killed his dog by "putting him on."

According to Jim this is exactly what he did, although I always suspected that he just dropped the dog off on the neighbors' lawn and ran like hell.

Discretion being the better part of valor.

The Squawk Box

In the early sixties when the telephone squawk box was being introduced, the office manager at the Leo Burnett Company, a man by the name of Ted Mendl, had one. He used it unmercifully. He would call any one of us at any time of the day and announce over his speakerphone, "This is Mendl." He then proceeded to complain about the amount of trash in our wastebaskets, the paper clips we were using, the number of black pencils we had taken from supply, the lights being left on in our offices, and so on.

Jim Hill and the office manager had had a running gun battle for years. It climaxed when Mendl installed his squawk box. Almost every day he called Jim on it, which for some reason enraged him. Finally one day Jim had had enough, and the next time Mendl called, Jim picked up his phone and answered, as all Burnett employees did, by giving his name. "Jim Hill," he said.

On came the squawk box at the other end saying, "This is Mendl." Jim said, "Hello, hello."

"This is Mendl." A little louder.

"Hello, hello," said Jim. "I guess no one's there," and he hung up... waiting.

Of course, thirty seconds later the phone rang again. The same thing happened. "Jim Hill," he said.

"This is Mendl" was announced via the squawk box.

"Hello," Jim said. "God damn it, something's wrong with this telephone. Someone keeps calling me and hangs up."

This happened three more times, whereupon Jim dialed the office manager and said, "Ted, there's something wrong with my phone. It keeps ringing, and no one's at the other end."

Mendl never again called Jim Hill using his squawk box.

The Fountain

Our offices on the southern side of the Prudential Building overlooked Grant Park in which was situated Chicago's pride and joy, the Buckingham Fountain. This fountain was turned on every morning precisely at ten o'clock by the City Works Department. One day one of the new P&G brand managers came to meet Jim Hill in his office, which, as befitting a V.P. and account supervisor, overlooked the park and the fountain.

The meeting started around a quarter of ten. At about five minutes of ten, this being his first trip to Chicago, the visitor stood looking out the window at the spectacular view.

Jim said, "See that fountain out there?"

"Gee, it's really beautiful. I've heard about it," Jim's guest said.

"Oh, really?" said Jim. (It was now four minutes of ten.) "Would you like to see it in action?"

"Are you kidding? Of course I would, it's really supposed to be spectacular."

"Well," he said, "that's no problem." He walked behind his desk, and *not* pressing down a button on his phone, picked it up and said, "Get me Mayor Daley." He waited a few seconds (it was now three minutes to ten) and said, "Dick? Jim. How are you?"

Another pause. "We're fine."

Stage wait. "How's your family?"

"Good...Terrific...You're right, it's been too long."

"Say, Dick, I've got a new client here from Cincinnati...Yeah, that's right, our Procter & Gamble client." (One minute to ten.) "You know, I wonder if you would mind turning the fountain on for him...You will? Aw, gee, that would be terrific, Dick." (Thirty seconds to go.) "Say, listen, Dick, I really appreciate it, and I know the fellow here will appreciate it...You're going to throw the switch right now? Fine! We're going to walk over and look out the window." (Ten seconds to go.) "Okay, Dick. We'll look and thanks a lot." (One second to go.)

Bingo! Bango! Ten o'clock and the fountain erupted. The client was floored.

"Wonderful, Dick. It looks terrific!" Jim said into the phone. "Anything I can do for you at the Leo Burnett Company, just let us know. Bye, Dick."

That night a very impressionable young brand manager returned to Cincinnati.

Goldfish Drink

One night as we sat at the bar in the Terrace Hilton, Jim Hill turned to the bartender and said, after I'd ordered my usual martini, "Oh, I don't feel like a martini tonight. Give me a Goldfish."

I didn't say anything, assuming it was some sort of arcane drink that only account supervisors drank. The bartender replied smartly, "Right, Mr. Hill, one Goldfish coming up."

Jim turned to me, winked, and said, "Watch this."

The bartender left his usual position and walked over to the other bartender and whispered something. The other bartender went to the third bartender and whispered something, and then the three of them went behind the bar and pulled out the ever-present *Seagram's Bartending Guide* and studiously leafed through it.

I asked Jim what was going on. He smiled and said, "For the hell of it, I just ordered a nonexistent drink to see how they'd react."

The bartender came over, turned to Jim, and said, "Gee, Mr. Hill, I must have made gallons of Goldfish in my time but I just can't seem to remember how to make them anymore."

Jim, without missing a beat, said, "Oh, it's very simple. It's just a martini straight up with an orange peel instead of a lemon peel." He obviously had invented this drink some time before and was waiting for the right occasion to introduce it.

The next time we came into the bar and sat down, the bartender came up to Jim and asked, "Your usual, Mr. Hill, a Goldfish? All the ad guys are drinking them. They are really very popular here now."

Ironically, years later there now is a drink called a Goldfish, which is vodka on the rocks with an orange peel. As far as I know, the only bar in the world that served the "famous" Goldfish in the 1960's was the Terrace Hilton Bar in Cincinnati.

S Sargeul B

The guiding principle behind staffing on the Procter & Gamble business was that we at the agency manned them (and I mean man—until the mid-sixties) on a one-for one-basis.

Further, we were trained to consider ourselves an extension of the brand group and hence equally responsible for all facets of the product; not limited to the normal agency areas of copy and media.

It was therefore not unusual for us to visit the various research centers located around Cincinnati when a product-related issue was being considered.

On one occasion, my account group and I were invited to the Winton Hill Technical Center where all product research for the toilet goods division was conducted. The particular project under consideration was a new fragrance for a Secret Deodorant line extension.

We had been going around and around with the technical people for weeks and had rejected all their offerings to date. This day they again presented their previous offerings: Summer Straw, Bluegrass, Ocean Mist, and Desert Rose. Again, after endless discussions and "sniffings," the agency and the brand group were totally confused. There was no clear winner and we had unanimously concluded that more work had to be done.

At this point the head R&D guy stood up and said, "OK, we really didn't want to have to use this one because we were saving it for another project, but we have to resolve this problem." He turned to his assistant and said with resignation, "Go into my lab and bring out the S Sargeul B sample."

The assistant shook his head but followed orders and soon appeared with a flask labeled "S Sargeul B – Secret" (that should have been the tip-off).

We sniffed it and to a man (again a man) were convinced that this was the answer to our prayers. It was perfect. We thanked the research types and departed. Another job well done.

On the way home on the plane, the Secret assistant account executive was writing up the meeting report and asked how to spell S Sargeul B. I told him and a few minutes later he said, "Those sons of bitches."

"What are you talking about?" I asked.

"They blew one by us. S Sargeul B is goddamn "bluegrass" spelled backwards. We just picked a perfume we've been sniffing and rejecting for three weeks."

And so it was.

Who ever said research guys don't have a sense of humor?

The Casting Book

In the early 1960's, the Leo Burnett agency maintained a Los Angeles office in the Capitol Records Building in Hollywood (the one that looks like a stack of records). It was from this facility that the agency did all of its West Coast TV commercial and program production.

Typically, agency account and creative people would meet their client counterparts for pre-production meetings at which all aspects of the commercial(s) were discussed. Not the least of the important items covered was casting. In those days it was not unusual to hold what was commonly called a "cattle call" (open casting). The part was posted with various agencies and all interested parties would show up.

On one occasion, I attended one of the sessions with my P&G client for an Ice Blue Secret commercial. There were about ten of us, all men, sitting in the agency's large conference room reviewing and sorting "head shots" of various young girls in order to winnow the group down to a small selection who would then do a reading.

We finally selected seven or eight actresses and began the torturous process of listening to them read the script with one of our production people.

After we had reviewed four candidates and rated them, the fifth appeared carrying large portfolio type book under her arm. She proceeded to read for the part and was absolutely dreadful.

Our producer began to politely give her the standard, "Very nice, don't call us we'll call you" routine, when she interrupted and said, "But you haven't looked at my portfolio yet."

He countered with, "That's all right, we don't have to see it."

After a little more back and forth, it became clear that she wasn't going to leave until we saw her book. The producer acquiesced and began to leaf through her scrapbook. It was obvious from his expression that this was no ordinary scrapbook. When he passed it to me, I knew why. It was totally filled with pornographic pictures of the young actress in many, many different poses.

Our P&G clients were equally shocked, but it didn't stop them from reviewing the book thoroughly.

Finally the P&G producer, Bob Roberts, turned to the girl rather sternly and said, "Has this book ever been responsible for you getting a part?"

"Oh no," she replied. "But I've sold fifteen of them so far."

Ain't show biz great!

Kimball Piano Factory Fire

In the 1960's, whenever advertising agencies visited Procter & Gamble at their 6th and Sycamore headquarters it was *de rigueur* to stay at the Terrace Hilton three blocks from the P&G building.

The TH was a rather unique structure as the first five floors were devoted to parking and offices, the hotel itself beginning with the reception area and restaurants on the sixth floor.

As the building was probably twenty stories tall, the rooms all had spectacular views of downtown Cincinnati and the Ohio River (in rereading I realize that the foregoing is probably an exaggeration, if not an oxymoron).

Because all of us spent between at least two or three days a week at the TH, we were well known to the staff from the bell caps to the manager and, in fact, had reserved tables in the dining room for breakfast: Burnett at one table, Y&R at another, Tatham-Laird at a third, and so forth.

One night we flew into Cincinnati on a late plane from Chicago (a Lockheed Electra, flown by American) and took a cab to the TH. Among others accompanying me on that particular trip was an account executive in my toiletries group named Tom Brennan. Tom stood about six foot two, was solidly built, and wore the map of Ireland on his face. Despite the fact that he worked on Ice Blue Secret, a lady's deodorant, he was the supreme macho male.

As usual, our arrival was accompanied by the standard obsequious greetings: "Oh, Mr. Bregman, how good to have you back," etc. And, even though we all traveled light and had been to the hotel dozens of times, it was SOP that a bell "boy" accompany us to our rooms. Tom was assigned a bellman named Roy, who we had all agreed, was probably gay, although that specific expression would not emerge for many years to come.

At the same time we were checking in, a major fire was in progress; the world famous Kimball piano factory was going up in flames not far from the TH.

When Tom and Roy reached Tom's room, Roy went through the usual procedure of turning on the air conditioning and opening the drapes. There, directly out his window was an eagle's eye view of the fire. Tom, not being able to identify the Kimball factory said,

"Where's the fire, Roy?" whereupon Roy plaintively replied, "In your eyes, Mr. Brennan."

This may have been the first time in recorded history that Tom Brennan was speechless.

The Bus Station

At one point in 1965, the Burnett Agency was asked to compete for a major slice of the Alberto-Culver account headquartered in Melrose Park, a western suburb of Chicago. While the account was large, there were problems. It was rumored that the company was skating on thin ice financially and that the owner, Leonard Lavin, was an impossible client to work with and for. (He was thought to be as bad as Ernest Gallo, a current client, but more about both gentlemen later.)

Notwithstanding all of the above, it was decided to compete for this account but only if the competition involved a marketing problem, not a creative one. The powers that be concluded that we could more readily divert marketing talent than creative time and thus I was chosen.

Sometime earlier I had explained to management (Ed Thiel) that I was "proctered-up"; after six years of nonstop Procter & Gamble doctrine, I was ready for a change. They reluctantly agreed and put me on the "repo depot" list (those available for a new assignment if it came up).

For the purposes of the A-C new business pitch I was to work with Marty Snitzer, a Philip Morris account supervisor, and we were to report to Len Mathews, the senior VP to whom marketing and media reported.

The project was to develop a unique media allocation and schedule for a brand of hair coloring called "Tresemme." We had exactly three days to do it while handling our own work at the same time. What we ended up with was a proprietary multiple regression analysis that had to be hand done on a Frieden calculator; naturally there were no computers to crunch the numbers.

Initially, it looked like we could conclude our calculations and make up the charts in time for the 9:00 A.M. presentation on Wednesday. The problem occurred when, just as we were finishing on Tuesday afternoon, I got a call from Seymour Banks of the media research department. He explained that he had just received new data on many of the magazines we were using for our reach and frequency calculations. All our work so far had to redone. If we had had a Lotus or Excel spreadsheet program it would have taken a half an hour. As it was, it was time for an "all-nighter." It may come as a shock to the latter day young lawyers and investment bankers that they didn't invent the term.

We repaired to Len Mathews' office, which was on the fifteenth floor in what was known as "fishnet row." The offices for the highest level of management, except Leo, Dick, and Bill, who had corners, were aligned along the south wall of the Prudential Building overlooking Grant Park. They were large and elegant with an all glass north wall opening onto the corridor. This wall was covered with a semi-opaque large weave curtain—thus "fishnet row."

We were using Len's office because it was big enough to accommodate our charts while at the same time it had a couch on which to catch a catnap. We toiled throughout the night sustained by pizza and hot coffee as we corrected our charts with multicolored magic markers. Len had gone home but came in at around six to go over our work.

By about eight Marty and I were totally out of gas; we still wore our clothes from the day before, we hadn't shaved, and we were as disheveled as it was possible to be. But we were proud that we had brought the project in on time.

At this point, General Bill Young arrived on the floor. He was an immaculate dresser who had all his clothes tailored by Sulka. This day he was wearing gray slacks, a blue cashmere blazer (he was the only one in the company who didn't wear a suit to the office), a light blue button shirt, and a matching repp tie and pocket square.

When he looked into Mathews' office he saw me slumped on the couch with my feet spread out in front of me, Marty collapsed in a chair, and the office strewn with paper pizza plates, half-filled coffee cups and, yes, ashtrays overflowing with butts.

He swept the room with an imperious glare and, without missing a beat, said in his southern drawl, "Jesus Christ, this place is getting to look more like a Greyhound bus station every day," and walked on.

Postscript: The presentation was a smash. We were offered a major portion of the account, but after reflection Dick Heath convinced Leo to turn it down on the basis that if Culver's financial base was as weak as rumored (Lavin would not answer questions about it) it could ruin us. As it turned out, McCann-Ericson took the account and successfully handled it until it was offered to me ten years later when I was president of Norman, Craig & Kummel.

Corporate Budgeting

My first assignment in account work was as the account executive on Camay for Procter & Gamble-Canada. During this period, I was introduced to the vagaries and intricacies of corporate budgeting. It seems that, based on the table of organization and equipment which P&G scrupulously followed, the Canadian company was not authorized their own aircraft; nonetheless, they had one.

The way this remarkable feat was achieved was simplicity itself. In the budgeting line items that were submitted each year to the accounting department in Cincinnati, the Canadian company had, for years, been listing an item called "ULO." No place in their budgeting did there appear a corporate aircraft.

Apparently, this item had been carried for so long that no one at the home office wanted to demonstrate his or her ignorance by asking what it was. And so it happened that the wily Canucks' corporate aircraft was cleverly disguised and hidden in the annual budget as "Unidentified Leased Object."

And thus, Procter & Gamble-Canada had a corporate aircraft for its President. It should be pointed out here that at the time, the president, Mr. George Williams, was, in fact, Neil McElroy's brother-in-law, but this has nothing to do with the story. It is merely an item of incidental interest.

Long live corporate accounting practices!

Expense Accounts

Probably no single item in the advertising workplace created more anxiety and controversy than the expense account. Because travel and entertainment was a way of life in the agency business, we were constantly filling out expense account reports and arguing about them with our bosses or worse, the accounting department.

As Marty Snitzer, one of my contemporaries at Leo Burnett, said, "Someday I hope to be paid enough to live as well at home as I do on the road." Filling out expense accounts became a profit center for some. My friend and boss, Art Hohmann, and I always played a game when we traveled together. He would pick up the check and say, "There's a number on the bottom of the check, odd or even. The winner gets the receipt and the loser pays the check!"

I

A small but important account handled by the Leo Burnett agency was the Tea Council. While the administrative office was in New York, the council basically represented tea growers from all over the world, and its avowed purpose was to increase the consumption of tea. Once a year the council met in New York for their annual meeting. This was a rather lavish affair and it was incumbent upon the agency to entertain the various Tea Council members. One year after a rather lengthy and expansive meeting the account supervisor returned to Chicago visibly shaken. He had apparently picked up the tab at a number of cocktail parties and dinners and found himself with a horrendous bill. It was clear to him that there was no way the accounting department was going to honor this incredibly large expense account.

He was shared his tale of woe with one of the other account supervisors, who offered a solution.

"How much do you say that bill was for?"

"It's around $1,700," the depressed Tea Council man answered.

"Well then put it in your expense account for $17,000."

"How the hell will that do any good?" he asked.

"It's very simple. When Jerry Ziegler (the hated accounting department manager) gets hold of your expense account he'll go crazy. He'll call you up and ask you if you are out of your mind turning in a $17,000 expense account for one week. You'll answer, 'Jerry, oops, there's been a horrible mistake, it must be my new secretary, my expense account was only $1,700.' He'll be so relieved that he'll approve it in a minute. Just don't try this more than once."

And you know something, it worked—once!

II

In the U.K. in the sixties, under the labor government, taxes were incredibly onerous. As a result, most executives of British companies relied heavily on their expense accounts and "perks" to make up the difference between the wage they should be making and the one they actually were.

Cars, club memberships, flats, and even clothes were often rented or bought by companies and given to the executives in lieu of wages and, of course, were not taxable. Lavish expense accounts were quite naturally another means of "making a person well." As in all situations like this, there was always someone who took advantage of the system. In our company, it was the Director of Client Service, a rather dashing divorced man who had quite a way with the ladies.

As managing director it was my job to approve his expense accounts, but as a "new boy" to the U.K. and the company I felt it proper to go easy. I therefore looked them over, but not as closely as I might have if I had been on more solid ground.

After four or five months, I felt more secure and began to scrutinize them a little closer. Other than the usual "padding" which I expected, I saw what was a reoccurring entry—one that had been present on every single report of his I had seen. It was "C.O.T.B." and varied from twenty to fifty pounds on each submission. I supposed it to be some kind of U.K. tax or levy. Finally, he resigned to join a competitor and in our last meeting, I figured my ignorance could have no effect on our relationship.

"Now that you're leaving Peter, will you tell me what in heavens name is this expense entry 'C.O.T.B.'?" I asked.

"Didn't you know, old boy," he replied with a wink. "It stands for "care of the body" and since I've been at Burnett I've had a jolly good time with ladies."

I didn't bother to warn the guys at Bates, his new company. I figured they could find out for themselves.

III

The Lilt account at Leo Burnett had a strategy of utilizing only "specials" for its advertising exposure (see Alice Faye). One of these events was the Miss Universe Show, broadcast from Miami Beach each July. Because the commercials were all produced "live" with amateur talent and because they had to be integrated into a live broadcast, it was necessary for a number of both agency and client personnel to travel to Florida and supervise the production. (Why else would anyone go to Miami Beach in July?)

The agency team consisted of Jay Levinson, a copywriter at the time; his boss, Bob Edens, the copy supervisor; several account executives; and myself, the account supervisor. In addition we had several brand, copy section, and production people from P&G and the contract director, Hal Tulchin and his retinue; in all about ten people.

As it was Levinson's first Miss Universe, we decided to play a little joke on him. As soon as we had signed in at the Fontainebleau Hotel, I found out his room number and passed this information on to our entire group. From that moment forward and until we checked out seven days later, we signed every single charge at the hotel to room 714, Levinson's room—every drink, every meal, every car park ticket, even the cabana we rented to have our meetings.

When we checked out everyone but Levinson had a bill for seven nights at the corporate rate plus charges for telephone calls and laundry (we couldn't figure out how to put these on Jay's room).

Jay on the other hand had an enormous bill that was at least two inches thick. (In those days, before computers, one received copies of all the checks they had signed attached to their bill). Being a creative person and not versed in the ways of finance, Levinson simply signed the bill, took his copy, and flew back to Chicago. When the master account billing landed on the much-feared Jerry Ziegler's desk all hell broke loose.

"How in the hell could you run up a bill like this in a week?" Ziegler thundered over the phone. "You apparently parked three cars a day, ate meals in all the restaurants, and had enough drinks to float a battleship not to mention your cabana and room service."

Slowly, awareness dawned. "None of the other people there ate or drank a thing. You, my friend, have been the victim of a cruel joke. From now on watch what you sign and what other people sign in your name."

Jay took this message to heart and the next year passed around the room number of Rod Stevens, the newest writer on the job.

The World's Worst Shoe Salesman

One of the most important accounts at the Leo Burnett Co. was The Brown Shoe Co. The account was important not only because of its prestigious name but also because it was one of the first accounts with which Leo had started the agency. It was located in St. Louis, Missouri, and required visits by account and media people on a regular basis.

On one of these occasions, a young media buyer by the name of Harry "The Hat" Madison (not his real name) had occasion to visit the client in order to present media plans for the upcoming year.

As it was only an overnight stay he brought with him a limited amount of necessary clothing and toilet articles. He arrived just after dinner and checked into the hotel. With nothing better to do he decided to visit some of the "watering spots" of St. Louis. After a number of drinks, he found himself in a bar talking to a lady who, in his degraded condition, he found to be quite attractive. One thing led to another and Harry found himself back in her apartment. According to his retelling of the story, he remembered nothing more until he awoke very early in the morning, stark naked in bed with a rather elderly and unattractive woman (she had looked pretty good the night before, he said).

He was beside himself. First of all, he had no idea where he was. Second, he had great trouble finding his clothes, and third he didn't want to wake up his hostess before he left. With considerable effort, he was able to locate his suit, underwear, shirt, and socks, but no amount of searching turned up his shoes. After a thorough re-inspection, he decided discretion was the better part of valor and very quietly left the apartment in his stocking feet.

His next project was getting back to the hotel. Not knowing where he was, he had to stand in the street at five o'clock in the morning and wait for a cab. Fortunately, a cruising yellow passed by within a few minutes and took him to the hotel. He then showered, shaved, and put on his clean shirt. Unfortunately, as this was only an overnight trip, he had not brought a spare pair of shoes. But he was in luck. The hotel was one of the old-fashioned ones that had a shopping area on the first floor with many different stores. Harry called the front desk and asked if they had a shoe store in the hotel and was delighted to find out that, in fact, they did.

"What time do they open?" he asked.

"They open at nine o'clock," the desk clerk replied.

Harry was delighted; his meeting was at nine-thirty and the Brown Shoe office was located rather close to the hotel. He could go downstairs, buy the shoes, and be at the meeting on time.

At precisely nine Harry presented himself at the hotel shoe store just as they were opening. The owner, seeing his first customer arrive in his stocking feet, decided to turn this sale over to his assistant, figuring that it shouldn't be too challenging to sell shoes to a man who isn't wearing any.

Harry sat down and asked for pair of brown wing tips in a particular style. He naturally followed the Burnett tradition and asked for Brown Shoes, his client's product. To his considerable displeasure he found that they did not carry the Brown Shoe products.

He abruptly rose and told the owner that because they didn't carry Brown Shoe products he would have to go elsewhere. This he did. Fortunately he found the shoes he wanted a few blocks from the hotel. As he told the story, the store was close enough so he didn't wear out his socks and he was able to show up at the client meeting properly shod.

There is no record of what happened to the unfortunate young salesman, but we believe the owner suggested that he pursue a career in some field less challenging than shoe retailing.

The Green Giant Contest

Of the many devices companies use to increase sales, one of them is "the contest." The Leo Burnett Co. had a fine promotion development department specifically charged with the task of, among other things, developing such contests.

Many of these contests involved rather elaborate artwork and copy which, of course, required art directors, copywriters, and lawyers. Always the lawyers!

One of the contests we developed was for the Green Giant Company. As I recall, it involved asking the customer to look at a large elaborate illustration which contained numerous little Green Giants distributed throughout (similar to the *Where's Waldo?* children's books). The contest was fully developed to include point of purchase material, special labels for the cans and, of course, final artwork to run in *Look, Life,* and many other large circulation magazines.

Everything was in readiness—the artwork had gone through final proof and the client had approved all the elements of the promotion. Unfortunately, one of the lawyers decided that there was something not quite kosher about the promotion and at the last minute the entire program was postponed.

Prior to the lawyer's intervention the agency had arranged with the Donnelley Company to handle the receipt and judging of the entries. Naturally with the delay of the program there would be no entries. At least that's what we thought.

A few days after the postponement, the account supervisor on Green Giant received a phone call from Donnelley. The caller announced that he had just received an entry to the contest. Not only had he received an entry, but it was a winner. Incredibly, the person who entered the contest had a perfect score.

"That's impossible," replied the astounded account supervisor. "We canceled the contest, we pulled the artwork from the publications, and none of them ever published the ad for the contest."

"Well that very well may be," replied the man from Donnelley, "but I've got an entry right here on my desk in four color and all the answers are perfect. By the way, it is a little strange, there's nothing printed on the other side of the contest ad and it's on sort of heavy paper."

When the account supervisor found out who had filled out the contest submission everything became clear. One of the art directors whose avarice clearly exceeded his intelligence had actually submitted an entry to the contest using a final press proof. Naturally, when the contest was canceled his entry was the only submission.

Not only was he greedy, but stupid as well, and that turned out to be a very bad combination.

Halloween in Lake Bluff

It may seem that many of the stories on these pages have a great deal to do with drinking. The simple fact is that during the period about which I'm writing drinking, unfortunately, played a major role in our lives. Unlike today, almost all of us had a drink or two at lunch, a drink after work, perhaps one or two on the train going home, and maybe one before dinner. I know this sounds unbelievable, but it is true.

Some of the biggest drinkers at the time were the media representatives. They were the fellows who sold time or space to the advertising agencies. Part of their stock in trade was to entertain the buyers for lunch, after work, or for dinner. One of the best at his job lived in the suburb of Lake Bluff, a very nice community on Lake Michigan about forty miles north of Chicago.

One Halloween, our hero returned home from the wars having had his usual complement of martinis. Because his wife had a meeting to attend and it was quite dark on trick-or-treat night, she asked him if he would take the children from house to house. He decided it was a very good idea but that he had to go in costume. As his mother-in-law was living with them and was a rather large woman, he had no trouble borrowing a long green ball gown, high heels, and tiara. He also borrowed his wife's wig (all the women were wearing them in those days) and amply made up his face with her makeup.

With his children in tow, he proceeded to visit all the neighbors, carrying a martini glass in his hand. While the children begged for candy and treats, he solicited for yet another martini. Everything proceeded smoothly as he went from house to house until he reached the home of one of his friends. Unfortunately, this particular friend had himself been imbibing to no small extent and thought it would be funny to play a joke on the "trick-or-treater."

After the "lady" in the green dress left, he called the local police and said, "I am a concerned citizen living on such and such street. I just looked out the window and saw what appeared to be a female impersonator walking down the street amongst a bunch of children. I think it's terrible and I think you ought to do something about it." He then hung up.

Shortly thereafter a police car appeared and pulled up to the curb next to where the media rep in the green grass was standing. Unfortunately, by this time, he'd had much too much to drink and became belligerent when the police stopped him for questioning. In fact, he took a swing at one of the officers and was promptly cuffed and hustled away in the police car, to the great alarm of his children.

After cooling off a while at the station, he told police that the whole thing was a terrible misunderstanding and could all be explained if only they would call his friend who lived in the last house he called on. When the police called the friend, who probably had had another drink or two since making his phone call, he denied all knowledge of the situation, apparently thinking his friend was trying to get back on his practical joke with one of his own.

Eventually everything was straightened out but the story had a very serious ending. When the "impersonator" came up in front of the judge at his hearing, the judge didn't think the story was very funny. In fact, he threw the book at him saying, "You people who commute in and out of our community and make the big salaries have got to take responsibility for your actions. There is never an excuse for drinking too much and attacking a police officer." The perpetrator was given a very heavy fine, many, many hours of community service, and a suspended sentence.

Needless to say he never talked to his neighbor again.

The Santa Fe Media Presentation

One of the most competitive aspects of local TV is the fight to sell sponsorships of the evening news. It is the highest rated local programming and usually the bell cow for the hometown media reps. The rivalry is particularly fierce to sell important resident corporations.

In Chicago in the sixties there were four TV stations: WGN-TV, WBKB-TV, WMAQ-TV, and WBBM-TV. When it became known that Burnett's client, the Santa Fe Railway, was in the market to use TV for the first time and to sponsor an evening newscast on "stripped basis" (all five nights a week), the sales reps for the stations engaged in a feeding frenzy. Each one labored to develop a reason beyond price why the A&T&SF would profit the most from sponsoring their news.

Elaborate presentations were developed by all four stations and scheduled to be presented in sequence to the Santa Fe and Leo Burnett personnel. Critical to the success in this encounter was the need to differentiate one's station from all the others. One station relied on its on-camera talent and sold hard on their strength and believability which would rub off onto Santa Fe. Another claimed a stronger signal which would not only reach "Chicagoland" but into areas in Indiana and Wisconsin as a free bonus.

The most memorable performance, however, was given by a station whose motto was "gets the news first and gets it to you first." This station had very identifiable couriers on motorcycles who whisked news film to the studio where it was processed in "state of the art" labs and put on the air before their competition. To prove the point, they scheduled their presentation at 4:30 P.M. with the plan of going through the obligatory background material first. Then, as their grand finale, a uniformed motorcycle courier would burst into the conference room with the film for that afternoon's news show. The station's team would string up the waiting Bell and Howell projector and *voila*, a "scoop" for the station and another victory for Yankee ingenuity and old-fashioned showmanship.

Everything went off like clockwork. The skilled presenter timed his routine to the second. Just as he finished his pitch on how his station always had the news first and was the first to broadcast it to its waiting audience, the courier arrived with the 16-millimeter film of breaking news. While it was being threaded the station manager built to his climax.

"And here is what all of Chicago's TV news audience will see this evening from the station that "gets the news first and gets it to you first," he proudly boasted. "Roll the film!"

When the screen lit up, the waiting audience was greeted with a shot of one of the station's news reporters standing in a cornfield who said portentously, "Behind me is the twisted wreckage of seven freight cars of the Santa Fe Railroad that were derailed just a short time ago. Fortunately, there was no loss of life; however, hundreds of pigs have escaped..."

By the time the shattered media exec had stopped the projector all the Santa Fe people were out of the room.

The station did not make the sale!

Upside Down Reading

Marty Snitzer was one of the brightest, most aggressive account executives at the Leo Burnett Company (see Bus Station). He had risen rapidly through the client service ranks from the P&G group to become the account executive on the agency's premiere account, Marlboro.

Marty had all the attributes of a great account man. He was smart, quick on his feet, a good presenter, and an excellent salesman. He could also read upside down. This particular talent stood him in good stead when he was in a client meeting and was able to read comments the clients wrote down as they viewed a presentation. He was thus able to prepare responses before the questions were asked. A neat trick.

Unfortunately for Marty, his little trick infuriated his boss, Owen Smith, who was V.P. of Client Service for the entire Philip Morris group. It drove him crazy to know that Marty could stand in front of him and surreptitiously read the memos in his "in" box as well as any other items on his desk.

Finally, when he couldn't stand it any longer, Owen hatched a plot. He called his secretary in and dictated the following memo:

CONFIDENTIAL

> *To: Owen Smith*
> *From: Leo Burnett*
> *Re: Marty Snitzer*

> *As we have discussed many times we have to do something about Marty Snitzer. I agree with you that the situation is very serious. I thought our last conversation was quite productive and hope we can come to a conclusion at our next meeting.*
> > *Leo*

He then had the memo typed, signed it "Leo" in green ink (Leo's trademark), and put it conspicuously in the "in" box on his desk.

Shortly thereafter, as was his practice, Marty strolled in and, as usual, glanced at the letter tray. According to Owen, Marty was, for the first time ever, speechless. His eyes popped open, but of course, he couldn't say anything. Delicious revenge.

Owen stirred the pot for a week by continuing the fake correspondence. He dictated replies from him to Leo. Marty was also adept at reading typescript off of a secretary's typewriter.

Finally, Marty could contain himself no longer and confronted his boss. He confessed that he had been "reading his mail" and just had to know what was going on.

Owen owned up to the "gag" and said he hoped that would cure Marty of his irritating habit.

It didn't.

Rosie

Marty Snitzer (see previous anecdote) had a very attractive wife named Rosalie. At one point, Marty was invited to represent the Leo Burnett Company by attending the 4 A's (American Association of Advertising Agencies) meeting at the Greenbrier resort in White Sulphur Springs, West Virginia.

It was a great honor and naturally they were both quite excited. Rosalie spent days putting together her wardrobe, mixing and matching to get just the right ensembles for the many activities.

Finally, the big day arrived and they traveled down to West Virginia and checked in at the world-famous resort. The first event was the standard "Welcoming Cocktail Party." As this was billed as informal, Marty chose a pair of gray flannels and an open shirt with a blue blazer. Rosalie wore a simple skirt and her favorite blouse of white silk with her nickname, "Rosie," tastefully appliquéd over the right breast.

Everything went beautifully for the first hour until one of the attendees, who had obviously been heavily imbibing the complimentary cocktails, walked up to her and closely examined her chest.

"OK," he slurred, "now I know the right one's name, what's the name of the left one?"

Marty later told me that Rosalie never wore that blouse again.

Ratner's Rats

There was something about the bar at the Cincinnati airport after a client meeting that was conducive to strange behavior. Maybe it was the release of tension after hours of pressure or maybe it was the double martinis served in brandy snifters. Whatever the cause, odd and wonderful things happened in these confines.

Perhaps the oddest was the Ratner Rat caper. One night a fairly large group of "Burnetters" were sitting around waiting for our delayed Delta flight and taking full advantage of the airport's "buy two get one free" martini special. We were at our usual large round table on the second floor by the window that allowed us to see the planes land. Thus, we could order a round when our plane was on approach and still not miss the flight.

Suddenly, a large airport tractor crossed the taxiway in front of us pulling two huge trailers stacked high with large aluminum shipping crates, on each of which was emblazoned:

RATNER'S RATS – THE WORLD'S BEST LABORATORY RATS

Jim Hill took one look and said, "OK, you smart agency types. There's a great new business opportunity for us. Those guys obviously need a new agency. We need to come up with a slogan better than 'The World's Best Laboratory Rats.'"

"You're absolutely right," Jay Levinson said immediately. "How about, 'I'd walk a mile for a Ratner Rat?'[5]

"Not bad," said Tom Hall. "But I like 'Gee, Dad it's a Ratner Rat.'"[6]

"Or," I replied, "'If you can find a better rat, buy it.'"[7]

"How about, 'Ho, Ho, from the land of the Jolly Green Rat,'"[8] chimed in Tom Brennan, mimicking a hugely successful Burnett campaign.

"Here's one," said Peter Husting, the Salvo account executive. "'The quality goes in before the rat does.'"[9]

---

[5] Camel Cigarettes
[6] Wurlitzer Organs
[7] I.W. Harper Bourbon
[8] Green Giant Foods

Bob Edens, our creative group head, added, "You guys are getting too complicated, keep it simple. 'Ratner Rats because....'"[10]

"I don't know, I like something with a little more human appeal like, "Try the friendly rats of Ratner,'"[11] added Mike Miles who one day would become the chairman and CEO of Philip Morris, Inc.

"We could also come up with a symbol for the company, say 'The Ratner Rat boy,'"[12] said Jim Hill.

"What do you think of, 'They laughed when I sat down with my Ratner Rat,'"[13] Levinson shot back.

"I'm thinking of a quality strategy," added Jack Stafford, who would become chairman and CEO of Pillsbury. "Like, 'When you care enough to test with the very best—Ratner's Rats.'"[14]

And so it went through another round of "white ones" till Art Hohmann said, "I think we should take the snob approach with something like, 'Ratner—The rats of the stars.'"[15]

And that ended the discussion because they finally announced our plane.

* * *

I had pretty much forgotten this incident until a year ago when my wife and I took our two sons and their wives on a cruise of the Greek Islands. Somehow, I brought the subject up over cocktails and my daughter-in-law, Trish, became the all-time champion of the Ratner Rat ad campaign development program with:

"Ratner Rats—the Other White Meat."[16]

---

[9] General Electric
[10] Modess Sanitary Napkins
[11] United Airlines
[12] Pillsbury Mills
[13] Steinway Pianos
[14] Hallmark Greeting Cards
[15] Eastern Airlines
[16] The Pork Association

Playboy Magazine

In the late 1950's the Leo Burnett Company had just about completed one of the greatest brand makeovers in the history of advertising. The brand was, of course, Marlboro. Today it stands as the foundation upon which the hugely successful Philip Morris company was built. Their subsequent acquisitions of General Foods, Kraft Foods, and Miller Brewing were truly fueled by the incredible success of "Big Red." The billions of dollars generated by the "Marlboro Man," the Marlboro song, the unique box packaging, and "Filter, Flavor, Flip Top Box" all stemmed from the creative and marketing minds at the Burnett Agency.

When LBCO (the Leo Burnett Co.) was assigned Marlboro the brand was best known for its effete packaging, ivory filter, and a major share of the male homosexual market. The package, product, and above all the Burnett advertising strategy was designed to make a 180-degree turn and create *the* manliest, macho, tough guy brand in town. Certainly the original "tattoo" and subsequent cowboy campaigns did just that.

For those of us in the media department (I was a spacebuyer on the Philip Morris account at the time), the challenge was to fit our media plan and execution into the same demographics as the creative. We wanted to target men between the ages of nineteen and forty-five with emphasis on the younger age groups—those with less well established buying habits.

TV was easy (yes, we could still run cigarette TV ads in those days). Sports—football, Friday night fights, baseball. etc. Action Westerns—"Gunsmoke," "Wyatt Earp." Cop shows—"Dragnet," "Michael Gunn." For print we, of course, used *Sports Illustrated* and other sports-related magazines.

At the same time that Burnett was doing the Marlboro makeover another phenomenon was taking place in Chicago. A minister's son named Hugh Hefner was publishing a new kind of men's magazine that not only showed gorgeous naked women but also included high-class story content by well-known authors.

The fact that the *Playboy* readership was perfect for Marlboro was not lost on the aggressive space salesmen from *Playboy*. At this point in the magazine's development, their ad revenue lagged their newsstand and subscription sales dollars because large national advertisers were afraid to take a chance. *Playboy* needed to get that "first olive out of the bottle" and decided that Marlboro was their best chance.

First, we were bombarded with invitations to the Chicago Playboy Mansion to meet "Hef" and his "friends"; next, we were offered unbelievable "loss leader" deals to get us in the book. They offered us the end rate and a backcover for the price of a B/W page. After a lot of soul searching and conversations with the client we decided that it was an offer we couldn't refuse. (At that time, the future CEO and chairman of Philip Morris, Hamish Maxwell, was in charge of their media department.) We all knew it was right for the brand and we had made a terrific deal.

Our elation was short-lived. It lasted only until the first issue was published. The geniuses at *Playboy*, in their zeal to impress Philip Morris, had sent complimentary copies of the magazine to all the executives. When Mrs. Cullman (wife of the then chairman and CEO) removed her copy from its plain brown envelope and saw the Marlboro Man on the back cover and a naked Janet Pilgrim on the front cover, she reached for the phone just before the smelling salts and called her husband.

Mr. Cullman's first act was to get Leo on the phone. As excrement rolls downhill, Leo called us in the media department and we were on the phone to *Playboy* in minutes. We cancelled all future insertions.

It would be quite a few years before Marlboro again graced the pages of *Playboy*.

The Comedy Routine

Every summer when we lived in Chicago and I worked at Leo Burnett, my wife took the children to the "Cape" to visit her parents. I would usually take a vacation and join them for a week or so, but during the intervening period I was a "bachelor." I typically filled the time by working late, eating downtown, and then driving back to our house in the northern suburbs.

On one occasion, Tom Hall, one of my fellow timebuyers, who was a *real* bachelor, invited me to go with him to a cocktail (read "beer") party at a friend's apartment on the near north side. As I was clearly not on the prowl for female companionship I asked him what the particular attraction was to this party.

"Well," he said, "I'm not quite sure but I understand that there is going to be a guy there that has a pretty funny comedy routine and he wants to try it out on a bunch of people. Besides, the beer's free."

After working till the requisite 7:00 P.M. (if you worked till 7:00 P.M. you received $3.00 for "dinner money") Tom and I drove in my VW bus over to the apartment where the party was being held. When we entered the room it was crowded with about twenty-five young men and women about our age most of whom were somehow involved in the advertising/media business.

As we sipped our beer I noticed a rather nondescript, balding guy with wire rimmed glasses whom I had never seen before. He seemed to be setting up an old Webcor tape recorder in one corner of the room.

A few minutes later, a fellow who I assumed to be our host put two fingers to his lips and blew a tremendous whistle. The room immediately grew quiet.

"Hey folks," he said, "thanks for coming. I hope you all have enough beer. I've got a real treat for you. Some of you know Bob from Arthur Andersen." (So that's why he looks like an accountant, I thought, he *is* an accountant.) "Well, he has a couple of routines he'd like you to hear—here's Bob."

With that, Bob, instead of getting up in the middle of the room and doing his "stand-up" routine, took out a secretary's shorthand notebook and sat down next to the tape recorder. Then, he turned on the machine and we were treated to the funniest half-hour of comedy I have ever heard.

As we giggled, chortled, guffawed, and cried with laughter, Bob sat calmly in the corner quietly taking notes. Not surprising, I thought, after all he is a goddamned accountant.

What we heard was the first public performance of the now famous "Abraham Lincoln and the PR Man," "Abner Doubleday Explains Baseball," "The Wright Brothers' Passenger Airline," "Sir Walter Raleigh Introduces Tobacco," plus several others.

The nondescript accountant was, of course, Bob Newhart. He was playing the tapes and taking notes, he later told us over a beer, in order to tighten up his monologues. He was listening for when and where the laughs occurred in order to eliminate the lines that didn't work and space out the ones that did work, so the jokes didn't "step on each other."

When he was finished with his methodical approach to polishing his routines, he had the closest thing to perfection there was in stand-up comedy.

Shortly thereafter Bob was booked into the original Playboy Club, situated about two blocks from where I first heard him. He was an overnight local sensation but the subsequent release of his first album, "The Button-Down Mind of Bob Newhart" and an appearance on "The Ed Sullivan Show" made him a national phenomenon.

To this day, I can't watch "Newhart" on TV without remembering Bob, the self-effacing balding accountant and his beat-up tape recorder and shorthand notebook.

Shipping Tape Heads

In the early days of taped TV, the technology was obviously quite primitive. The only equipment that was available was a two-inch Ampex tape deck onto which content was recorded, edited, and played back. Actual editing was done the old-fashioned way, with a razor blade and scotch tape. When a program or commercial was completed, the finished tape was shipped along with the specific tape heads on which it was recorded to wherever it was to be played back and/or broadcast. The heads were not interchangeable. Playback on any but the original tape heads resulted in zigzag video lines and audio "hash."

On one occasion, we had just completed taping a very important Lilt commercial in Chicago and had to get it to New York for a network telecast. After the client and agency had "signed off," the producer called down to the mailroom and asked for someone who could a) be sent to New York on an important assignment and b) be trusted to follow instructions to the letter.

Soon an earnest young man appeared and reported that he was to be the messenger. It was, after all, a good deal for him. He was getting an all-expense paid trip to New York and all he had to do was deliver the tape and tape heads to our production office.

"I want you to know," the producer started out, "that this is a very important delivery that you have to make. This taped commercial cost twenty thousand dollars" (a lot of money in 1963) "and it is irreplaceable."

This was true. We could make dupes of the original but in those days the "generation loss" between the original and the copies made the latter unusable for broadcast purposes.

"Further, these tape heads are critical for the proper playback of the tape. You must deliver the total package (tapes and tape heads) to our office first thing tomorrow morning. Here are your tickets. Take a cab out to O'Hare and don't let this box out of your sight."

At this point, he handed the by now thoroughly frightened young man a sealed cardboard box measuring about eighteen inches square by three inches high. Because of the heavy tape heads it weighed about ten pounds.

The next day we checked with New York and found out the package had arrived on time for broadcast by CBS.

It was only a few days later that we found out, as Paul Harvey would say, "the rest of the story."

Our valiant messenger had no problem getting to the airport or boarding the plane. This was, of course, before metal detectors and full body searches. He found his seat, which happened to be in the front of the tourist section, and carefully stowed his precious cargo under his seat.

Everything went fine for the first hour or so of the flight until he felt the need to use the men's room that was located in the back of the plane. Remembering the producer's speech, "...don't let this box out of your sight," he reached under his seat and removed the box. He then picked it up and carried it the full length of the plane into the lavatory with him.

One can only imagine the reaction of the other passengers upon seeing a nervous young man carrying a heavy taped box into the bathroom with him.

It wasn't very long before there was a loud insistent knocking on the lavatory door. The young man opened the door to find a very large, very serious co-pilot who inquired just what the hell was he doing with that box in the john.

It was only his fear of the producer and not making the delivery that produced a satisfactory explanation from the terrified messenger. Fortunately it was persuasive enough to keep the officer from confiscating his package and making an emergency landing. A subsequent announcement by the lead stewardess calmed the nervous passengers.

Who says life in the mailroom is dull?

Leo's Farm

Old Macdonald had a farm and so did Leo Burnett. Leo's was in Geneva, Illinois, and was a good hour and a half commute from his office via the Northwestern Railroad. Each day Leo would arrive from the farm at the downtown Chicago railroad station clutching his huge, scarred and battered briefcase, the kind that opened at the top in an accordian fold and was held together with wide leather straps.

As the station was about a mile due west of our offices in the Prudential Building, it was Leo's habit to jump into a cab and continue working on whatever had been his project on the train. One morning he is reputed to have mistaken a blue and white Chicago police car for a taxi. He hopped in, ordered them to take him to the Prudential Building, and went back to work. Mythology has it that the shocked policeman did just that.

My neighbor, two houses down in Highland Park, was the agency's most talented art director, Gene Kolkey. Had he not tragically died from cancer in his forties, there is no doubt that he would have ultimately been the agency's creative director. Gene was responsible for almost all of the wonderful characters the agency produced such as Snap, Crackle and Pop, Tony the Tiger, The Keebler Elves, The Pillsbury Doughboy, and many more. He was simply a genius.

(His genius did not, however, extend to things mechanical. One day he failed to show up at the office. He called in and reported that due to a power outage he was unable to get his car out of the garage. He did not know that the little disengage/manual handle that dangled from the opening mechanism would have opened his door.)

Gene and his wife Gilda were extremely proud of their house and their own original artwork with which it was decorated. To show it off they had an open house cocktail party one Saturday and invited all the "brass" at the agency including Leo and his wife, Naomi. My wife, Robbie, and I were invited because we were neighbors.

During the tour, Robbie struck up a conversation with Naomi and asked her where she lived. She replied, "We live on a farm in Geneva."

"Oh, that must be nice," my politically correct wife commented.

"It's not nice, it's awful. I hate it," Naomi snapped back. "I wish I'd known Leo was going to make all that money before we bought the dumb farm. Now I can't get him to move."

Not knowing what else to say, Robbie said, "Oh, that's too bad."

"You know," Naomi went on, "a few years ago, for my birthday, Leo had a big area off our little river dredged out and filled with water. He called it "Lake Naomi." So for his birthday, I had a dam built on the lake and called it "Dam Leo."

Apparently, Leo didn't have a monopoly on creativity in his family!

Green Ink

Leo Burnett died on June 7, 1971. I hadn't seen him since Jay Levinson and I left Chicago in December 1965 to join the Leo Burnett Company in London. At that time we were hardly chums but at least he knew who I was and hosted a small farewell lunch at his private club on top of the Prudential Building.

On the day after his death, I was flying out to the West Coast for a major new business pitch in my capacity as president of Norman, Craig & Kummel. I was leafing through the *Wall Street Journal* and there it was. Leo had died. It was a funny feeling. Although we never really worked together in any sense, he had had a profound influence on my advertising career. His work habits, his professional ethics, his aphorisms—"Always reach for the stars, you may not touch them but you won't get a handful of dirt" —were all part of the mosaic that became me.

As I sat on that plane I was overcome with a deep sadness and sense of personal loss for a man and an era that had passed. I asked the stewardess for some stationery and an envelope (airlines still supplied them in the seventies) and began to write a condolence note to Naomi.

I wrote to her from the heart and told her what Leo had meant to me: his personal style of leadership when we only had 100 employees in 1958; the memos he sent congratulating me on the birth of our sons and the memo he sent on a particularly good analysis (which he no doubt had read on the train) and then scolded me for several grammatical errors; the inspiration I gained and lessons learned while watching him in the many CRC's (creative review committees) I had attended.

How I treasured the copy he sent me of *The Elements of Style* by William Strunk Jr. (I had made a particularly egregious error, mixing up "effect" and "affect") and most of all, how proud he made me to be an "ad man."

My letter flowed on for many pages fueled in part by the copious martinis I was being served by the attentive stewardesses. I knew Leo above all would understand how the judicious application of vodka and vermouth could sharpen the creative edge.

I finished my letter and, as I was addressing the envelope, was suddenly horrified. I had written the whole damn thing using my regular writing instrument, a classic Schaeffer fountain pen given to me by my father-in-law when I graduated from college. The problem was that it was written in green ink!

Leo's trademark was green ink.

When I joined the Burnett Agency and filled out a requisition for supplies, I had indicated that I needed ink for my fountain pen and had received a bottle of green ink. Apparently the only person other than me who used a fountain pen was Leo and I got a bottle of his ink, but didn't know it. As the most junior member of the media research department I figured that was all they had so I went ahead and used it. Oddly enough I continued to use green ink and no one said much about it. In later years, after I had left Burnett for NCK I continued the practice without much thought.

But now, I had written a long letter to Naomi Burnett using her deceased husband's personal trademark. How would she take it, as an insult or a tribute?

I couldn't take a chance. I asked the stewardess for some more stationery and an envelope (and another martini), borrowed a ballpoint pen from her, and copied the whole letter over in blue ink.

P.S. To this day, in my retirement, for luck, I mark all my golf balls with a green magic marker.

PART II: THE LONDON YEARS

On December 1, 1965, I departed Leo Burnett Chicago, never to return again. I was sent to the London office of Burnett to bring some "Chicago advertising" to England.

For the next year I would work on the Burnett accounts in London: Green Giant, Burlei Mills Foundation Garments, Players Tobacco, Irish Linen, and others. Pretty thin gruel, as the English say. In the meantime, we prospected for new business from our U.S. clients such as Kellogg and Procter & Gamble.

In November of 1966, my old friend Art Hohmann, who by now had left Bates in New York for Norman, Craig & Kummel in London, convinced me to join NCK as managing director of the London office. Within a year I would replace Hohmann as president of NCK Europe when he returned to New York.

During the NCK Europe years I led a twelve-country network of agencies and represented Colgate-Palmolive, Chanel, Chesebrough-Ponds, Fiat, Aspro-Nicholas, IWS, Nestle, Grant's Whiskey, and a myriad of European national accounts.

In August of 1970, my family and I returned to the United States where I took on the job of president of Norman, Craig & Kummel U.S.

The King's English

It has often been said that the United States and the United Kingdom are two countries separated by a common language. Nothing could have proven the wisdom of this saying more than the following story.

At the end of 1965, I was sent to England by the Leo Burnett Co. to become Vice President of Marketing and Client Service. Accompanying me was Jay Levinson, a copy group supervisor I had worked with in Chicago, who was to become creative director in England. He was young, bright, funny, and extremely creative (see The Goldfish Near-Pack). Like me, he was a Chicago native and had spent little time out of the country.

We arrived in London around the first of December 1965, and went right to work. One of the accounts that we handled in London that we also handled in the United States was the Green Giant Food Company. It wasn't a big account in London but, because of its American parentage, was very important to the London branch of Leo Burnett.

The project they assigned to us was to develop some competitive print advertising that would introduce Green Giant to the English housewives and explain the high quality for which the company was famous.

Jay immediately set to work and his facile mind quickly produced what he thought to be the perfect headline. It was so perfect, we failed to consult our English coworkers before we rushed off to present his idea to the client.

As Green Giant always illustrated their advertising with a picture of the fictional Green Giant and a large picture of the product (in this case corn niblets) it was also unnecessary to consult the art department. Jay merely pasted his new headline and body copy over existing artwork.

We showed up at the client's office and after the usual preliminaries wherein I meticulously went through the marketing and creative strategy, Jay stood up to present the creative work.

"And here we have what the agency considers to be an extremely compelling headline," he announced. "We have no doubt that every housewife in the U.K. will be 'stopped' by this ad."

He then turned around a large cardboard poster holding the ad. What they saw and caused the entire assembled client personnel to virtually fall off their chairs in gales of laughter.

The headline read, *"DON'T SPEND A PENNY TILL YOU TRY GREEN GIANT."*

Little did we know that "spend a penny" in England means to go to the lavatory.

That was absolutely the last time we ever presented advertising to our clients without checking first with the U.K. personnel.

The ad never ran!

Rolls-Royce and Baseball

Shortly after we moved to the United Kingdom, I bought a wonderful ten-year-old Rolls-Royce Silver Cloud. It was my pride and joy and I drove it everywhere.

At that time, London was an incredibly exciting town, being famous for Carnaby Street, the Beatles, and Mary Quant. It was also at the height of the U.S. filmmaking era. The English had adopted the so-called "Edie plan" which made it extremely favorable for American film companies to produce their movies in the U.K. As a result, the city was inundated with American movie stars.

In the spring of 1966, two big movies were being shot at the same time. One of them was *Grand Prix* starring, among others, James Garner. The other one was the classic, *Dirty Dozen*. This particular film starred Lee Marvin, Charles Bronson, Telly Savalas, Trini Lopez, Jim Brown, Ernest Borgnine, and many others.

On the weekend, it was the habit of the American community to stage a baseball game in Hyde Park. (You may have seen clips of it in the movie *Touch of Class* which launched Michael Caine's career.) Because my cousin, Buddy, the director of musical entertainment for BBC 1, was a good athlete, he was a regular at the game. I was invited to play as a legacy.

For my sins, I had been a catcher in high school (this is a position that no one wants to play; the equipment is not called "the tools of ignorance" by accident). At any rate, Charles Bronson was a particularly excellent fastball pitcher and we made up the battery for two games on this particular Saturday morning.

As I was leaving after the game, he asked if he could take a look at my Rolls-Royce, as he had never seen the engine of a Silver Cloud before. I was naturally quite flattered and immediately lifted the "bonnet" so he could take a look.

I thought nothing more of the matter until Monday morning when my secretary, Faye MacDonald, announced on the intercom that I had a call from a Mr. Chalmers of Rolls-Royce. I had no idea why he was calling, but I took the call anyway.

"Mr. Bregman," he said, "this is Chalmers from Rolls-Royce. Did you have a bit of a bother with your car on Saturday?"

"No," I answered, totally at a loss.

131

"Well, sir," he went on, "you were observed in Hyde Park with the bonnet raised on your Silver Cloud and we wondered if you had a breakdown."

"Not all," I replied proudly. "As a matter of fact, I was only showing the engine compartment to a friend of mine who is an American movie star." I figured this would get me off the hook.

"I see," he said sternly. "Actually, Mr. Bregman, this is really not done. We would appreciate it if the next time you open the bonnet for inspection, you do so in the privacy of your garden."

Now I realized what happened. By opening the engine compartment I had alerted the world to the possibility that I had a problem with my Rolls-Royce. Someone from the RR image patrol had snitched on me. I had displayed unspeakable bad form and besmirched the escutcheon of Rolls-Royce.

From this incident I learned when one buys a Rolls-Royce, one takes on a certain amount of responsibility.

The Dinner Jacket

In early 1966, I was living in the London Hilton and eagerly awaiting my family's move to the U.K. We had found a house and my wife was winding up the loose ends in Chicago. I was working hard during the week but was rather lonely, especially on the weekends. You can imagine my delight when our real estate agent, Anne Neville-O'Brien (I was not used to "double-barreled names"), invited me to a charity party to be held in the elegant ballroom of the Dorchester Hotel.

I naturally accepted immediately. She was pleased I could make it and signed off with, "And of course, Walter, it is black tie." She had hung up before I had a chance to tell her that my tuxedo (as we called it back home) was in Chicago. I really wanted to go to the party so I figured I would splurge and buy a new one. Little did I know that I could have easily rented the whole kit and caboodle from a London institution named Moss Bros.

At any rate, I stopped into my boss's office for advice. Hubie Sinclair had been in England for over a year and I figured he knew the ropes. He did. He suggested at lunchtime I walk over to Simpson's, "a wonderful clothing store," and buy my dinner jacket. He had recently purchased a suit there and had seen hundreds of dinner jackets on their racks.

He was right. When I arrived on the third floor I saw literally ten or twelve double swing out racks of dinner jackets. I wandered around for a few minutes before a salesman approached me. He looked and talked like he had walked off the set of *Goodbye Mr. Chips*. He was tall, skeletal, with receding wispy hair to match his receding chin. An exceedingly long neck and protruding Adam's apple topped off his visage.

Approaching me he said in his best Oxford accent, "And how may I help, sir?"

"Well, I'd like to buy a tuxedo, oops, I mean a dinner jacket," I replied. "I'm a U.S. 42 long."

He looked me up and down and after what seemed an eternity said, "Oh sir, I'm terribly sorry. We have nothing to fit you. It's the shoulders, you see, while they are physically commendable, sartorially they're a pity."

I was crushed. Trying to appear smaller, I slunk out of the store and returned to my office.

I told Hubie what had happened.

"That's absolute bullshit," he said. Being a Canadian he shared their trait of cutting right to the heart of the problem. "They've got dinner jackets up the gazoo; they can fit every size in the world. We're going back there right after work."

And so we did, although I was less enthusiastic than he was. We went to the same floor with the same racks, but this time an older, quite distinguished-looking salesman greeted us.

I told him what I wanted. "You look like a U.S. 42 long," he said.

I prepared myself for the worst, but he simply walked over to a rack, plucked a dinner jacket from it and said, "I think this will fit the bill nicely." He was right. I tried it on and it fit like it was made for me.

As I was paying the bill, my curiosity got the better of me. I related my experience of that afternoon and described the young salesman who had refused to fit me.

"Oh," he replied, "that must have been young Smith-Wallace, he hates Yanks."

This was my first, but not last, exposure to the fact that all was not sweetness and light between the UK and its former colonials.

Repp Ties

In the weeks before I moved to the U.K., one of my activities was to fill out my wardrobe with what I thought to be appropriate clothes. Naturally, I had suits, ties, and shirts that I wore in Chicago and Cincinnati, but I felt that perhaps I needed a few extra items.

Fortunately, the Harvard Coop (pronounced as in "chicken coop") winter catalogue had just arrived and announced a sale on button-down shirts and repp ties. I purchased four shirts (buy three get one free) and five ties (buy four and get one free). This, I thought, would do nicely in London.

Upon my arrival, the first order of personal business was to find an estate agent and begin looking for houses. The plan was for me to roughly screen areas, neighborhoods, and houses after which my wife would fly over for the final decision making.

Thanks to my boss, Hubie Sinclair, I was introduced to a very capable agent named Anne Neville-O'Brien (see The Dinner Jacket) who showed me many houses throughout London and the suburbs. In the course of "looking" we became quite good friends and she seemed genuinely concerned for my welfare, particularly on the weekends.

One Friday afternoon after viewing some properties she said, "I say, Walter, do you have plans for the weekend?" Knowing full well that I had none.

"No," I responded. "Nothing in particular."

"Well, Mummy and Daddy are having a Sunday brunch at their home in Hove on the South Coast. Perhaps you'd like to pop down there with me." (She really did talk that way!)

Naturally, I agreed. After telling me to wear "country casual" (sportcoat, tie, and slacks), she also told me that she would pick me up at my hotel, the London Hilton, at 10:00 A.M. Sunday morning in her Mini Cooper (the "in-car" of the mid-sixties).

I dressed quite carefully in my gray J. Press Harris tweed sportcoat, new repp tie, blue button-down shirt, gray flannel slacks, and cordovan loafers. Looking in the mirror, I saw myself as the personification of "country casual."

The drive to Hove was beautiful, quick, and uneventful during the course of which Anne told me that her father was really Brigadier Neville-O'Brien who had had a "good war" and was now retired to golf and gardening. She also explained that many of the guests at the brunch would be "chaps Daddy served with in the forces." It turned out that Hove was a community almost totally composed of retired military.

In time, we arrived at a huge, brick house near the water named "Thistle Cottage" or some other self-deprecating name and I was introduced to her parents who looked like they came out of a David Niven movie. Her mother was rather thin and birdlike in a flowered dress while her father was erect and florid with a trim white mustache and wore a jacket with leather patches on the elbows and shoulders.

Similarly, their friends were variations on the "central casting" theme; all about the same age and background.

We began the party with "champers" and strawberries and progressed through white and red wine with brunch after which the ladies retired to "powder their noses" and the gentlemen repaired to the study for cigars and brandy.

It was at this point that my world collapsed.

As we entered the library, one of the guests, a Colonel something or other, said, "I say, Harold," addressing one of the other guests, "did you notice that young Walter must have been seconded (temporary duty assignment) to the old regiment? How else could he be wearing the tie of the 29th Fusiliers?"

I looked down at the "bargain" repp tie I had bought from the Coop—black, silver, and red stripes —and thought, "Oh shit, now I've really stepped in it."

Without allowing me to reply, someone else chimed in. "Is old Bluesy still in the mess?" and another said, "How about Malcolm, the wonderful Sargent Major?" and "What happened to Freddie the faggot," etc. They were really grooving now, peppering me with questions about people who must have been dead or retired for at least ten years. Clearly, the prodigious quantity of champagne, wine, and brandy had them in a time warp.

In the end, I shamefacedly confessed that the closest I ever was to the 29th Fusiliers was the Coop's tie catalogue and solemnly promised never to wear it again. Fortunately, they took it all with good nature or were too drunk to care.

The first thing I did when I got back to the Hilton was to bundle up all the repp ties (Brigade of Guards, Naval Air Arm, Scots Guards, Royal Engineers, *and* 29th Fusiliers) and put them in the bottom of my dresser, not to see the light of day until my permanent return to New York in 1970.

Michael Caine

In mid-1966 there was no more popular screen star than Michael Caine. His movie *Alfie* had been an international box office hit and propelled the young Cockney actor from the London docks to instant stardom.

Meanwhile in London, the Leo Burnett Agency was tussling with the problem of how to advertise Tipped Weights, a brand of "working-class" cigarettes from Players, our biggest client (yes, that is the way they were categorized in those days). The product was skewed to blue-collar workers and sold in fives and tens, and in some kiosks you could even buy a single for a few pence. We had to talk to our market in words they understood.

It suddenly hit us that Michael Caine (alias Maurice Micklewhite), son of a fish peddler and charwoman, was the perfect person to endorse Weights. Who better but a man from a working-class environment who'd made it big but never forgot his roots? Our customers would love him. The production department contacted him and to our surprise he agreed to do the commercial. The problem was that he wanted 20,000 pounds! This far exceeded our budget and at the time was an exorbitant amount of money. On the other hand we really wanted him.

Through a series of discussions we learned that he didn't necessarily want the 20,000 pounds. What he really wanted was a fast speedboat that cost about 5,000 pounds to use on the Italian Rivera. The problem was that British taxes were such that he would need more than 20,000 pounds in order to end up with the 5,000 he needed.

I told the client of our problem and they instantly agreed to handle the "details" through the Italian subsidiary of their parent company, Imperial Tobacco.

In no time the deal was struck. Caine's boat was delivered to him on the Riviera, we had a great commercial for Tipped Weights, and I learned a big lesson in how business is done by international companies.

English Justice

Perhaps the strangest incident of my advertising career consisted of a case of industrial espionage wherein the London office of Leo Burnett was the victim and Jay Levinson and I were unwitting and innocent bystanders.

It started one afternoon when Jay was interviewing a candidate for a copywriter position. At the same time, I had a client on the phone and needed an answer from him about the scheduling of a pending creative presentation. I walked over to Jay's office, excused myself, and asked him to step into my office and get on the call with the client to iron out the details. This, as I remember, took all of five minutes at the most.

Jay returned to his office and concluded the interview, deciding in the end that the applicant wasn't right for the job. That was the end of it—we thought.

Not so. A week later I got a call from Brigadier Sir John Anstey, MBE. DSC, "mentioned in dispatches '44-'45," etc. This was unheard of. The Brigadier was the Chairman of John Player and Sons and was at such a lofty level that agency flunkies like me only saw him on ceremonial occasions such as lunch in the Chairman's dining room. (Yes, at Players the executives ate in dining rooms according to rank.)

"Good afternoon, Walter," he said. "We have a rather ticklish bit of bother on our hands and I'm afraid it involves you and your Mr. Levinson."

"I'm sorry to hear that, sir. What seems to be the problem?"

"Well, it seems that somehow a young chap who was in your offices saw some secret material and tried to sell it to Gallagher's." (Gallagher's was a major U.K. tobacco company and an archrival of Players.)

My blood ran cold. Players was our biggest account by a mile; this could destroy the London office. "I see," I said, thinking of no other intelligent reply.

"Yes, he somehow contacted my counterpart at Gallagher's in Newcastle and offered to sell him this very valuable secret information all about our new product program. Well, as you can imagine their chairman was outraged but carried on and asked him to call back in a little while. He then, of course, immediately called me.

We both belong to the Army–Navy Club, you know" (also called the "In and Out" because of its prominent signs on the Club's driveway).

The seeming non sequitur made it clear to this dumb Yank that fellow clubbies don't steal secrets from each other. It just isn't done.

"We then called Scotland Yard and they suggested the Gallagher's chairman set up a meeting with the caller. They sent over an officer with some money marked with fluorescent dye and a tape recorder."

Holy shit, I thought, this was sounding more like an episode of "Rumpole of the Bailey" (a popular BBC police drama) than "My Life in the Agency Business."

"The chappie showed up as scheduled and proceeded to give my friend about six product sketches of new Players cigar products all with the Leo Burnett stamp on them. The money was exchanged and shortly thereafter the culprit was apprehended. He's now in jail and will be tried shortly. My question is, how did he obtain this secret material?"

"I have no idea, sir, but I'll find out and get right back to you," I stuttered and hung up.

In a short while Jay and I pieced together what had happened. The crook was the unsuccessful copywriter candidate. Jay had shown the "boards" to him as an example of what we did, telling him they were rejects. When I called Jay out of his office to take the phone call, the thief must have rifled through the material on Jay's credenza and slipped some of the cigar concept boards into his attaché case.

Of course, the stuff he stole was totally worthless. True, we had been working on new product ideas for small cigars, but because the material he had stolen had been rejected internally, they had never made it up to Nottingham (Players headquarters). The Players people had never seen them.

With great relief, I quickly reported our side of the story to Brigadier Anstey. Although we had been guilty of an egregious lapse in security, nothing of any value had been stolen and offered to our competitors. He took the whole thing with great aplomb as, I suspected, someone who had been "mentioned in dispatches" would. He told me we would be hearing from the Crown's lawyers.

Sure enough, in a few weeks, Jay and I were asked to go up to Newcastle to testify in a case of industrial espionage. We dutifully boarded the train at King's Cross Station and journeyed to the North of England.

The courtroom looked as we expected it to look. Gloomy, all dark wood, drapes, and lots of people wearing wigs and robes—all that was missing was Alfred Hitchcock. There was no jury, just an elderly judge sitting far above us behind a huge desk.

Soon our case was called and after the Gallagher's chairman testified, and the police detective showed the money and played the tape, Jay and I were called to tell our part of the story.

"Mr. Levinson, can you positively identify these sketches as the ones that were taken from your office?" asked the wigged and robed Crown lawyer.

"Yes sir, they are definitely the ones that were in my office when I was called out by Mr. Bregman," Jay replied.

"So there is no doubt that this is stolen merchandise."

"No doubt."

"What is the value of these items?"

"Well, they really have no value because they had been rejected. I'd probably have thrown them out in a day or so."

Up jumped the defense attorney who, up to this point, had been totally dispirited.

"If it please your lordship, I call for a dismissal of all charges. My client is accused of industrial espionage which presupposes that he attempted to take something of value from one party and sell it to another party, thus providing the buyer with a competitive advantage."

He was really warming to his subject. "As Mr. Levinson and Mr. Bregman have now testified, the items the accused attempted to sell were worthless, there can be no case of industrial espionage against him. Thank you, your lordship," he smugly concluded and sat down.

Even as it happens in the movies, an audible murmur swept the courtroom.

The judge thought for a minute or two, adjusted his glasses, and said, "Quite so. It appears that because of the lack of worth of the items stolen there is no reason to charge the accused with industrial espionage." Big smiles from the defendant's side of the courtroom.

"However, because the defendant attempted to sell something which he knew had no value he is guilty of fraud." With this he banged his gavel and said, "He will be confined in Her Majesty's prison for not less than four years. Bailiff, take him away."

Before I could turn around the thoroughly shaken felon was being led away by a couple of huge policemen as his wife wept uncontrollably.

Such is the swiftness of British justice.

The Greek Cruise

During my entire agency career I never started and ended a scheduled vacation with my family. Our cruise through the Mediterranean was no exception. In the spring of 1968 we booked a two-week cruise on a Greek line from Venice that would take us throughout the entire Med. We'd visit Greece and the Greek Islands, Cyprus, Crete, Egypt, Israel, and Yugoslavia. The cruise was particularly exciting as the "Six Day War" had only recently ended and we were to be the first tourists into Egypt since the war.

As usual, my work prevented me from accompanying my family for the start of the cruise from Venice, but I did meet up with them in Athens. I told Robbie I would catch a flight from London in time to meet her and the kids at the Acropolis. I don't know what I expected it to be but certainly not as big and spread out as it was. The fact that we met up at all was a most fortuitous happenstance. The sight of me carrying my suitcase around the Acropolis looking for my wife and kids must have been hilarious.

The next few days on the ship and ashore were exciting but uneventful. When we left Crete for a sail across the Mediterranean it got interesting. Several swarthy gentlemen boarded the ship and we were informed that they were Egyptian immigration officials who would be reviewing our passports. We had been told in advance that if we had an Israeli stamp in our documents our landing privileges would be automatically denied. Our English friends who regularly traveled in this part of the world always carried two passports—one for Arab stamps and one for Israeli ones.

From time to time the loudspeaker would ask that a guest report to the main lounge, where the Egyptians had set up office. As in "Will Mr. and Mrs. Goldberg report to the main lounge?" We got to know that that meant they were to be denied landing privileges and kept on the ship. I guess Bregman didn't sound sufficiently Jewish because they never called me. We were permitted to disembark in Alexandria after a harrowing harbor approach during which we were led through the minefields by an Egyptian Navy motor torpedo boat.

We were bused to Cairo and spent two days viewing the city itself, the pyramids, and the sphinx. It was rather spooky being the only tourists at every place we went. At the end of our Cairo tour we again were bused back to Alexandria to rejoin the ship and the shipmates who not been allowed to disembark.

Before we had to board our ship we had a few minutes to sightsee on the dock. Robbie, our two sons, and I strolled down the waterfront to see and film the usual collection of beggars, sword swallowers, fire eaters, and other assorted harbor riffraff. I had with me a German 8mm movie camera that dated back to our service days in Germany. It had an unusual feature. There was an optional viewer that allowed one to hold the camera sideways yet film straight ahead. Thus, I could essentially face away from my subject while filming. It came in handy for impromptu shots of the local population. At this particular moment I put it to good use shooting the dockside scene.

I also noticed that a rather large ship had tied up near us since we had originally landed at Alex two days before. It appeared to be Russian. Hundreds of sailors, dressed in what looked like their pajamas, were hanging over the rails smiling and waving at the crowd on the dock. I thought it was rather interesting so I employed my special viewer and shot quite a few feet of film panning back and forth on the ship. While there were guards on the dock, they took little note of me because I was with my wife and little kids and was apparently not even facing the big gray warship.

We then went on to Israel and Dubrovnik and my memory of the afternoon on the dock faded away. That is, until two weeks later when my secretary, Faye MacDonald, telexed me in Paris and reported that a Lieutenant Commander something or other had called several times and was very anxious to talk to me. I told her to tell him that I had already contributed to the Navy League and brush him off.

The next day she called me and said, "This Navy chap is very insistent that he talk to you. He says it's very important."

"Tell him I'm busy and I'll call him when I get back to London," I said and promptly forgot about the whole thing.

The next Monday morning I was in my London office quite early. First thing, Faye buzzed me, "It's that Navy bloke again and he sounds really upset. You'd better talk to him."

"Walter Bregman," I said.

"Good morning, Mr. Bregman," he said. "I'm Lt. Commander Robinson and I work for Admiral McCain. I understand you recently took a trip through the Mediterranean."

Now I was really confused. "Yes, that's correct."

144

"Did you by any chance take any movies while you were on your trip?" he asked.

What an odd question, I thought. "Well, yes. As a matter of fact I took quite a lot of pictures. Why would you ask?"

"We're only interested in the pictures you may have taken in the harbor of Alexandria. Do you have them available?" the Commander continued.

What the hell was he driving at, I wondered. "I have them, if that's what you're asking. I wouldn't exactly say that they are 'available,' whatever that means," I said. "Look I'm very busy and I have to be on an airplane to Milan in an hour. Let's talk some other time," I said, hoping to brush him off.

He wouldn't give up. "I'm afraid we really have to see those movies. When can we get together?" he asked with a hint of desperation in his voice.

Who was "we"? What was the big deal? Why me?

"I'm afraid I'm out of the country all the rest of this week and next. I simply won't be available for at least two weeks. Sorry," I said, figuring this would get rid of him.

"How about this weekend?" he said. "I know you live in Camberley and belong to Wentworth (my golf club in Virginia Waters). Could you and your wife possibly come to a cocktail party at Admiral McCain's house? It's very near your club."

How the hell did he know so much about me?

I knew that the Admiral lived in Romany House, a gorgeous Georgian mansion on the club grounds. It was the official residence of the Commanding Admiral of the Atlantic fleet. I also knew that invitations to his weekly cocktail parties were few and far between for ordinary mortals. He had me!

"Well, I guess we could make it," I said.

"Wonderful," he said with relief. "We'll expect you at 1600 (4:00 P.M.) sharp. And by the way please bring your movies. They're 8mm, aren't they?"

The next Sunday I played golf as usual with my ex-pat friends at Wentworth and told them about my odd conversation and invitation. One of my golfing partners, Bob Montgomery, who had joined us on the cruise with his family, was a Navy veteran and active in the Navy League. He never admitted it, but I suspect he was the source of the Navy's information about me.

145

That afternoon, my wife and I dutifully showed up at the Admiral's house at precisely 4:00. A blond, crew-cut young man in civvies, wearing a big blue and gold ring, greeted us at the door. He introduced himself as the Admiral's aide.

"Good afternoon and thank you for coming. The others are in the lounge hall," he said.

Apparently all the other guests had been invited to arrive before us as the driveway was full of cars and I could see a number of people from where we stood in the foyer.

"Before I introduce you to the Admiral, I have to tell you that the McCains received some rather bad news this morning. Their son, Johnny, has been shot down over Hanoi and is missing. They're waiting for more information."[17]

"My God," I said, "that's terrible. Why not cancel this party? We can come back some other time."

"I thought Lt. Commander Robinson told you. The admiral said he wants to see your movies. He *really* wants to see your movies. I assume those are they," he said gesturing toward the film can I was carrying.

"Yes, they are," I replied and handed them into his outstretched hand.

"Good," he said, "I'll have them strung up after I introduce you to the McCains and the others."

At this point he guided us into the main room where a number of attractive and fit young men and women were surrounding an older couple. The man was short and stocky and smoking an enormous cigar, the woman petite and extremely attractive. Both looked tired and strained.

"Admiral and Mrs. McCain," our escort said, "allow me to introduce you to Mr. and Mrs. Bregman. They're the people who took the film."

I really didn't know what to say but I tried. "I am terribly sorry to hear about your son," I said. "We hope he will be all right."

---

[17] It wouldn't be till the following day that the McCains would find out that their son had been taken prisoner.

"Thank you very much, we appreciate your thoughts," the admiral said. "But he's a navy pilot and he has to take his chances like all the rest."[18]

In short order, a uniformed Filipino mess steward gave us a glass of champagne and another offered canapés.

"Let me introduce you to the others," said our guide. "This is Mr. Jenkins," he said as we walked up to another tanned crew cut with an Academy ring. "He's in charge of the library at the embassy on Grosvenor Square."

Right, I thought and they gave him that ring for excelling in library science.

We then met several other "recruit poster" specimens whose "duties" ranged from agricultural attaché to public information officer. But all wore the tell-tale ring.

At precisely 1630 the Admiral looked at his watch and called out to Lt. Commander Robinson.

"Commander, I think it is time to see the movies." He then led us into his study that had been darkened by curtains. A projector was set up facing a screen at the opposite end of the room and chairs had been arranged in a semi-circle facing the screen.

"Mr. Bregman," Admiral McCain said, "you sit here next to me and describe what we are seeing. It would be most helpful."

I was dreading this moment from the time the Navy said they wanted to see the movies. I didn't know exactly what they wanted to see, but I sure as hell knew what they didn't want to see. The problem was that 8mm film came in 50-foot rolls. After I had them developed, I had assembled them into chronological 200-foot rolls. The part the navy wanted to see (the big Russian ship) was unfortunately buried in the middle of my third roll. This is the one I had given to the Ensign to "string up" on the projector.

Well, as I had learned in my own service career, an order is an order.

After everyone (not the ladies) had assembled in the study and the lights had been turned off, I began my narration.

---

[18] Brave words and I suppose what an admiral has to say. It was only when I became involved in Senator John McCain's presidential primary campaign that I repeated this conversation to him. "Well, that may be what he said, but believe me, he was torn up inside."

"What you are about to see are movies I took in Alexandria Harbor about three weeks ago." And the movies started. "Now you're looking at my sons, Mark and Jim, talking to a juggler, and there is my wife, Robbie, trying to get rid of a beggar. Now they're walking over to a fire eater and some people selling trinkets." On and on it went.

I could feel the admiral shift in his seat and knew I wasn't showing him what he wanted to see, but this was long before videotape and there was no fast-forward. Everything had to be shown and viewed in real time. My narration went on for what seemed like an hour but was in reality only two or three minutes. I'm sure Lt. Commander Robinson saw his entire career going down the drain as this idiot civilian rambled on about buying marzipan for his family. My next commentary saved him.

"And here is a big Russian boat that was tied up next to our ship in Alexandria harbor."

The room came alive.

"That's a Smirnov class cruiser, Admiral. We've never seen one in the Med before," said the "librarian" from the embassy.

"That gun training radar is brand new, sir. We don't have any good pictures of it," said the "agriculture attaché."

And so it went around the room, all the "ring knocker spooks" making a pithy comment as to how my random pictures had added to their intelligence. We must have run the same 45-second sequence backwards and forwards ten times; to freeze the frame would have burned out the film.

Finally the Admiral said, "Well done, Bregman. You've done a great job. May we borrow this film for a week or so?" Naturally, I agreed. Obviously, I had successfully completed a mission I didn't know I was on.

As we were leaving Robinson came over and said, "Your pictures were really important. You know, this James Bond stuff is baloney. We get most of the really good intelligence from civilians like you. Did you know that before D-day the British solicited the public for all their holiday pictures taken on the beaches of France? They laid them out on the floor of a huge aircraft hangar and pieced together a pretty good topographical map of the Normandy beaches. By the way Mr. Bregman, where are you taking your next trip?"

I pointed out that most of my travel was to friendly countries and besides, I didn't think I was cut out to be a spy.

Two weeks later my film arrived by mail, without a note, in an unmarked envelope, postmarked London.

And this would have been the end of the story except for a chance encounter fifteen years later.

In 1982 I was attending the Esmark Annual Meeting at the Drake Hotel in Chicago.[19] The night before the meeting, the CEO, Don Kelley, hosted a dinner for the executives of the Esmark companies and the Board. By chance I was seated at the same table and next to a director, the former Chief of Naval Operations, Admiral Elmo Zumwalt.

For some reason, I related how I had met Admiral McCain and the story of my movies.

When I finished Zumwalt put down his fork, looked me in the eye, and said, "So you're the guy who took those pictures."

I was astonished. "You know about my pictures of that Russian ship?" I asked.

"Know about them! Those pictures of yours were on my desk in Washington the next day! McCain had copies and blowups made and they were flown over by the fastest jet the Navy had."

"Why were they so important? I asked.

"Well, you see, those were the days long before satellite reconnaissance. We didn't have any really good way to keep track of the Russian navy. As far as the Med was concerned, we and the Russians had a sort of gentlemen's agreement that neither side would send in any ships larger than a destroyer," the former CNO said.

He continued, "We suspected that a Smirnov class cruiser had snuck past Gibraltar in the fog but we didn't have any evidence to prove it. Your pictures caught them red-handed. Not only did you provide hard evidence that they were cheating on our agreement, but you also handed over close-ups of some of their newest radar and sea-to-air weapons. It was a real coup. A little while later, State "back-channeled" the Kremlin that we knew what they were up to and the cruiser was removed in short order. You didn't know it, but you played a major part in the Cold War."

---

[19] Esmark was the parent company of International Playtex.

So now my grandchildren will know that their granddaddy was a spy!

The Nestle New Product

During the late sixties, Norman, Craig & Kummel Europe was desperately trying to obtain another international client in addition to Colgate. Nestle was our major target. Finally, after great perseverance and many new business presentations, we were invited to their headquarters in Vevey, Switzerland, to be briefed on a major new product assignment. Needless to say we were thrilled. We eagerly flew to Geneva, drove down the beautiful road to Vevey and finally arrived at Nestlé's fortress on the lake.

For those who have never been there, the first floor is totally glass, the second supported by pylons built up some twenty fleet. Apparently the local residents would only give permission for the building to be built under the proviso that the first floor would be constructed so they could look through it to the lake. Clever, these Swiss!

After a confrontation with a receptionist who obviously studied humanity from Ilsa Koch, we were announced and brought into the great briefing room. Following the usual introductions, a humorless Swiss marketing director began the presentation. After droning on for a few minutes, my creative director, Edgar Marvin, turned to me and said, "Is it any wonder that the Swiss Comedy Hour only lasts twenty minutes?"

It was subsequently revealed that the new product that was to be our assignment was an imitation, nonalcoholic Campari made from "a jungle root found in one of our South American subsidiary countries." This mysterious root was not identified to us, but its magical powers were soon to be revealed.

They next told us that they were about to show us some remarkable films documenting the rejuvenating and invigorating power of this miracle beverage. The serious Swiss pushed a button on his podium and a movie screen majestically lowered from the ceiling.

"Now," he said after a pregnant pause, "on the left-hand side you will see some laboratory animals that have not had the privilege of drinking this miracle beverage, and on the right you will see those who have."

At this point the lights dimmed and the film rolled. On the screen we could see two groups of rats swimming in a divided glass pond with tiny lead weights strapped to their backs. Via the miracle of time lapse photography numbers appeared on the top of the screen—five minutes, ten minutes, fifteen minutes, and so on. Slowly but surely the poor little devils in the left section of the tank began to roll over and drown, drifting quietly to the bottom of the glass pond. Those on the right happily paddled away until the film ended.

The lights came up, and while my creative group was trying to keep from both laughing and vomiting at the same time, the proud and emotionless Swiss unequivocally stated, "And so you see, our beverage does, in fact, work." He went on to say, "Now in the next sequence of films, you will see the same effect as it is tested on our famous Swiss Army."

At this point, our creative director, Edgar Marvin, could not contain himself. "Oh, my God," he whispered to me, "they're going to drown those poor sons of bitches too!"

Alas no, instead we were treated to split screen film of two groups of Alpine troops climbing up a mountain. One group, as you would expect, quickly fell by the wayside panting in exhaustion (they were the ones who drank the placebo), while the others (who drank the miracle juice) happily sang and effortlessly marched together all the way to the top.

Unfortunately, after an unsuccessful test market in the U.K. (the product tasted terrible and we couldn't figure out how to show either the rats or mountain troops in our commercials) Nestle quietly killed the project. We suspect that what actually happened was that they found out that the "mysterious South American root" was, in fact, a controlled substance.

Obviously, they had been "tripping out" their subjects to a point where the rats would have swum the English Channel and the Alpine troops would have climbed the mountain even if it hadn't existed.

And so ended our first attempt to break through at Nestle.

The Chanel Yacht

For Norman, Craig & Kummel the Chanel fragrance account was one of most important ones that we handled. Not only was it extremely prestigious, but also we serviced it throughout the world. Because it was our showcase account, and I suspect, because it was headquartered in Paris, our leader, Norman B. Norman, was personally involved in almost every presentation.

Each year the agency would travel to Paris to present the new advertising for the forthcoming year. Clearly, this was a major event and required that the most senior creative and account personnel be present.

The Chanel Company was owned entirely by the Wertheimer family under the iron-fisted control of the "old man," Pierre Wertheimer. While we presented to a number of staff members, we all knew that there was really only one real vote and it was Pierre's.

Frequently, however, after we had presented to Pierre Wertheimer, who at the time was well into his eighties, he would pick up the telephone and say, "Send in the Bubba." This meant that he was asking that his son, Jacques, join us. (In Yiddish *Bubba* means "little baby.") In this case the "Bubba" was over sixty years old.

When Jacques would arrive at the meeting the old man would bark out, "What you think of this advertising?"

Jacques would make some sort of comment after which his father would usually say, "How idiotic, get out of here, you stupid boy."

Clearly, the son had no love for a father who humiliated him in front of not only company employees but the agency as well.

Finally, sometime in the late 1960's Pierre Wertheimer died, leaving the company to Jacques. As the story goes, on the way back from the cemetery, Jacques fired every single employee that had made fun of him.

One of Pierre's favorite possessions was a huge yacht, docked in Monte Carlo; it was reputed to have been a French minesweeper during the war. He had it lavishly furnished, manned by a full crew including his personal chef, and available for his use at any time.

Naturally, stemming from his antipathy towards his father, Jacques also hated the yacht.

A year or so after Pierre's death, Norman and Jacques happened to be in Monte Carlo on some sort of a combined business and pleasure trip. One morning, Norman looked out the window of the Palace Hotel and said, "Jacques, isn't that your father's yacht out there at the dock?"

"That's impossible," Jacques said. "I had the damn thing sold right after he died."

"Maybe so, but it sure looks like it to me," Norman replied. "Let's find out."

The two of them went down to the harbor and sure enough there was the Chanel yacht in all its glistening chrome, polished brass, and eye-shattering whiteness.

As they walked up the gangplank the captain saluted Jacques smartly and said "Welcome, Mr. Wertheimer. We'll be ready to put to sea in a moment. What would you like for lunch? We have a wonderful fresh turbot and have, of course, Crystale champagne on ice."

Jacques was livid. Suddenly, he realized that for the last year the yacht had been sitting in Monte Carlo burning up an incredible amount of cash as the crew polished brass and prepared daily meals that only they ate.

It turned out that while he thought he'd given instructions to sell the yacht, they had never been carried out and someone in the accounting department had been paying the bills for over a year.

Upon his return to Paris he had the yacht given to Israel, where it became a gunboat in the Israeli Navy. We later heard that it had seen action in one of the Arab-Israeli wars.

It must have seemed to Jacques that his father continued to torment him even from the grave.

Yankee Ingenuity

While I was living in England, we frequently had visitors from the United States. On one occasion I was joined by a good friend of mine named Pat Sullivan (not his real name). Pat fancied himself as quite a lady's man and, in fact, he was.

On one particular night several of us were having dinner at the White Elephant Club on Curzon Street in London. The White Elephant was an exclusive dining club that catered to the "show business" element of English society, having been founded by an executive of the BBC. It also had a large number of members who were American film and TV stars. For this reason, it was not unusual to have a quite a few attractive young ladies in the club at any given time. This particular evening I was sitting at the bar with Pat and several friends when, not uncharacteristically, Pat struck up a conversation with a particularly attractive young lady. One thing led to another and she agreed to join us for dinner.

Pat was obviously in fine form and put all of his best moves on his "target of opportunity." Not surprisingly it seemed to be working. Around eleven-thirty he decided to move in for the kill and asked her if she would like to join him in his "suite" at the Dorchester. She said she would love to but had to get home to Brighton, which was several hours away. In fact, in order to make her train, she had to be leaving for Waterloo Station within a few minutes.

Pat appeared broken-hearted, but was not willing to give up so easily. He excused himself from the table and went to the headwaiter's desk. I saw him talk to the headwaiter and look at his watch after which he gave him what appeared to be a five-pound note.

Shortly thereafter, he said to the young lady, "OK, I'll take you home." I naturally thought he meant he would take her to the station and expected to see him back at the table shortly. This was not to be the case.

After waiting for the better part of an hour, I went to the headwaiter and asked him what he had done for Mr. Sullivan. "Oh," he said, "I hired transportation for him to go to Brighton. It appeared awhile ago and left with him and the young lady." I figured that Pat had magnanimously hired a limo and had driven his new friend home. Wrong!

155

The next morning at breakfast, he explained. "I figured it was about an hour and a half to Brighton and why waste the time. I hired an ambulance. The two of us got in back and had a wonderful time together. (I knew what that meant!) I drove her up to her parents' door, let her out, kissed her goodnight, and slept on the gurney all the way back to the Dorchester."

I guess the morals of the story are:

1. You can't beat Yankee ingenuity and,
2. Where there's a will there's a way.

Room 506

From 1966 to 1970, when I held the position of president of Norman, Craig & Kummel Europe, I supervised our offices in twelve countries ranging from Norway, Sweden, and Denmark in the north to Spain and Portugal in the south and all the European countries in the middle.

I was also required to fly back to New York once a month for a meeting of the Board of Directors of the parent company. I guess I was one of the original road warriors and didn't know it.

My normal routine was to spend approximately one week a month in my office in London and the rest of the time visiting our offices and clients on the continent. Typically, I would fly into a location the night before a meeting, have dinner with the agency or client principles, attend a meeting, and then fly off to the next location. At the beginning of each week my secretary, Faye McDonald, would type up my itinerary on a card so I would know where I had to be and when. At first, I gave these cards to my wife so she could find me but the itinerary changed so frequently that she abandoned the cards and just called Faye whenever she needed to talk to me.

On one occasion, I arrived in Madrid at my normal hotel, the Ritz, checked in, and had dinner with the managing director of our company and the manager of the Colgate-Palmolive subsidiary. After a pleasant evening, I returned to my room and proceeded to order breakfast for the next morning. As I recall, I had an early morning meeting and I needed to have breakfast precisely at seven-thirty.

I called room service and said, "This is Mr. Bregman in room 506 and I would like to order breakfast for tomorrow morning. I would like orange juice, coffee, scrambled eggs with bacon, and toast." I went to sleep secure in the knowledge that the Ritz would produce my breakfast as ordered and on time.

The next morning I was very disturbed when seven-thirty passed without my breakfast arriving. I called downstairs and said, "This is Mr. Bregman in room 506. Where is my breakfast?"

The answer was, "But Mr. Bregman we delivered your breakfast and you sent it back."

"That's impossible," I shouted. "I've been sitting here the whole time and no one showed up with my breakfast. Please send it up right away."

Again I waited fifteen minutes and no breakfast. Again I called and asked where my breakfast was, becoming even more irritated.

The response was the same, "But Mr. Bregman, we again brought the breakfast to your room and you again sent it back saying you never ordered it."

I muttered something to myself about "stupid Spaniards" and said, "God dammit, I'm sitting here in room 506...." At that point I looked at the telephone and to my horror saw the number 307.

Room 506 had been the room I stayed in the night before at the Lombardy Hotel in New York.

Naturally, I apologized profusely but I know to this day somebody in the Ritz Hotel room service department tells stories about the "stupid Americans."

The Lombardy Hotel

For reasons now lost in antiquity, the Lombardy Hotel became my hotel of choice whenever I was in New York. Located on 56th between Park Avenue and Lexington, it was basically an apartment/hotel. Long before it became *de rigueur* in the hospitality industry, every room in the Lombardy had its own kitchen and cable TV and was decorated with real books and paintings. I later found out that most of the rooms were owned or on long leases and rented back to hotel guests when unoccupied by the long-term tenants.

The best rooms looked across 56th street and had balconies with stone railings decorated with very ugly gargoyles on the corner of each balustrade. On one occasion, Art Hohmann and I shared one of the large suites that had two bedrooms and a very large living room. The night before we had overindulged to a monumental degree and I had the granddaddy of all hangovers. To avoid what I thought to be imminent sickness, I stepped out on the balcony for some fresh air.

Unbeknownst to me Art went into his bedroom and dialed the room's other phone. After listening to incessant ringing I staggered into the living room and picked up the phone to hear, "Hello, I live across the street and I just wanted you to know that I think your middle gargoyle looks very sick!"

On another occasion, Art and I flew into New York from London for the regular monthly NCK board meeting. Again we had been upgraded to a huge suite (being a frequent guest does have its rewards). I decided to have a party and called up all the usual suspects including Bill Eldridge, Pete Conway, and other assorted friends and acquaintances. We ordered the liquor and the deli plates and soon our guests began to arrive. The party was really going strong when the doorbell rang and in walked what turned out to be a five-piece Cuban band. Now the party really got into high gear. I was really pleased that one of our guests had hired the band. That is until an hour later when the manager called and complained that another guest was missing a Cuban band and it appeared that it was performing in my suite.

It turned out that Pete Conway was out on the famous balcony having a cigarette and saw the band getting out of their cabs. He yelled down to them, "Come on up we're in suite 710." They, not knowing any better, thought it was their "gig," got in the elevator, and came on up. We ended up keeping them and paying them as, by then, the original host had lost interest.

Somewhat later in the year, I again flew in from London for a board meeting. The cab ride was longer than usual because of traffic and by the time I arrived at the hotel I had a dire need to use a bathroom. The desk clerk checked me in and gave me my key. As I only had carry-on bags and didn't need a bellman, I quickly took the elevator to my floor and rapidly walked down the corridor to my room. The particular room I had been given was entered via a long hall. On one side was the kitchenette and on the other the bathroom.

My condition was desperate. I rushed through the door, dropped my bags and flipped on all the light switches. In a few seconds I heard very strange sounds emanating from the bedroom.

"Oh, I love it when you do it that way."

"Do you, how about when I kiss you here? Does that turn you on?"

"Oh God, don't stop. Please keep it up and do it harder."

What the hell had I stumbled in on? Obviously, the room was occupied. The occupants were "getting it on" and I was trapped in the bathroom. Clearly nothing good could come of this. As I desperately tried to figure out an exit strategy, the lovemaking became more passionate. The dialogue was now interspersed with "Oh God, oh God," punctuated by rapid inhaling and exhaling.

I finally decided that I would do the only manly thing, pull up my pants, quietly open the door and run like hell.

Just as I was about to execute my brilliant plan I heard, "We hope you have enjoyed tonight's performance of "Sex in New York" on the Blue Channel and will tune in next week."

I walked into the bedroom and found that the TV set was on. Obviously it was triggered by one of the wall switches. The previous occupant had left it tuned to what was the first public assess porno channel in New York and I was the jerk that got fooled.

The Vier Jahreszeiten

Someone once said that the best practical joke is one where you never really see the end and can only imagine the result.

Art Hohmann and I perpetrated just such a joke one night at the Vier Jahreszeiten Hotel in Hamburg (see Jogging in Germany). Like all great continental hotels the Vier Jahreszeiten prided itself on its wonderful service and staff. From the time your car pulled up at the covered portico till you checked out, the hotel staff coddled you in every possible way. The check-in process was effortless, the room service waiters appeared instantly, and the maid and turndown service was impeccable.

In keeping with their high standards, the hotel also had a complimentary shoeshine service every night. All a guest had to do was to leave his or her shoes outside of the room door when they retired and the next morning, as if by magic, the newly shined shoes would be waiting along with a copy of the newspaper of choice (*The Hamburger Zeitung* for Germans, *The International Herald Tribune* for English speakers and so forth).

One night, Art and I were returning from another evening of injudicious imbibing when, spotting the many pairs of shoes lining the hall corridor, he had a brilliant idea.

"Let's swap them around," he said. "This ought to cause an uproar tomorrow morning."

In my liquorish state I agreed. We proceeded to move the shoes from in front of one set of doors and replace them with others from another door. Thus, the high-heeled black pumps from in front of room 510 were replaced by the cowboy boots from room 525 and the Gucci loafers from 517 got the pumps, and so on. As there were at least twenty rooms on the corridor and most of them were availing themselves of the courtesy shine, "Operation Big Switch" took a considerable length of time. Miraculously no one came along and caught us.

The next morning we arose, dressed, and briskly walked through the angry crowd that was rapidly forming in the hallway.

We never did find out how long it took to untangle the mess we had created.

Jogging in Germany

Long before it was popular, Phil Beekman, president of Colgate-Palmolive International, took up jogging. He was a remarkable individual who claimed to sleep only four hours a night and spent the rest of the time as a workaholic and health nut. When at home in suburban New Jersey, he would arise at 4:00 A.M. to do two hundred sit-ups and push-ups and then run through the hills for an hour or so. Then he would take the first train into New York and be at his desk by 6:30, much to the chagrin of his subordinates.

When he traveled, Phil always took exercise clothes with him and worked out and ran at every opportunity. Remember, we are talking about the late 1960's. No hotel had a gym or workout area. Our exercise regimen consisted of walking from the cab to the office and bending our elbows at every opportunity. Not Phil!

On one occasion, we had all gathered in Hamburg, Germany, for a major meeting on laundry detergents. Phil had flown in from New York with some of his staff and I had traveled from my headquarters in London with my group. We had all registered at our usual hotel, the very elegant Vier Jahreszeiten. The hotel, established in 1897, was reputed to be the very best in Hamburg, if not all of Germany. It boasted several wonderful restaurants, spacious rooms, and a location on the beautiful Auben Alster, a small lake in the middle of Hamburg.

After a wonderful dinner together, the two groups agreed to meet in the hotel dining room for breakfast at seven-thirty the next morning. The C-P Germany subsidiary was to send transportation for us at eight-thirty to take us to the company building for a nine o'clock meeting.

All of the NCK and Colgate team showed up for breakfast except for Beekman. We waited awhile and then ordered. Still no Beekman. Finally one of his assistants left to call his room on the remote chance that he had overslept. He returned wearing a concerned look.

"There was no answer," he said. "And I let it ring for a full minute in case he was in the john. Then I called him five minutes later. Still no answer."

"Maybe we should ask the assistant manager to check the room," I said. I was worried that the health nut had had a heart attack on his two hundredth push-up.

Reuben Mark, future CEO of Colgate-Palmolive but then European marketing manager, went into the lobby to seek out the assistant manager. In a little while he returned looking very worried.

"We checked his room and it was empty. The bed had been slept in and his stuff was there, but no Phil," he said.

By this time it was almost eight-thirty, the time our transportation was due to arrive.

"Look," I said, "maybe he forgot about breakfast and because he gets up so damn early, decided to go out to the company and talk with Hank Arnold (the C-P German general manager) for a while before we got there. He sure as hell isn't here. We might as well go out there ourselves."

My suggestion was accepted. We paid the bill and walked out through the spacious lobby to the front steps where several black Mercedes awaited us. Just as we were about to climb into our limos, a Hamburg police car pulled up and out climbed a disheveled Phil Beekman clad only in running shorts, sneakers, and a T-shirt.

After the shock wore off, Reuben asked, "What in the world happened to you?"

"You won't believe this. About five-thirty I went out for a jog around the lake and everything was going great until these idiots picked me up," he said, gesturing toward the policemen.

"You'd better watch your language," I cautioned. "You don't want to piss them off."

"Oh, don't worry, they don't speak any English. That was the whole problem." Beekman continued, "I was minding my own business jogging along in the dark when the Gestapo here flashed a spotlight in my eyes, yelled a bunch of stuff at me in German, and then threw me in the back of the car and took me to the station house.

"Naturally, none of the morons there spoke English either. I guess they figured I was some kind of pervert running around in my underwear so they locked me in a cell till they could find a translator. Finally, around eight someone showed up and I had to explain to him that I was not a sexual predator but just an American businessman out for a run. Believe me, it took quite a while to convince them, particularly because I couldn't remember the name of the goddamned hotel and I had no I.D. or money."

"How did you finally get here?" Reuben asked.

"Well, after I convinced them I wasn't public enemy number one, they put me back in the squad car and we have been driving around the friggin' lake to all the hotels looking for one that looked familiar. Thank God you guys were standing outside or I don't think I would have recognized this place."

And so an international incident was avoided and Phil Beekman learned to carry I.D. and know where his hotel was located. However, it didn't stop him from running around strange cities in the dark.

Hotel Meurice

In order to maintain solidarity in and enthusiasm for NCK Europe, I held quarterly "partner" meetings. It was at these meetings that all of our multi-national founder/owners would gather and discuss mutual problems and opportunities. We would also plan strategy for our attack on various new business opportunities and listen to presentations by New York executives on both the state of the company, and new creative and marketing techniques.

The idea was that each subsidiary company would, in turn, host a meeting in their headquarters city and thus allow them to entertain their partners and for the partners to visit the agency offices. Naturally, after the first few meetings each successive get-together became increasingly more elaborate as the eponymous owners tried to outdo each other.

Finally, it became France's turn to host a meeting. Along with the U.K. agency, France was wholly owned by NCK, Inc. It therefore, became my obligation to host the meeting although the planning was totally left in the hands of my general manager, Andre Bouebant.

I did tell him that we would need ten or twelve hotel rooms and a suite big enough to hold our business meetings. Because the agency was located in Clichy, a fair distance from the center of Paris, I thought it best to hold our conferences and presentations at the hotel and only visit the offices for "the tour." I also told him that my usual hotel, The Lancaster, was too small to accommodate our group so he would have to look elsewhere.

A few weeks later he called and told me that everything was organized. He had booked a large suite and the necessary rooms at the Hotel Meurice on the Rue de Rivoli. The elegant Hotel Meurice was founded in 1835 and has been in continuous service since then. Its location is fantastic—facing the Tuileries Gardens, between the Palace Vendome, Place de la Concorde, and the Louvre Museum. It is clearly the epicenter of Paris.

The day before our meeting was to begin, I flew to Paris and, with Andre, inspected the large suite in which we were to have our meeting the next day. It was on the second floor, grandly decorated with period French furniture, the windows hung with opulent drapes and the floors covered with thick burgundy carpets; clearly the best the hotel had to offer.

This alone was certainly impressive, but what took my breath away was the view from the balcony that ran the full length of the suite. Across the Rue de Rivoli stretched the Tuileries Gardens, the view only interrupted by the huge French Tricolor that hung from a large flagpole affixed to the balcony railing.

I was transfixed and then shocked. I opened my attaché case and removed the book I was currently reading.

One of the peripheral advantages to traveling around Europe fifteen or twenty days a month is that one does a great deal of reading. Unable to understand local newspapers, magazines, radio, or TV, the non-polyglot traveler either consumes alcohol or books in great quantity.

Coincidentally, my book of choice was *Is Paris Burning?* by Larry Collins and Dominique Lapeirre. It is the true narrative of how Paris was spared destruction in August 1944, when the Nazis withdrew to the East, despite Hitler's orders that it be "burned to the ground." A further twist of fate was the fact that the Hotel Meurice was the headquarters of the German Army Commander, General Dietrich von Choltitz.

What caused me to momentarily lose my breath was the fact that I believed I was actually standing in the very room that had housed von Choltitz's primary office and reception room. I quickly opened my copy of the book, and sure enough, there in the photo section was a picture, taken from the street, of "my" suite, the caption of which read in part:

"General von Choltitz's troops (above) parade past the windows of his Paris headquarters in the Hotel Meurice on the rue de Rivoli opposite the Tuileries..."

Prominently hanging from "my" flagpole, now carrying the French tricolor, was the infamous black, red, and white Nazi swastika additionally emblazoned with an Iron Cross indicating the headquarters of a General Staff officer.

I was deeply shaken and swore to quickly read through the rest of the book after dinner.

What happened next is as unbelievable as it is true. After dinner with Andre Bouebant and his wife and a few postprandial brandies, I went upstairs to bed and settled in to read my book. After about a half an hour I came to Chapter 34, page 224, which said in part:

"At room 238, Mayer paused, opened the door, set down the tray, and parted the blackout curtains. As the first shafts of light pierced the darkness, Choltitz stirred in his bed. He opened his eyes and looked at Mayer. Then, as he had done almost every morning for the past seven years, Choltitz asked the genial Corporal, "What's the weather like?"

It was dull and gray, and it was exactly seven o'clock, Thursday, August 24, the last day in his life Corporal Mayer would bring Dietrich von Choltitz his breakfast."

My God! I was sitting up in bed in room 238.

I was in the very bed from which General von Choltitz had arisen that August day and, the date for our Partners' Meeting the next day was August 25, 1968.

I was reading about an event that had occurred exactly twenty-four years ago to the day and in exactly the place where I currently resided.

Truth is stranger than fiction!

The Armoire

During my five-year tour of duty as president of Norman, Craig & Kummel Europe, I had many memorable experiences. One of them was at a new business presentation in Gothenburg, Sweden. A subset of our network, the Scandinavian agencies (Denmark, Sweden, Norway, and Finland), was in the finals for the International Wool Secretariat (IWS) account. Because it was such a huge opportunity for NCK Europe, both the chairman of NCK Europe and of our Danish and Norwegian agencies, W. G. "Graham" Lockey[20] and I traveled north for the meeting.

We planned on spending three days in Gothenburg and had so registered in the Grand Hotel. As usual, I had to leave my wife in the habitual lurch and had flown up from a vacation in Marbella to make this all-important presentation. The IWS was a not only an extremely prestigious account but was a wonderful showcase for an agency in that it utilized very high-quality "slick magazine" print to be presented in four different languages. (There was no commercial television in Denmark, Sweden, or Norway at that time.)

The work and the presentation were extremely complex and required the combined efforts of three of our agencies plus our correspondent agency in Finland. Nonetheless, after the three-day ordeal of endless rehearsals and presentations, we thought we had done very well. We had! The judges eliminated J. Walter Thompson, Young & Rubicam and McCann-Erickson; it was down to the finals between Norman, Craig & Kummel and Foote, Cone and Belding. That was the good news. The bad news was that we had to stay over for one more day while they continued their deliberations.

---

[20] Graham Lockey was an extraordinary man. A wonderful athlete, he had been an "international" footballer for England. On a trip to Denmark before the war he had fallen in love with a Danish girl and married her. Her father owned a small advertising agency and Graham went to work there. When the war came along he remained in Denmark and spent the war years smuggling Jewish refugees to freedom across the North Sea in his small sailing boat. He received many medals and awards for his heroism but was never known to talk about it. In 1963, his agency, Lockey, became Lockey-NCK and Graham moved to London to become chairman of NCK Europe.

Unfortunately, we had only reserved rooms for three days. When we went to the hotel manager to extend our stay we found that they were unable to provide us with the number of rooms we needed. Everyone would have to double up. And so it happened that Graham Lockey and I were forced to share a room.

We had a wonderful meal together but I was terribly nervous about the day to follow and kept Graham up quite late talking about all the possible permutations and combinations. Who had blinked and who had smiled, who liked us and who didn't, and what tomorrow's outcome would be. But Graham, the pro that he was, was confident all the while and said, "Don't worry, Walter, we've got the business." Clearly, I was a little less sure.

We went up stairs to our spacious double-bedded room around midnight, donned our sleeping attire, performed our ablutions, said goodnight, and went to sleep. About two hours later, a tremendous racket, a very loud banging and knocking, awakened me. In my drowsy state, I turned the light on and saw that Graham was missing from his bed, but I could not identify the source of the sound. I looked around and realized that the strange sounds were coming from the large ornate armoire on the other side of the room. I then heard a muffled British voice saying, "I say, Walter, are you out there? I seem to have misplaced myself."

I opened the armoire and found Graham standing there in his pajamas, his fly open, obviously looking for the urinal. It seems that in the darkness, he had mistaken the door of the armoire for the door to the bathroom and had walked in and closed the door behind him. Armoires do not have handles on the inside. He was trapped.

Graham looked down at me from his stance in the armoire and said with great dignity, "Thank you so much." Whereupon, he walked around behind me into the bathroom, proceeded to perform his necessary function, turned off the light, and went back to bed, leaving me standing, staring at the empty armoire.

Postscript: We got the account. Graham was right all along and always the proper English gentleman.

Friends Forever

One bathroom story leads to another. In this particular instance, we were having our quarterly NCK Europe partners meeting in Brussels; our new Belgian partner had offered to host the gathering.

The morning meeting had dragged on and, at about ten-thirty, we elected to take a break for those who wished to use the facilities and/or make phone calls to their offices. We agreed to reconvene twenty minutes later in the meeting room to cover some important aspects of new business.

As we all sat at specified places with quite impressive name plaques in front of each seat, it was immediately clear when we re-assembled that one of our Swedish partners, Arne Leon, was missing. We assumed, naturally, that he was on the phone to his office, and went on with our business. But we became concerned when fifteen minutes, a half an hour, and finally forty-five minutes went by without a sign of Arne.

His partner Krister Luning said that he would go and look for him. Arne and Krister had been inseparable friends since the first day of grammar school. In the Swedish schools of that era, students were always seated in alphabetical order, and thus Arne Leon and Krister Luning were fated to be side by side throughout the whole of their formative years. Afterwards, they remained friends and formed an advertising agency in which Normal, Craig & Kummel subsequently took a minority interest, and thus they became our partners.

Krister left the meeting and went upstairs to Arne's room, knocked on the door, got no response, and became very concerned. He found the housemaid and had her open the door. He walked in, called for Arne, and heard a mumbled voice in the bathroom. He opened the door and there was Arne, fully clothed, sitting on the toilet seat, the bathroom door handle in his hand.

We were very concerned when Arne finally reappeared in the meeting room until he explained about the broken door handle.

I then asked, "What did you do?"

"Well, nothing," he explained quietly. "I knew that sooner or later Krister would come for me and find me."

Such are the bonds of friendship in Sweden.

Norman in Marbella

At another NCK Europe partner's meeting, this time in Marbella, Spain, the great man himself, Norman B. Norman, and his charming wife, Gail, came over to attend the festivities. The agenda consisted of very important and detailed reports covering all of our international accounts, the status of our new business efforts, and a discussion of the financial status of all of our partner agencies individually and the international company in general.

Norman, ever acquisitive, also led an in-depth discussion about the possibility of expanding further by purchasing agencies in countries where we were not currently represented. In total the meetings were highly intensive and very serious, but there was always time for recreation.

One day after the meeting, I was standing on a bluff overlooking the Mediterranean and happened upon Gail Norman.

She turned to me and said, "Have you seen Norman?"

And I said, "Oh, yes, he's down at the beach."

Knowing her man, she said, "Oh, is he walking on it or buying it?"

I am not sure whether or not he did buy the beach that day.

Spanish TV

One of the continuing and nagging problems I had at Norman, Craig & Kummel Europe was my inability to get our Spanish agency going, to truly make money in this important and vital country. We had small pieces of very fine international clients, Chesebrough-Ponds, Vick Chemical, Colgate-Palmolive, Chanel, and several others, but for one reason or another, we had absolutely no local Spanish business.

I therefore made it my business to spend a disproportionate amount of time in Spain and try to sort out the problem. After about two weeks in the market, talking to our clients and talking to our prospective clients, it became clear to me that our biggest problem was that our Spanish agency was viewed as a branch of our Portuguese company, Ciesa-NCK. We had compounded the problem by putting Portuguese management into Spain.

Being gringos we figured, "What the heck—Spanish, Portuguese—they're all in the Iberian Peninsula; they're pretty much the same, they must like each other, and that'll be fine."

What we didn't know was that we were trying to put out a fire by throwing gasoline on it. In fact, the Portuguese and the Spanish did not get along. They did not like each other, and the worst thing we could have done was to put a Portuguese manager into our Spanish operation.

And so it became clear that I had to find a new *consulero delegado* (managing director) for our Spanish agency. I hired Spencer Stewart, the best headhunter in town, and I interviewed endlessly until I found a bright young fellow who was everything I was looking for. He was currently with TWA, he was a *don* and hence politically well connected (somewhere in Madrid there was a fountain named after his family), and most important, he had worked in New York for an American agency. He had more chutzpah than anybody I had ever met. His name was Enrique Martin. He was tall, handsome, intelligent, and very, very clever.

I told him what his assignment was and I told him what our problem was in terms of getting new business. He asked, "Well, first of all, what has been your television allocation?" At that time Spanish commercial television was allocated on the basis of a lottery wherein all of the agencies applied for the amount of time that they wanted for their clients and the Ministerio de Informacion held a drawing.

I told him that we really had been extremely unlucky in the drawing. Of course, being unlucky in the drawing meant that we were unable to attract new business. New business always went to those agencies that had an overabundance of time available and therefore could make it available to their new clients. He said that this was the first problem he had to solve and I said, naively, "Well, how do you solve the problem of being unlucky?"

He smiled confidently and said, "Well, we'll just have to change our luck. I'll get back to you tomorrow."

I went back to the hotel, and the next morning when we met at the agency, Enrique said, "Here's some good news. As luck would have it, the Ministerio de Informacion discovered that there was a problem with the last television lottery. They're going to have to redraw and I think our luck is about to change."

As it happened, we were very lucky. As it also happened, the fellow in the Ministerio that did the drawing was one of Enrique's cousins. And for the next few years, we were always very "lucky" and our business and new business in Spain prospered.

Spanish Taxes

Having solved the television time problem, the next thing that we had to attack was, of course, the financial stability of the company. Enrique took one look at the books and said, "Oh, my God, how come you're paying so much tax?"

"Well," I said, "they operate on the 'global system' in Spain as, of course, you are aware." The "global system" meant that each industry was taxed on the basis of an assigned amount of money that, prima facie, the government decided it should pay; then the individual companies within the industry were apportioned their split of that particular pie on the basis of the size of their businesses.

Enrique immediately identified this as a basic problem and asked, "And what billing numbers have you been reporting?"

"What do you mean?" I responded. "We've been reporting whatever they were as they come off the books."

He looked at me as an adult would look at a very stupid child and said, "A-ha, there's the problem. But, of course, in Spain nobody ever admits what their real billings are and you dummies have been paying tax for all the other agencies in Spain!"

From that day forward, we attacked the problem in true Spanish fashion. We reported half our actual billings, reduced our taxes substantially, and our bottom line improved from that day forward.

Needless to say, Enrique remained our general manager in Spain for many years. Our agency prospered, our new business grew, and at the time I left NCK Europe in 1970, we were the second or third largest agency in Spain—all thanks to Enrique's local knowledge, relatives, and inborn chutzpah.

Golf in Portugal

It was not all work and no play in the advertising business in Europe. Because of the many holidays granted in various European countries, I frequently found myself with a day off whether I liked it or not.

On one such occasion I was in Lisbon with Tom Myers, our marketing director from New York, to meet with Colgate, when we found that the next day was a birthday of some obscure saint. As a result, the office would be closed, our clients would be closed, and we had nothing to do.

Tony Beja, NCK's representative in Lisbon, was a native Portuguese and from very fine family. Before he joined the agency he had been a Portuguese bullfighter. In Portugal, they don't kill the bulls, they have teams of young men who run out in the arena and try and throw the bull on his back. Only the socially prominent are allowed to "play" this nutty game and the most distinguished and dangerous position on the "team" is that of *fucador*. This guy is sort of the quarterback. He directs all the others and then, at some fleeting moment of perfection, throws himself between the horns of the bull, grabs them, and attempts to wrestle the bull to the ground. The plan is that wherever the bull's head goes, the rest of the body will follow. Tony had a rakish four-inch scar across his left cheek that bore witness to the fact that the bull didn't always follow the script.

Fortunately, Tony was also an excellent athlete in other sports, one of which was golf. To fill in the time on the saint's birthday, Tony invited Tom and me to his club, the most exclusive golf club in Portugal, Club de Golfe de Estoril. He picked us up at eight o'clock at our hotel, the Ritz, and we drove to Estoril. The club was situated on a gorgeous piece of property overlooking the ocean, with flowing lawns, manicured polo fields, and clay and grass tennis courts. As we drove down the long winding driveway to the club, I was surprised to see a jumpsuit-clad young boy with a rake standing erect next to every sand trap. Tony told us that these *mozos* (young boys) were there to rake the traps so that the players and their caddies didn't have to. It was a pretty good job. Such was the condition of the Portuguese economy under Salazar.

After we had dropped off our clubs at the bag drop and were about to enter the men's changing room, Tony grabbed my shoulder and stopped me.

"When you get inside, you might be approached by a good-looking young fellow who'll ask you if you have a game. He'll want to join us," Tony said. "Just say 'thank you, we already have a game.'"

This seemed rather odd and mysterious, but after all I was a guest so I just nodded.

Sure enough, while I was changing my shoes and putting things in the commodious locker to which I had been assigned, an attractive Latin man walked over. He was about six feet tall with erect posture and wavy black hair, wearing incredible alligator golf shoes and a tan cashmere cardigan sweater.

"Good morning," he said in excellent, though accented English.

"Good morning," I replied.

"I see you're about to go out on the course. I wonder if I might join you?"

Remembering my instructions, I said, "I'm terribly sorry but we already have a game."

This seemed a rather absurd statement as in five minutes he would see us on the first tee and realize that we were, in fact, a threesome.

As we walked over to the putting green, my curiosity got the better of me.

"By the way, Tony, who was that guy in locker room and why won't you let him play with us?"

"Oh, he is a Spaniard, his name is Juan Carlos. Everybody knows that the Spaniards are all cheaters so no one will play with him."

"You don't mean *the* Juan Carlos, do you?" I sputtered.

"Yes, that's the fellow, the crown prince of Spain. Franco sent him over here to get him out of the country so he spends most of his time at the club," Tony replied matter-of-factly.

"Wait a minute. You mean to tell me that we had a chance to play golf with the future king of Spain and you turned him down because you think he cheats?"

"*All* Spaniards cheat," he insisted.

Despite their geographic and ethnic proximity, or maybe because of it, there existed great antipathy between these Iberian neighbors.

"I don't care, let him cheat me! I can tell all my friends about the time I was cheated by the prince of Spain," I entreated.

But Tony was adamant and no amount of arguing would change his mind. And thus I missed the chance to observe royalty at play.

Perhaps Juan Carlos was just ahead of his time. I seem to recall a recent American president who made a habit of shaving his strokes and he got plenty of games.

A Lesson Learned

When I was appointed president of NCK Europe, I was thirty-three years old and had been in Europe for less than a year. The organization I was to "run" was a conglomeration of nine independent national agencies in which Norman had purchased minority interests.

As a result of our minority status, I really couldn't *tell* our "partners" what to do; rather I had to *sell* them. The problem was further complicated by the fact that every single partner was at least fifteen years my senior and, for the most part, had founded their own agency after service in the war (on one side or the other).

For example, our French partners were a couple who had been "Heroes of the Resistance," our German partners had been in the "Unterseeboots" and the "Africa Korps," our Danish partner had been decorated for sneaking Jews out of Denmark in a small boat, and our Portuguese partner had sat out the war in Lisbon doing God knows what. Needless to say there was little love lost between them. The Danes and the Norwegians felt that Sweden's neutrality was a joke and that they "let the Germans through to kill us" and, of course, the Spaniards and Portuguese totally mistrusted each other (see Golf in Portugal).

I often said that the only thing that united our partners was their total dislike of Americans in general and me in particular. In truth, we had bought our way into Europe and they quite properly resented it. Until we could bring them business that they wouldn't normally have a chance of getting, we were just an annoyance.

With the above as background, I had to walk very softly and use all my powers of persuasion to get anything done.

One day I had a meeting scheduled with our Portuguese partner, Fernando Faria. Fernando was a short, swarthy, jovial man given to three-piece suits and elevator heels. From the beginning, he was, of all the partners, the one that was most civil towards me.

It was his first visit to NCK Europe headquarters at Greater London House. I thought he would be impressed with our suite of offices and particularly the rather grand one that I had been assigned. It had large windows overlooking Regent's Park, a conversation area with a couch and coffee table at one end, and a beautiful mahogany desk at the far end, behind which I sat in solitary splendor.

Fernando walked across the room and I rose and walked around the desk to greet him. After going through the customary Latin embrace, I sat down again and asked him to pull up a chair.

What he said next stunned me.

"Wally," he said, "you're making a big mistake with that desk."

I had no idea what he was talking about so, uncharacteristically, I kept my mouth shut.

"I'm a lot older than you and so are all the other partners. The last thing you need is to put up artificial barriers between us."

I was still at a loss as to what he was getting at.

"I walk in here as an equal but the first thing that happens is that you sit down behind a big desk and I have to pull up a chair like some sort of supplicant. From the beginning, I am put off and on the defensive; you are the superior and I am the inferior. That works fine if you are a king or a prime minister but you're not, you need to solicit our cooperation, you can't command it. We're all on the same side."

Wow, did that make sense.

The next day I had my desk placed against the wall so that I faced into it. When guests arrived I was able to walk over to greet them with no interference and, more importantly, when we sat to talk, *nothing* came between us.

From that day forward, some thirty-five years ago, I have never had a traditional office desk arrangement. My desks at NCK New York, Gallo, International Playtex, and the one I am using to type this manuscript all face the wall.

Somehow I think this setup markedly changes the way one thinks about people and relationships.

The Italian Agency's Colgate Presentation

During the late 1960's, globalization of advertising was becoming a reality. Several agencies took the lead in expanding the handling of their clients via their international subsidiaries. Specifically, McCann-Erickson, J. Walter Thompson, Young and Rubicam, Ted Bates, and Norman, Craig & Kummel were at the forefront of this effort in Europe.

Our biggest client both in the United States and Europe was a Colgate-Palmolive Co. for whom we had developed the White Knight, the White Tornado, and the House of Ajax concept. Clearly it was in our best interest to have the advertising we created run in every country where Colgate did business. It was not in our interest to have other agencies run our advertising and get the billing for it. Hence I was asked by Norman to expand as rapidly as possible throughout Europe by buying small agencies and quickly getting the Colgate business for them.

Like many things, this sounds good if you say it fast enough. In reality, bringing a highly sophisticated client like Colgate into a small provincial agency frequently caused more problems that it was worth.

Specifically, we had acquired a small agency in Milan that owed its existence to the fact that the president, Jonmarco Morati, was the son of the Esso distributor for Italy; this large and profitable account was the only one the agency had. Handling it was rather easy as they took the advertising developed by the agency in the United States, translated it into Italian, and made a tidy little sum. Unfortunately, one couldn't handle Colgate that way because Colgate had a very large, very sophisticated operation in Italy fully staffed with marketing, sales, and promotion people.

I had begun preparing my tiny little agency in Milan for the Colgate business by hiring an absolutely wonderful managing director named Alfredo Reinis. Alfredo had spent several years in the United States, had attended Northwestern University, and subsequently worked for McCann-Erickson in New York. He was a great beginning but we had a long way to go before we had an office staffed to handle Colgate.

Unfortunately, just after I hired Alfredo I got a phone call from Bill Miller who was the president of Colgate Europe. He informed me that he wanted to make a major agency change in Italy and that it would be in all of our best interests if the business went to NCK. In two weeks, he wanted us to provide them with a full presentation of our personnel and accomplishments.

I thought to myself, "This won't be hard, we only have three employees (the son and daughter of the Esso distributor and Alfredo) and we have absolutely no accomplishments." I knew we could not possibly handle the business if we took it. The client in Milan would be furious with us in no time at all.

I called Alfredo and told him the problem. He told me not to worry but to go ahead and schedule the presentation. He would take care of everything else. I told him I thought he was nuts but it was his company to run and his funeral.

The day before the scheduled presentation I showed up at the office in Milan and found Alfredo and Jonmarco Morati and his sister Betti, his "vice president," sitting in our cavernous quarters as if they didn't have a care in the world.

"What are we going to do, Alfredo?" I asked. "The Colgate guys will be here at 10:00 tomorrow morning and we have nothing to show them. This is going to cause a huge problem and Norman is going to beat the crap out of me."

"Oh, Wally, don't worry," Alfredo said. "There is no problem and everything will be fine." He then went back to a rather animated telephone conversation in Italian.

The next morning when I arrived at the agency I was absolutely stunned. There were at least twenty people sitting at desks typing, there were artists frantically working at easels, messengers running back and forth with papers and even a couple of people editing film on a flatbed Moviola. Furthermore, more and more people seemed to be pouring into the office followed by people carrying furniture, files, and all the accoutrements of a full-service advertising agency.

"Who the hell are all these people and where the hell have they come from?" I asked Alfredo.

"These are some of my friends who took the day off from their regular job to come in and help us out with the Colgate presentation," he said. "They brought along some of their work so they would look busy."

I didn't have any time to question him further because the receptionist (who I'd never seen before) announced that the Colgate people had arrived.

"Show them into the conference room," Alfredo said.

"What conference room?" I asked. I knew that we didn't have a conference room—at least we didn't have one yesterday.

Alfredo met Miller and his staff in the reception room and led them down the hall past the furiously working "employees" into what had been a huge empty storeroom. To my shock and amazement it had been converted into a sumptuous conference room complete with a credenza holding coffee, fruit, and pastries. Sitting around the table in the conference room were several total strangers immaculately dressed and clearly at ease.

Because I didn't have the foggiest idea of what was going on, I naturally led off the presentation.

"As this is to be a presentation by NCK Italy I think it would be presumptuous of me to take a major part. I would only say welcome to our Italian office. I hope that this will be the beginning of a long and fruitful relationship between our two companies. I will now turn over the rest of the meeting to Alfredo and his people." Pretty good, I thought, considering I didn't know what he was going to say or who the people were.

"Thank you very much, Wally," Alfredo said, standing. "I would like now to introduce the executive personnel of our agency. First our creative director, Mario Belli; our executive art director Johnny Pozzi, and your account executive, Jonni Pincalli. As he made each introduction a new stranger would stand up and smile at the client. He went on introducing our putative media director, research director, office manager, etc.

After the introductions, he asked each of the newly introduced executives to talk a little bit about the work they had done in the past and where they had done it. Each one was more impressive than the last. All of them had worked for U.S. agencies, all of them had worked on sophisticated accounts and, to hear them talk, all they ever wanted out of life was to work on the Colgate-Palmolive business for NCK Milan.

Not surprisingly, the Colgate people were knocked out and after about an hour and a half of the presentation, Bill Miller said to me, "Wally, this is the finest collection of agency talent I've seen in a long

Spray the Bear

time. There's no question that with your organization you can more than handle all of the difficult problems we have here in Italy. We were going to split the business down the center and give half to you and half to Ted Bates."

This was a huge assignment!

"But after seeing your organization," he went on, "I think we ought to consolidate the whole account at NCK."

I staggered through some sort of a thank you, and followed Alfredo as he escorted them out of the office.

In twenty minutes all of our "new employees" had followed the client out the door and others were loading up the furniture and carrying it out, including the Moviola editing machine and its operators.

Soon, there was just the four of us again. Alfredo, the children of the Esso man, and me.

I had the horrible thought that if one of the Colgate people had forgotten his hat and come back for it, he would realize that he been the victim of one of the greatest "stings" in the history of the agency business.

"Now what are we going to do, oh great one?" I said to Alfredo. "Now we've got the business and no agency. How can we possibly handle the business?"

"Not to worry," he replied (he obviously had spent some time in the U.K. as well as United States). "All those guys will be here to work on Monday. I told them I'd hire them if we got the business and they agreed to quit their current jobs and come with us."

Sure enough the next time I went to Milan I found Alfredo, Mario, Johnny, and all the rest of the people from the presentation hard at work on the Colgate business. Except this time they really did work for us.

Salazar's Legacy

During the period of my Norman, Craig & Kummel Europe experience, we went through many political shocks, not the least of which was when, in 1968, Portugal's strong man and dictator, Antonio de Oliveira Salazar suffered a "stroke."[21] The government panicked. Troops were immediately dispatched to all borders, and transportation of all currency was blocked. At that time, our Portuguese agency was extremely profitable. We had literally thousands of dollars in escudos in local banks that we could not now get out of that country.

The official story was that Salazar had a stroke but had not died and, in fact, he "lingered" for months. During that period it was problematical as to whether the Communists would take over, whether there would be a revolt, or whether as it turned out, there would be a smooth transition of leadership.

Because of the continuing uncertainty, it became clear to me that we had to try and get our money out of the country any way we could. Coincidentally, at this time, Edgar Marvin, our NCK Europe creative director, was about to take a vacation to the Algarve area of Portugal with his wife, Arleen, and three small daughters.

As he was about to leave, I casually said to him, "By the way, Edgar, if you're going to be in Lisbon, you might stop by the office and see if you can pick up a few of the escudos we have stuck there and bring them back to England; but be very careful."

Edgar was an extremely diligent fellow and quite dedicated to the company but politically totally naïve. And so, when he visited our Lisbon office, he told the manager, Fernando Faria, that he would take all of the escudos they had and bring them in to England. Of course, he did not realize the terrible danger he was facing and the penalty that the Portuguese government would inflict if he were caught.

What he did was to tell his three little daughters aged four, six, and eight to split up the escudos and stuff them into their underpants

---

[21] The gossip at the time was that Salazar had been the victim of a political coup and was under house arrest in the Presidential Palace. The country was in turmoil and rumors of a possible Communist takeover were rife.

under their skirts and bring them out that way. One can only picture the three little girls boarding the airplane with their panties stuffed with escudos as Edgar and Arleen prayed that none of them would slip out and fall on the runway.

The story did, in fact, have a happy ending in that all the money was brought out safely—some $20,000 worth, which was probably ten million escudos. The little girls were none the worse for wear, and no one was arrested.

That's called dedication.

The Green Dress

Edgar also had an adventure in Paris, where I frequently sent him to help our French agency with creative work. Edgar professed, as I believe most creative people do, to be helpless in terms of the simple, logistical acts of life.

This may have been true. After Edgar had been in England for months it happened that David Smith was boarding the same British rail train bound for their homes in Virginia Water. Edgar started to get on a coach car. Smith pointed this out. Apparently, Edgar didn't know the difference between coach and first class. While he always bought a first-class ticket, he had been riding coach as he failed to look for the Roman numeral one or the gold painting above the windows denoting first class.

He apparently convinced Arleen of his absence of practical skills because she always packed and unpacked for him. On this particular occasion his wife packed for him as usual. He went off to Paris, stayed at the Hotel Lancaster as he always did, attended his creative meetings and flew back. What Edgar reported to me later, however, was that when he arrived at home and his wife opened his suitcase to unpack for him, there was a green lame ball gown in it for which he could obviously not account.

To this day, we do not know how that green dress got into his luggage, and Edgar isn't telling. I suspect that there was some mix-up at the airport, but who knows?

PART III: THE NEW YORK YEARS

In August of 1970, by which time our family was fully prepared to spend the rest of our years as ex-pats in the U.K., Norman called me to New York and offered me presidency of the New York company. To be the president of a Madison Avenue ad agency at age thirty-seven is an offer one can't refuse.

Thus for the next five years I worked for NCK in New York. Our agency was a "jewel box" of major accounts: Colgate-Palmolive, Chanel, Vick Chemical, Shulton, Chesebrough-Ponds, Grant's Whiskey, International Playtex, Kellogg, Liggett & Myers, TWA Cargo, Dow, and several others.

New York was *the* place to be if you were in the agency business in the seventies and I was in the middle of it.

I stayed on Madison Avenue until March of 1974, when I left New York for Modesto, California, and the E & J Gallo Winery.

I Can See 1,000 Miles

During my NCK (Norman, Craig & Kummel) days, I was president and chief operating officer of the company but, at the same time, supervised our biggest client—namely, Colgate-Palmolive. One of the "House of Ajax" products we had developed for them was Ajax Window Cleaner, designed to go directly against the market leader, Windex.

Our creative group had developed a marvelous commercial shot off the Monterey coast utilizing a helicopter and a spectacular cliff-side home. You may remember the commercial—it opened on a woman standing in front of a huge plate glass window cleaning it with Ajax and in the background the audio track carried the popular folk song "I Can See, I Can See, I Can See a Thousand Miles," at which point the helicopter shot zooms in on the woman and reverses behind her as she continues to clean the window. The spot ends as she looks rapturously out across the pounding surf and the blue Pacific.

After the campaign had been running for a few months and sales began to take off, Windex obviously became concerned. As luck would have it, the National Association of Broadcasters Committee on Truth in Advertising contacted us. They suggested that our advertising claims exceeded the bounds of "allowable puffery" and were, in fact deceitful. They urged us to take the ad off the air immediately or come in for a hearing.

Because the Colgate account was vital to NCK and because the commercial was one that we were truly proud of, I asked my leader, Norman B. Norman, to accompany me to the NAB hearing. As we walked over from our office at 919 Third Avenue I repeatedly asked him how he thought we should handle the problem. He merely waved a dismissive hand and said, "Don't worry, it's no big deal, I'll take care of everything."

Anyone who has worked with Norman knows that (a) he was probably right, and (b) it didn't make much difference, anyway, because he was going to do what he was going to do.

After being kept waiting for fifteen minutes in the outer office, we were finally shown into the commissioner's office. With hardly any of the usual pleasantries, the commissioner angrily pointed to our storyboard and said, "Here is an egregious example of how you people in advertising use excesses, use exaggerations, and use words to deceive the public and don't truly conform with the principles of truth in advertising. Everybody knows that it is impossible to see a thousand miles."

Norman, imperious, six-foot-six, silver crew cut bristling, marched rapidly to the office window, pulled the cord to raise the venetian blinds, and pointed a skeletal finger out the window.

Without raising his voice he said, "Is that so? I believe I can see the sun."

The commissioner blanched, cleared his throat, smiled sheepishly, and, fully abashed, turned to us and said, "Get out of the office."

The commercial ran for two more years with great success.

Abe Plough, Head of the Table

One of the most memorable clients we had at Norman, Craig & Kummel was Abe Plough, the founder, president, and chairman of the highly successful eponymous Southern patent medicine company, Plough Incorporated. On one occasion I flew down to Memphis with several other people to meet with the venerable Mr. Plough (nobody called him anything but "Mister") and to discuss the advertising for several of the brands we handled.

We all assembled in the boardroom and seated ourselves around the table; after a few minutes the great man himself appeared. As usual he was coatless, wore his patented red suspenders, and adopted the true "good ole boy" manner for which he was justly famous.

The staff people that had followed Plough into the room suddenly became very nervous when they saw us. Something was terribly wrong. One of them turned in horror to my account executive and whispered, "Oh my God, you're sitting in Mr. Plough's seat at the head of the table!"

Our man jumped up immediately as if from a high-voltage electric shock and said, "I'm awfully sorry, Mr. Plough, I seem to have taken your place at the head of the table."

Abe looked at him and, addressing the entire room, said, "Don't you worry none, sonny, wherever I sits is the head of the table."

Boy, was he right!

Abe Plough in the Elevator

After we finished our copy meeting, I was "invited" into Mr. Plough's office along with his son-in-law, who reported to Abe but was the putative head of the company. The purpose of our meeting was to renegotiate the agency's remuneration contract covering the millions of dollars of billing we handled for Plough Inc. Abe Plough *never* paid "retail" for anything and that day was no exception. Abe's style was to continue the "country boy" pose and interject into his negotiating phrases like, "How can a poor country boy like me compete with you slick New Yorkers?" Irritating but effective.

The meeting went on till about six o'clock. We went round and round on how NCK would be rewarded for all the work we were doing on five or six brands which billed multi-million dollars of measured media. We negotiated hard and tough and finally struck a deal just as Abe said, "My doctor said I had to go home every night at six. I can't keep working these long hours." (I believe he was close to eighty at the time.)

I said, "Fine."

We had concluded our business and NCK was signed on to receive close to a million dollars in commission for the next year. The old man locked up his office and walked with us to the elevator. When we got to it, there was a very old colored woman standing inside of it cleaning the ashtrays.[22]

Abe said to her, "Bessie, how are you and how's the family?"

"Fine, Mr. Plough, how are you?" she replied as she continued working.

It was clear to me that they had known each other for longer than I had been alive.

"Bessie," Abe said, "I came in this morning at seven o'clock and I noticed that you hadn't turned the light off in the elevator last night. Do you know how much it costs to run a light bulb in an elevator all night long? You've got to be more careful, Bessie, or you'll be sending me to the poor house."

---

[22] Historical note – In 1972 people of color were called "colored" and elevators had ashtrays.

"Yes sir, Mr. Plough," the contrite cleaning lady replied. "It won't happen again."

This was the mark of the man with whom, minutes before, we had been negotiating over millions and millions of dollars in commission. He was as tough in those negotiations as he was regarding the light bulb in the elevator in his building.

I learned, if your "name is on the door" it makes one helluva difference!

Sam Bromfman and His Amex Card

The story goes that Samuel Bromfman, chairman of Seagram, never carried money and never, ever carried credit cards. (Such was the way of commercial nobility.) Finally one time, when he was on his way to Europe, one of his underlings said, "Mr. Sam, you really ought to get an American Express Card, it will come in quite handy." (This was in the days when plastic was just coming in, long before credit cards were common.)

Mr. Sam was dubious but said, "Well, OK, if you think I ought to have one."

The executive assistant then called an American Express executive who was just leaving for the weekend, but was overjoyed that Sam Bromfman wanted an AMEX card. He learned that Bromfman was flying to Europe on Sunday night and therefore had to "fast track it" to get a card in time. The card was produced at a facility in New Jersey on Saturday and then sent by special messenger to Bromfman's house on Sunday morning.

Mr. Sam flew to Paris as planned and the first night hosted a huge dinner for his international managers and staff at La Tour d'Argent. The meal was, as usual, sumptuous, fabulous, and *very* expensive. After the meal, as opposed to the normal procedure, Bromfman decided that this night he would pay the bill; he would use his new and wonderful toy, the American Express Card.

Thus, when the headwaiter brought the check, Bromfman waved him over and majestically produced his new green card (this was before the Gold card). He handed it to the headwaiter who walked off smiling. A few minutes later, he came back this time with a puzzled expression on his face, and whispered, "I'm so sorry, Monsieur Bromfman, there is a slight problem, sir. Your card has been denied, it seems it has a five hundred dollar limit." Five hundred dollars wouldn't have paid for the hors d'oeuvres for this dinner.

What had happened was that all new American Express Cards in those days carried a maximum credit limit of five hundred dollars. The limit was then increased progressively during ensuing years as credit was established. In the rush to produce the card, no one had bothered to tell the people in New Jersey who had "cut" the card that this particular card was for a very important person and multi-millionaire—namely, Mr. Sam.

History does not divulge how the dinner bill was finally paid.

The Barbados Vacation

During my NCK years I was under a great deal of pressure to succeed, both self- and Norman-imposed. As a result, I kept a feverous pace of client meetings, new business presentations, creative and marketing review meetings, and "doorbell ringing" research trips. Frequently I would put in twelve to fourteen hour days and six and seven day weeks. Even though I was relatively young (late thirties) and in good shape, this pace caught up with me and I finally had to have a break.

Norman agreed and on short notice arranged for my wife and me to borrow the Barbados vacation home of our lawyer, Leonard Biscoe. We flew down, picked up our rental car, and quickly found the charming waterside house. It was gorgeous. The house itself was set on a small lot facing the Caribbean and was four stories high. The first floor held the reception area; the second, the kitchen and dining areas; the third, a living room; and the fourth, bedrooms. Our room, the master bedroom, with an A-frame roof and terrace, faced the sea and had a spectacular view.

It was after sundown when we arrived but the combination of tropical air and full moon made me drop off the bags and jump into my swimming suit for a quick dip. My wife, Robbie, who doesn't like to swim anyplace where she can't see the bottom, demurred.

I ran down the steps from our room to the ground level and found another flight of steps that led to the water. I was somewhat surprised to find that there was no beach, but merely a landing that stood a foot or so above the water. Nevertheless, I looked up and saw Robbie unpacking, took a look at the moon-drenched sea and waves and, not being sure how deep the water was, executed a shallow dive into the warm water.

It was glorious. I swam out a hundred yards or so and again looked up at my dutiful wife. I was in paradise. I continued to leisurely swim for about ten minutes and then, feeling guilty that Robbie was doing all the unpacking, began to swim back.

Now I had a problem. The waves that looked so gentle from the landing were in reality pretty big. Every time I swam toward the house I could feel the undertow pulling me back. I was making zero progress and getting tired and close to panic. The first thing I did was to yell up to Robbie who, of course, couldn't hear me. The second was to yell for help—to no avail. The third, being first and foremost an adman, was to compose headlines for *Ad Age*:

"Ad Man Perishes In Freak Drowning Accident,"
"Caribbean Claims Promising Agency Head," and finally,
"Bregman's Barbados Burial."

Finally, I got a grip on myself and swore that I wasn't going to succumb. I reasoned that I had to conserve my strength and figure out how to get away from the waves. I decided to tread water for a while and get my strength back.

I flipped over to execute my plan and hit the bottom with my knees!

Shocked and relieved I stood up and found that I was in three feet of water. The reason for the excessive undertow was that the water was shallow for five hundred yards out.

Ad Age was gypped out of another headline: *"Moronic Executive Gives Up the Ghost in Three Feet of Water as Wife Looks On."*

PJ Clark's Cops

Norman, Craig & Kummel's offices were at 919 Third Avenue, the building distinguished only by the fact that on the corner stood the venerable PJ Clark's. In the late 1960's the owners had refused to give up their property when the entire block was demolished; thus it sits in solitary splendor as an island of old-fashioned New York surrounded by the black glass and faux marble of the 919 Third Avenue building. Apparently they made the right decision because to this day PJ's remains a famous watering hole for the "glitterati"— advertising types, socialites, show business, and sports figures, and wanna-be's. It is also one of the biggest liquor "pouring accounts" in New York.

NCK occupied the top four floors of 919 and we frequently stopped in at PJ's for a drink after work or after a meeting. One night Mike Chappell, our creative director; Tom Myers, my executive vice president; and I had been working on a new-business presentation quite late and decided to have a nightcap.

Without being intentionally rude, I should point out for the sake of clarity that Mike Chappell was quite imposing—round faced, round bodied, and generally quite large. Tom Myers also had a pretty good gut on him, and I was not exactly slim and trim in those days.

The three of us entered PJ's around ten o'clock and bellied up for a drink(s). We were standing just at the corner of the bar inside the door. Sitting over at the end of the bar in the far corner on the left-hand side under the clock was a little fellow whom we'd seen there several times before. He always sat in the same seat and was distinguished by the fact that he was the only person I'd ever seen who, upon getting bald, actually sprayed the top of his head with black spray paint in order to disguise the fact. Also, he was always nattily dressed in a black suit with a rose in his buttonhole and drank himself into oblivion almost every night.

This particular night he spotted the three of us and apparently mistook us for some detectives from the 17th Precinct, located just across 3rd Avenue on 55th Street. At first we didn't know to whom he was talking but it became increasingly clear as he pointed his beer mug at us and yelled at the top of his voice, "You Goddamn cops!

You SOB's! You lousy rotten flatfoots, get out of this bar! Why don't you go back to the Precinct, you dirty friggin' cops!"

We ignored him for a few minutes and then Mike Chappell nudged me in the ribs and walked over to the little man and said, "Shut up, buddy, you can't talk to police that way." Chappell was into his police impersonation routine, which I had seen on several occasions.

But the guy couldn't be silenced and began using every four-letter word in the book. Now, Tom Myers got into the spirit of the thing and started to reach underneath his coat. I joined in and grabbing his arm, said, "For God's sake, Tom, you can't pull your piece out in here!"

Tom said, "I sure as hell can. I'm going to kill the son of a bitch. He can't talk to cops that way."

I said, "Don't, Tom, don't take your gun out!"

"Screw you," Tom said. "I'm going to blow the little bastard away."

Mike and I held Tom back so he wouldn't pull his finger out of his coat pocket while the little drunk screamed all the more. Finally after we'd "subdued" Tom, Mike said, "Okay, Goddamn it, I've had it! Get off that bar stool. Get up against the wall and spread 'em!"

The little fellow finally got the message and semi-panicked when he realized he was surrounded by the three of us. Meanwhile, for once, PJ's was silent. The drunk leaned up against the bar and Mike and Tom, having seen enough police movies, did a reasonably effective job of frisking him.

Turning to me, Tom said, "Okay, Lieutenant, he's clean."

We really sounded like Edward G. Robinson, Jimmy Cagney, and Pat O'Brien in that scene.

Mike let the fellow get back on the bar stool, and said to him, "Listen buddy, we've had our eye on you for some months, and now you're in big trouble. Where do you work?"

The guy, somewhat sobered and shaken, said, "I'm a singing waiter at Flannagan's, an Irish bar over on the west side."

Tom growled, "Why should we believe this son of a bitch? He's got to prove it." Turning to the drunk he said, "Give us a song."

Whereupon the "singer" got off his bar stool, raised his tenor voice, and proceeded to sing several choruses of "My Wild Irish Rose" to the complete delight of everyone in the place. Not only that, but he did three encores: "Danny Boy," "The Rose of Tralee," and "Galway Bay."

To this day, he probably believes he avoided the 17th Precinct drunk tank because of his musical ability.

The Account Executive and the Tollbooths

Our creative director at Norman, Craig & Kummel, Mike Chappell, had a wonderful sense of humor (see the Pine Valley story) and was one of the greatest practical jokers in the world. He demonstrated his skill one day when he was escorting a new, young account executive to the offices of the Shulton Company in central New Jersey. At that time, we handled all of their men's fragrance advertising and particularly Old Spice; hence, weekly trips to the client's offices were in order.

It seems the account executive needed to go someplace after the meeting so Mike agreed that the young man should follow him in his own car to the client's office. Mike was very careful to instruct the account man to "stay right on my tail and follow me all the way to their offices."

When they were about to leave the underground parking lot in our office buildings at 919 Third Avenue Mike said, "Wow, that's a Buick Electra you're driving, isn't it?"

"Yes it is," said the flattered young man. "Why do you ask?"

"Only because I guess today is your lucky day. I just read in the paper that the New Jersey Tollway Authority has a major joint promotion with General Motors going on today. Anybody driving a Buick Electra gets through all the tolls free."

"Thanks for telling me. That's amazing," replied the naive young man. He proceeded to get into his car and follow Mike.

Naturally, whenever they approached a tollbooth, Mike would tell the attendant that he was not only paying for himself but for the car behind him. As a result, when the account executive drove up, the booth attendants smiled and waved him through.

This continued through the tunnel and all the tolls until the two cars arrived at the Shulton office building. You can imagine how appreciative the young man was of Mike for having told him about this special promotion.

You can also imagine how disturbed the AE was on his return to Manhattan when the "stupid idiots" in the northbound tollbooths professed no knowledge of the special Buick Electra promotion and made him pay up.

Another victim of Mike's weird sense of humor bit the dust!

Pine Valley

Next to Augusta National, Pine Valley Country Club is perhaps the most prestigious and famous in the United States. It is located in New Jersey, close to Philadelphia, and boasts one of the most exclusive memberships in all of golfdom. An invitation to play Pine Valley is considered a command performance and no golfer worth his wedge would ever turn one down.

In 1973, I was so honored. For some months, NCK and I had been wooing the Scott Paper Company and by the late spring we were getting very close. We had gone through the usual "mating dance" of presentations and visits but, thus far, to no conclusion. Finally, I got a call from the then marketing director, Phil Lippincott (who in later years went on to be a very successful president of the company).

"Hi, Wally," he said, "we really enjoyed our last meeting and would like very much to have your top team come on down to our place at Pine Valley for a day or so. We want to really get to know you guys over dinner, drinks, and a game of golf."

This was it. I knew that the final test for an agency appointment at Scott was a trip to their house on the grounds of Pine Valley. As the story went, if we didn't get drunk at dinner and trip all over ourselves on the golf course, we were in.

"Great, Phil," I replied. "Any time that is convenient for you folks is fine with us." We set a date and prepared for the trip.

From our side would be my executive vice president, Tom Myers, a solid ex-Colgate marketing guy, and myself, plus our corpulent creative director, Mike Chappell, who like many of his ilk could most charitably be described as an unguided missile. I was nervous about bringing him, but our prospective client had specifically requested him. My hands were tied.

The three of us drove down to Pine Valley together. All the way, I coached Mike on his behavior and believed that he really understood. The "Scott House" was lovely, tastefully furnished and manned by a couple who catered to our every wish. Drinks and dinner went very well and after brandy in the library, we all repaired to our beds to get a good night's sleep in anticipation of our early morning golf game.

The next morning, Mike, who sported a walrus mustache, showed up in a faded nondescript golf shirt, bulging khakis hitched up at the waist by a frayed belt, down-at-the-heel golf shoes, and a canvas "Sunday golf bag" containing a completely mismatched set of antique clubs. He was smoking an eight-inch long cigar, which perfectly set off his round moon face and "Prince Valiant" haircut.

One can imagine the attention he received from the members waiting to tee off behind us. As I recall, Phil, Tom, and I hit adequate but undistinguished tee shots and then Mike strode up to the tee. The first thing he did was to balance his huge smoking cigar on the tee ball, much to the consternation of the bystanders. He then hitched up his sagging pants across his ample middle, selected a most disreputable driver from his bag, and teed up his ball. He took a mighty swing and proceeded to shank his shot directly into the crowd of golf carts filled with members.

I saw my whole life passing before me and as was my habit instantly wrote a mental headline for Ad Age—*"Agency Man Kills Pine Valley Founder in Freak Golfing Accident."*

Mike was undisturbed. Without missing a beat he reached into his pocket, teed up another ball, and sent a perfect drive screaming over 275 yards straight down the middle of the fairway.

He picked up his bag and cigar, tapped off the ash "Groucho" style, and said to the assembled bystanders, "Just trying to get your attention."

He ended up shooting just over seventy-five and later told us that a) his mother had been a golf pro back home in Iowa, b) he had attended Iowa State University on a golf scholarship, c) his best friend and boyhood golf partner was Raymond Floyd, and d) when he was low on money he would take his "act" to the Playboy Golf Club in Atlantic City and "hustle the rubes."

We got the business, but to this day I'll never know whether he shanked that ball on purpose or was just making the best out of a bad shot.

It's even money.

The Elephant and the Volkswagen

At Christmas time, before the payola scandals, it used to be the custom of suppliers to give gifts to various agency personnel with whom they had done significant business. The TV stations and publications gave presents to the timebuyers and the printers, engravers and photographers gave to the art directors, and so forth.

One holiday season, an art director at NCK by the name of Louie Musaccio was particularly well taken care of when an engraving company gave him a case of Johnny Walker scotch.

Louie was thrilled and decided to take the liquor home immediately rather than risk leaving it in the office. As he was going to make a stop at a local watering hole before driving home to Long Island, he stowed the case of scotch in his bright red Volkswagen Beetle's trunk, located in front of the driver's compartment.

His stop was a sports bar very near Madison Square Garden. While Louie was having his "going home drink" with his cronies, little did he know what strange activities were taking place around his car.

At that time of the year, Madison Square Garden hosts a Holiday Circus complete with wild animals, acrobats, jugglers, and so forth. Among the "wild animals" are elephants, which are housed across the street from the Garden and brought over by their trainers twice a day to perform. On this particular night one of the trained elephants mistook Louie Musaccio's red Volkswagen for his stool and proceeded to sit on the hood.

When Louie came out of the bar he found his crushed hood and a distraught trainer waiting for him. The trainer told him that the circus would take care of all the costs if he would call them in the morning. As the car was drivable, Louie proceeded to the Long Island Expressway for his trip home to Garden City. This night the traffic was unusually heavy because of a major accident on the expressway. For his part, Louie was in a great hurry as he had found that the circus accident had caused some scotch from a broken bottle to leak through the trunk compartment onto his pants.

In an effort to get around the tow trucks, ambulances, and police cars at the accident site, Louie swung onto the shoulder of the road and tried to drive around the tie-up. Unfortunately for him, a police car spotted his smashed-in front end and pulled him over. The officer obviously thought he had discovered a scofflaw fleeing the scene of an accident. What he found was poor Louie redolent in Scotch fumes.

The police officer quite naturally said, "OK, buddy, what's going on?"

Without thinking Louie said, "Look, officer, it's not what you think, I had nothing to do with the accident. This elephant sat down on the front of my car and broke the scotch, which spilled on my pants. I'm innocent."

Twenty minutes later, while in the holding tank for drunks, he was allowed to make one phone call. Unfortunately, he hadn't learned his lesson because when he called his wife to come and get him he began, "Honey, I'm at the police station and I need you to come and get me. This elephant sat on the front of my car and…"

That's as far as he got when he heard a deafening and heartbreaking "Click!"

Louie spent that holiday night in jail and it was some time before he and his lawyer got everything straightened out with the authorities. It took even longer to convince his wife.

The Playtex Sales Meeting

While I was president of Norman, Craig & Kummel, one of the accounts we handled was International Playtex. Its president, Joel Smilow,[23] was an old friend from P&G days and I'm sure our relationship was helpful in NCK's obtaining the account.

At any rate, NCK maintained a house at the Ocean Reef Club on North Key Largo and I had invited Joan and Joel Smilow to join my wife and me for a week in the sun. It conveniently coincided with the Playtex bra/girdle division's sales meeting being held in Nassau.

Joel and I chartered a plane and flew from the Ocean Reef airstrip to Nassau for the meeting at the big convention hotel on Paradise Island. That night we attended a small dinner hosted by Meshulum Riklis (known by some as "Reckless Riklis"), the chairman and principle owner of the company. It was quite elegant and attended by the key divisional sales and marketing executives. It provided no hint of what I was to experience the next morning. Further, my experience with sales meetings, while considerable, had been limited to very "straight" companies like P&G, Colgate, Kellogg, Pillsbury, etc.

I should point out that despite the fact that Playtex sold 100 percent of its products to women there were at that time (1972) no women in the sales force. Thank God!

The next morning we were awakened at seven o'clock by the Nassau Police Band in full regalia marching through the hotel's interior courtyard playing the bra and girdle division's theme song, which started out, "I'm glad I made the decision, to join the bra and girdle division...."

After coffee and donuts in the ante room of the conference center we filed into our seats, again accompanied by the stirring strains of the bra and girdle division's march (this time played by a large on-stage orchestra) to which most of the salespeople sang the words,.

When all were seated, Mr. Riklis walked down the center aisle and sat in the first row along with Joel Smilow and the rest of the

---

[23] Joel E. Smilow had been my copy section client at P&G. He subsequently left and joined Glendenning Consulting and in 1969 became president of Playtex. In 1979 he hired me away from Gallo to succeed him as president of Playtex, where I remained until 1985.

"brass." I was relegated to the back of the room with the agency types.

It was now eight o'clock in the morning.

With out further ado, the band struck up an overture and a very beautiful woman strode out on stage in complete eveningwear. She then proceeded to perform a complete, and I mean complete, striptease, which would have curled the mustache of the most jaded Frenchman on the Place Pigalle. To say I was shocked is a major understatement. The guys in the front row really got an eyeful but seemed unperturbed and certainly not surprised.

After her performance, the meeting continued seamlessly with normal sales meeting content: past accomplishments, success stories, new products, goals and objectives, and impassioned speeches by sales executives.

It ended at noon and we all repaired to the pool for lunch. I was invited to dine with "Rick," Joel, and some others. We were joined by a very attractive young lady to whom I introduced myself. She was startled and said, "You know me, didn't you see my act this morning?"

I stammered and stumbled and said, "I'm sorry, I didn't recognize you with your clothes on." (A line I was to use years later—see Nancy the Model.)

"That's OK," she said, "it happens all the time." She then gave me her card which, I believe, read—

ROTTEN RITA – ENTERTAINER

The Golf Tournament

The next spring I was invited to play in a very prestigious and weird golf tournament held at the Sleepy Hollow Country Club on the Hudson River. The attendees were almost entirely from the advertising and media fraternity. The tourney was famous for its format.

Each player was given a certain amount of money in scrip and would then proceed to bet with fellow competitors and sponsors on scores and shots throughout the round. The players with the most scrip would win truly extravagant prizes.

At the same time, the tournament wasn't really serious. Some holes had the flag stick stuck in the green nowhere near the cup and on another hole six or eight holes were cut in the green. Further, sponsors would jump out from behind trees just as players were about to hit and make bets with fellow competitors. Needless to say the USGA rules did not apply.

The day of the tournament was extremely cold and blustery, a result of the cold wind blowing in off the Hudson. All of those playing were bundled up in sweaters and raingear and still were uncomfortable.

Somewhere in the middle of the round my foursome approached a short par three with an elevated tee and a full carry over water. It seemed a little odd at the time that so many members and sponsors were surrounding the hole, but I took little note of it.

I was the first to hit, and as I addressed my tee shot several sponsors suggested rather large bets that I wouldn't hit the green. As it was only 150 yards or so downwind, I accepted.

Little did I know.

Just as I began my backswing, someone pulled on a rope and a stark naked woman appeared in a canoe just below the tee on my right side. Needless to say I lost all my bets.

On the other hand, I got the last laugh when she looked up at me and said, "Hey, it's Wally, the guy from Playtex, how the hell are you? It's Rotten Rita and I'm freezing my ass off out here."

She then wrapped herself up in a blanket and they pulled the canoe back into position for the next "performance."

18-Hour Girdle Circles

In 1971, my good friend Joel Smilow assigned Norman, Craig & Kummel New York some Playtex business. Our first assignment was the 18-Hour Girdle, which had been running the famous "My Girdle Is Killing Me" campaign, but the client decided it needed refreshing.

As a first step, the agency held that the only way to really understand any product was to get down to the technical aspects of it and learn what makes it tick. So the account group, the creative group, and I planned a trip to Paramus, New Jersey, where Playtex had its technical center.

Once arrived, we went into a large room, much like a boardroom, sat down, and met with Jack Locasio, who at that time was the head designer, Joel Coleman, the corporate legal counsel, and several others. We had come up with a claim that noted the 18-Hour Girdle and only the 18-Hour Girdle stretched 360 degrees—two dimensions —up and down and left and right, whereas the girdles sold by our unscrupulous competitors only stretched in one dimension, that is, 180 degrees up and down.

But how to prove it? Thus the reason for being in the room.

This being my first meeting, I didn't know what to expect. Shortly, the door opened and a model came in wearing the 18-Hour Girdle, which in and of itself was sort of shock; but we got over that as she proceeded to walk around, bending and stretching and so on, to show us how the garment performed.

We then asked her to put on the competitor's product, which she did. At this point, we had no visible proof of our superior stretch claim. So, I suggested that she put the 18-Hour Girdle back on and we draw a circle on one of her buttocks and had her bend over a chair. We could easily see how the circle stretched evenly, making a larger circle. Then when we put the competitive girdle on her and drew the same circle, and had her stretch, we got an elongated oval.

This idea was greeted with cheers from all sides and we proceeded with the plan. Barbara, the model, came back in wearing the 18-Hour Girdle. She stood in front of me. I then squatted behind her with a magic marker and a round-circle template and proceeded, basically, to draw a circle.

As I worked with the pen, I looked around the room and thought to myself, "Thank God my parents can't see me doing this; to know that all the money they spent to send me to Harvard College has finally come down to me crouching behind a girdle model and drawing a circle on her ass."

The result was that we created a new 18-Hour campaign known as "I Forgot I Had It On." The "circle" demonstration was used successfully and legally for three or four years.

I guess my college education paid off.

Linda and the Condoms

My niece, Linda Taft, came to work for NCK in 1972. She had never worked for an advertising agency before and was fresh from graduate school in special education in Boston. She decided she wanted a change of scenery and applied to me for a job. I told her I couldn't show favoritism but would arrange for an interview. (I wonder how objective people are when they are interviewing the president's niece.)

In due course, she was offered a junior account executive's job on the Vick Chemical account. We handled several of their cold remedies, Lavoris mouthwash, and several other minor brands. For a while everything went very well and Linda did a fine job. Unfortunately, she did too good a job and fell in love with her client, Michael Solomon, who would subsequently become her husband.

When I got wind of the romance, I told her that while I was in favor of close client/agency relations, I didn't think it should go as far as it had. We would have to reassign her to another account. She understood and asked where I thought I could use her. As it turned out I had only one opening for someone with her limited experience. It was on the Young Rubber Company account. Young Rubber was the largest manufacturer of prophylactics in the United States. Naturally, she was a little squeamish about this assignment but ultimately took it with good grace.

As one can imagine this position precipitated many jokes and Linda was the butt of them all:

"Hey Linda, want to have an R&D session together on your new products?"

"We're having a sales meeting, how about a product demonstration?"

For Linda this was nonetheless a quite interesting job as the client was very creative in developing new products. For example, one was packaged in glow-in-the-dark wrappers: *"You'll never have to turn on the light..."*

On another occasion, they developed another new product and packaging, which Linda had to take into test market. The product was called "Fiesta" and consisted of five condoms packed on a little cardboard tray, each in a different color (much like the old candy called "Chuckles"). The condoms came in red, green, yellow, blue, and orange. The idea was that "Fiesta" provided a high-end novelty product which had strong display value in the stores that would carry them (remember this was 1972) and worked well in the print advertising the agency developed for *Playboy* and *Esquire*.

As a joke, the creative department decided to make Linda the Betty Crocker of condoms and, in all the advertising, they ran a line that said, "For information and customer service on the Fiesta product, contact Linda Taft" and gave her office phone number.

Unfortunately, the product had a tragic flaw, which wasn't discovered until the brand entered the test market. It seems that the dye used for the red product had a unique property. Under heat and pressure, i.e., normal use, the dye would transfer from the condom to the skin, from which it was almost impossible to remove. Obviously, under use conditions in the sanctity of marriage this was an inconvenience, but when used for extramarital purposes it was a tragedy: "Gee, honey, I can't imagine how this happened…"

As one can imagine, Linda was deluged with calls from all sorts of irate customers and had to explain how to remove the dye. "Don't use nail polish remover or Lava soap." After that experience nothing much ever fazed her.

The Fiesta product was pulled from the market and to the best of my knowledge never reappeared.

Thank God!

Cold Power at Macy's

One of the standard devices used by the advertising agencies in the sixties and seventies was to enlist the recognition and stopping power of a celebrity. This was a common practice and we at Norman, Craig & Kummel were no different from the rest.

Cold Power was a detergent made by Colgate-Palmolive, which we had introduced and handled for many years. It was quite a success considering the fact that we were competing against the mighty Procter & Gamble.

A practice we employed to stretch our advertising budget was the development of cooperative advertising with other manufacturers. In one instance, we decided to do some work with a company called Tiny Tots Togs, a producer of children's play clothes.

For some reason, it was decided to use Craig Stevens, the actor who had played Peter Gunn so successfully on TV, in this commercial. The idea was that Stevens would stand in front of Macy's, walk through the swinging door, and recite the line, "Here we are at Macy's, world's largest department store, where on the second floor they sell Tiny Tots Togs."

What we didn't know was that while Stevens was incredibly photogenic he was totally incapable of retaining a line. In fact, we subsequently learned that the entire Peter Gunn series was shot in what is called "reaction," meaning that Stevens rarely had a line looking at the camera. All his lines were delivered off-camera so he could read them off the script.

For our purposes, we had to shoot our commercial at night after Macy's had closed because obviously we couldn't disrupt the store's business with our crew, lights, and paraphernalia. So it was that we all showed up one freezing night in front of Macy's waiting to shoot the establishing shot from which the whole commercial stemmed.

Stevens emerged from his Winnebago and look great, deeply tanned and beautifully groomed. He was given his instructions, which were quite simple. All he had to do was to walk through the revolving door of Macy's, look into the camera, and say, "Here we are at Macy's, the world's largest department store, where on the second floor they sell Tiny Tots Togs."

I admit Tiny Tots Togs is a mouthful but the fact is Stevens could never get through the first line.

Finally the director decided to drop the second line, which would be added in voice-over later; hence, all Stevens had to say, was, "Here we are at Macy's, the world's largest department store."

After twelve takes it looked like Craig finally had it right and we were about to go for the final take. At that point Stevens walked through the swinging door, passed in front of the camera, continued all the way around until he was outside again, and delivered the line flawlessly.

That was the end of the shoot; the director decided to "loop" the entire audio portion in voice-over by shooting Stevens in a long shot to which we added his lines in postproduction.

The moral, if any, is that you never know the problems you're going to encounter until you get on the set.

Walter W. Bregman

The Kodachrome Plant

As everyone knows, research can be very tricky. It is particularly difficult to analyze raw data and to ensure that the proper results have been obtained. The following story, while perhaps apocryphal, does make the point.

Some years ago, the Kodak Company was interested in building a new Kodachrome processing plant in the state of Georgia. In order to ascertain whether or not the geographical area surrounding the plant had sufficient potential, they hired a well-known research company to go into the field and find out.

The company dutifully developed a probability sample of the surrounding five states and fielded an extensive questionnaire, the purpose of which was to develop projectible numbers on color photography.

When the results were tabulated, analyzed, and sent to the main office in Rochester, NY, the executives there were ecstatic. It appeared that the future for color photography in the South was even higher than that in the North. The research results had more than justified the marketing department's recommendation to build the new plant.

Unfortunately, after the factory was built and put online, sales results were extremely disappointing. In actual fact the incidents of sales of Kodachrome film fell far below the national average and the plant turned out to be an extremely expensive white elephant.

How could this have happened?

During the postmortem the marketing department discovered a fatal flaw in their research technique. The critical question buried among a number of other questions in the research was:

"What percentage of your photography is colored photography?"

You can probably guess the answer. In the five surrounding states, which had a disproportionately high black population, the answer of course was:

"All of my photography is colored photography."

And so perhaps even before the computer revolution, the phrase "garbage in, garbage out" proved to be true.

The Business Card

One of the most famous and successful television shows in the 1960's was "Rowan and Martin's Laugh In." The show starred, among others, a crazy young actress named Judy Carne. She was bubbly, perky, unpredictable, and, hence, extremely well-known by the television audience.

She was most famous for the line "Sock it to me," which she shared with Goldie Hawn. They would shout the line at odd moments in the show after which the subject (sometimes themselves) would be drenched with a bucket of water. Many famous celebrities participated in this running gag including John Wayne, Frank Sinatra, Elizabeth Taylor, and even Richard Nixon.

In a word, Judy personified Andy Warhol's claim that everybody has fifteen minutes of fame.

At Norman, Craig & Kummel, we were casting about for a way to introduce a new Playtex padded bra designed for small-busted women. Someone in the creative department decided that Judy Carne would be perfect for the role in that a) she was extremely famous at the time, and b) she had small breasts and was well-known on the show for her lack of endowment.

In due course we contacted Judy, she agreed to do the commercial, and we proceeded to Hollywood for the production. The night before the shoot we were all invited to a party at the director's bungalow on the property of the Bel Air Hotel. When I joined the party it was in full swing and the room was jammed with agency and client personnel. (Everyone wants to go to a celebrity shoot.)

After a few minutes, I wandered over to where Judy was standing and proceeded to introduce myself.

"Hi," I said, "I am Wally Bregman, the president of Norman, Craig & Kummel. I just wanted to stop by and introduce myself."

She looked at me for long time and said, "Bullshit! You're much too young to be president of an agency." (Judy was known for her salty language.)

I protested to the contrary and told her that I really was president of the agency, but she would have none of that. She remained unconvinced. Finally I reached in my pocket and pulled out one of my business cards, which I handed to her. She looked at it for a long time and said, "Listen kid, if Mr. Bregman ever finds out that you're passing his cards out at parties you're going to be in a shit load of trouble."

I finally had to get the director, Hal Tulchin, to come over and convince her that I really was who I said I was.

The commercial was sensational and was the hit of the Playtex sales meeting in Nassau (see story relating to this meeting).

The Padded Bra Film

In addition to Judy Carne's qualifications as a small-busted semi-celebrity was her water drenching routine, which tied into the Playtex Padded Bras' claim of "will withstand at least thirty washings."

We created a commercial that opened with Judy just coming off stage after being doused with water, having said the famous "Sock it to me" line. She then turned to camera and said something like, "When you get soaked as many times as I do, you have to have a bra that will withstand at least thirty washings; and my bra is the Playtex Padded Bra," and so on.

Interestingly enough, the commercial was turned down by network continuity on the basis that NBC had trademarked "Sock it to me," and therefore we couldn't say it. As it turned out, it didn't really matter all that much. We constructed a set that looked just like "Laugh In," had her soaked with water and walk off stage to great applause, and then do her copy line. But we couldn't say "Sock it to me."

After we completed the successful shooting of this commercial, we decided that we wanted to put something on film to introduce the padded bra to the Playtex sales force, who were meeting in Nassau that year. Judy agreed and I, along with one of our copywriters, quickly wrote a "brilliant" sales meeting script.

Judy agreed to be soaked one more time, but she made it very clear that this was going to be a "one take" shoot because it wasn't in her contract and she was really doing it as a "friendly." Because Judy clearly hadn't time to memorize the script, we printed out my sales meeting speech on idiot cards. Hal Tulchin heated up the cameras, and we knew we had only one chance to make it work.

The cameras came on, the lights lit up, sound rolled, and we soaked Judy with water.

She turned to the camera, and said, "Hi, there, all of you folks out in Playtexland and all you Playtex salesmen." (We had no women in the sales force in those days.) "Wally Bregman, the agency fink, wrote me a really dumb script but I won't read it. I'm just here to tell you one thing. Big tits are out, and little ones are in, as long as they wear the new Playtex padded bra."

I don't know what she said after that because I was completely convulsed, as was everyone else on the set. All I know is that when we showed her tape at the sales meeting in Nassau, at the end of the first line, the sales force was on its feet stamping and screaming and left the room ready to do or die for the Playtex Padded Bra.

Milton Biow

One of the true giants of the advertising business in the 1960's was a mad genius named Milton Biow. His agency at its height handled P&G, Schlitz, Pepsi, and Philip Morris, among others. (See P&G Sales Meeting). He was also responsible for creating the $64,000 Question for Revlon. His agency was truly a jewel box and a money machine.

As the story goes, Milton was having drinks at the Hotel New Yorker with Alfred E. Lyon, the legendary advertising manager of Philip Morris, when they heard a bellboy calling a guest for a phone message. It was through this chance happening and their inspiration that the famous line "Call for Philip Morris" was born and a four-foot-tall Italian named Johnny Roventini became an advertising icon, as well as rich and famous.

One wonderful story about Milton has to do with his new business skills. It is reputed that after a presentation at the agency, Milton would invite the prospective clients back to his lavish Fifth Avenue apartment for dinner.

The dinner was served in his beautifully appointed Regency dining room. After dinner, Milton would take the prospect on a tour of his penthouse to show off his priceless collection of French Impressionist painters. After visiting his Matisse, Van Gogh, Cézanne, and Toulouse-Lautrec collection, the tour would end in his gorgeous paneled study overlooking Central Park. He would offer Napoleon brandy and Cuban cigars and then, standing in front of his carved marble fireplace under a priceless Monet, survey the room and say, "And so gentlemen, you see, it *does* pay to advertise!"

Another story deals with the way Milton handled the inevitable problems that occur in the agency business. It seems that buried in the mailroom of the agency was a very attractive elderly man. This man served as the scapegoat for any and all mistakes made by the agency.

For example, if a client's insertion missed a publication and the client complained to Milton, he would get on his phone and say to his secretary, "Send Fred Williams up to my office immediately."

Dutifully, Williams would appear at the door, immaculately dressed in a blue blazer, gray flannel slacks, button-down shirt, and repp tie.

"Williams, are you responsible for handling the print insertions for XYZ Company?" Biow would ask.

"Yes sir, I am," Williams would respond.

"Well then you must be responsible for missing this week's insertion in *Life*. You know, at the Biow Agency we can't tolerate that kind of mistake. You're fired. Pick up your pay and get out."

On cue, Williams blubbered some sort of lame excuse and pleaded for another chance.

At this point, the client would usually join in and plead leniency, but Milton would be unyielding. "No, we can't make an exception. Your business is too important to us to accept anything but perfection. I'm sorry, Williams, but you must go."

Williams, of course, would go back to the mailroom and resume his normal duties.

Supposedly Williams was fired for everything from bad artwork to billing errors and everything in between. Further, he was reputed to have kept a log detailing for which clients he was fired so that he never showed up twice.

Milton Biow was truly a genius.

Famous Sons – I

In 1973, I was elected president of the New York chapter of the American Association of Advertising Agencies. The position was far from honorific and covered everything from dealing with the networks and the National Association of Broadcasters to handling public relations on behalf of the industry. As a result, I was a frequent visitor to the association's New York office.

Our executive director at the time was a tall (six-foot four), distinguished, and experienced advertising man. One day after we had finished our business, I said to him, "John, you just don't seem yourself today. You seem distracted and not quite with it."

"You're right, Wally," he replied. "It's my son. As you know, he graduated from Harvard a couple of years ago with honors and is now finishing up at the medical school. The problem is after all this effort, he doesn't want to practice medicine."

"Well, what does he want to do?"

"You're not going to believe this," John said. "He wants to become an author. In fact, he's almost finished writing his first book. It's a science fiction medical thing about a virus that attacks the population; some sort of a strain that starts with an "A." I can't remember. His mother and I are really troubled that he would spend all that time and money to become a doctor and now he's going to be a starving author."

As I recall, I commiserated with him and suggested that the young man would surely come to his senses in due time, once he got this "wild oat" out of his system.

Thankfully, he never did. That young man, the would-be doctor, went on to become one of the most successful writers and producers in history. His father was John Crichton and he was, of course, Michael Crichton.

221

Leonard Lavin

In early 1970, my wife and I were preparing to take my recently widowed mother on a trip to London and Paris. My mother flew to New York from her home in Palm Springs, spent a few days with her grandchildren, and prepared for our flight to the continent.

The morning of the day of our flight (we were to take an overnight plane) I received a call from the legendary Leonard Lavin, founder and CEO of Alberto-Culver.

"Walter Bregman," I answered.

"Walter, this is Leonard Lavin. I am in New York for a few days and I'd like to see you about NCK handling some of our business."

This was the often dreamed of but seldom received "transom business." No competition, no new business pitch, no travel, no entertainment—no nothing!

"Certainly," I answered. "When would you like to meet?"

"How about two o'clock today at my suite, number 1111 at the Dorset Hotel?" he responded.

"I'll be there. Is there anything or anybody else you'd like me to bring along?" I asked.

"Nope. See you at two," and he hung up—a man of few words.

My next call was to my wife who was putting the finishing touches on her packing. My mother was already packed; her suitcases were in the front hall awaiting the airport driver.

"Honey, I have bad news. I can't get away today. You can go with my mother and I will meet you in a day or so, or we can put it off a couple days and go together."

Having been through this routine before, she chose the latter option, figuring if they left without me I'd never join them and she'd be stuck in Paris with my mother. My mother was thunderstruck. This had never happened to her in her forty years of marriage to a scrap iron broker.

That afternoon, I showed up at the Dorset and met Leonard. He didn't waste any time on the niceties.

"I'm going to fire J. Walter (Thompson) today and I want to know what part of the business you can handle," he said and proceeded to hand me a typed sheet that listed all of the Alberto-Culver brands and the approximate billing.

This was an unbelievable windfall. JWT Chicago handled the entire account—fifty million at least. The problem was that I had terrible conflict problems between Alberto-Culver brands and Colgate-Palmolive, Chesebrough-Ponds, Plough, Clairol, and Shulton.

In the end I sat across the coffee table from Mr. Lavin and went down the list. I crossed off those products that were direct conflicts with brands we already handled. As it was, I knew I was in for a rough time clearing some assignments with my clients. When it was over, I ended up with about thirty million dollars in potential billing and suggested that Lavin give the rest to the Compton agency, which didn't have much H&BA (health and beauty aids) business.

"OK, we have a deal," he said and shook my hand. "I'd like you to be out in Chicago when I get back in three days. You can meet our people and get a briefing on all the products you're going to be handling—it'll probably take a couple of days."

I took two thoughts away from his last remark: 1) "You" was not used in the generic sense. This guy had just given me the majority of his advertising budget without ever meeting one other person from NCK. "You" meant me! 2) Bye, bye European trip. This deal was going to take all of my time for the next month.

Well-run agencies don't have a bunch of people waiting around for new business to show up. In this case I was going to have to reassign some existing staff and hire a lot more account people, writers, artists, etc., and do it fast. We had to hit the ground running.

My wife took the next call in stride and began to unpack. I think she was half expecting it anyway. My mother, who was all packed, simply took the next flight back to Palm Springs after telling my wife that she thought we were both crazy.

A week later, after our briefings at the Melrose Park headquarters of AC, I got my next shock. Our CFO stopped into my office and said, "You know any reason why we would be getting a check for a quarter of a million dollars from Alberto?"

"No, but deposit it and I'll find out," I replied.

I called my counterpart at JWT in Chicago, Wayne Fichinger. In the event of an account turnover, the agencies are supposed to meet and work out a smooth transition even if they are archrivals. Sort of like the surrender ceremony on the battleship Missouri.

What he said shocked me.

"Oh, I guess Leonard never got around to telling you. Unlike any other client you or we've ever handled, AC does not believe in the standard ninety-day notice clause. When you get the account you get it from day one and similarly when you lose it, bang! The checks you're getting are the results of ads we created and media we bought: you're getting the commission as from your meeting in New York, after which Leonard called me and fired us."

What followed was the most bizarre experience of my advertising career. For the next four months NCK churned out literally hundreds of storyboards and scripts, which were presented to AC in Chicago practically every week. We presented on shampoos, on deodorants, on food products, on hair care, on body care—you name it, we worked on it. I had three creative teams working full time on the ten or twelve brands we were assigned.

We never sold one single ad to the client.

In the meantime, torrents of money continued to flow into my accounting department. Even with all the creative work and travel, AC was the most profitable account we handled. No media buying, no commercial production, no marketing, no entertaining, and only motel rooms in Melrose Park.

Finally, I called Leonard up. Despite several requests for a meeting, I had not set eyes on him since our encounter at the Dorset.

"Leonard, this relationship just isn't working. We obviously can't please your people and my creative teams are in revolt. Frankly, I can't get anyone else to work on your business so rather than destroy my agency, we'll either have to find a different way to work together or I'll have to resign the business." I figured he'd a least allow me to show him our work—wrong!

"OK, Wally, if that's the way you feel, we'll just call it off," he said and he hung up.

The next day it was announced that the NCK portion of the Alberto-Culver business was being reassigned to Compton-Chicago. The same day the money stopped flowing in.

Thus ended the only client-agency relationship on which I made money and never ran an ad.

Raquel Welch

Clairol was a very important client of NCK, not because of its size but because of the opportunity it represented. Further, the chairman and president, Dick and Bruce Gelb, were friends of Norman's. Upon my accession to the presidency of NCK, I also became friendly with these two very nice gentlemen (more so with Bruce). At any rate, we were an "agency of record" but handled a fraction of their business and were eager to improve our position.

Finally, I got a call from Bruce to come over to their offices in the Seagram Building for a briefing on a new hair color product. I was thrilled; hair coloring was the mother lode and a new brand in this highly competitive field would mean multimillions in billing. I was also delighted to have beaten out Foote, Cone and Belding, their major agency.

At the initial meeting, the client explained that the new product was a semi-permanent hair-coloring product, exclusively for brown-haired women, called "True Brunette." This could be huge. Despite what the public thinks, the biggest market for hair coloring is not "Blonds Having More Fun" but everyday brunettes who either want to enhance their highlights or cover gray.

In due course I assigned a creative and account team to the project but kept in very close touch with developments as Bruce had made me promise to do (the extraction of such a promise is *de rigueur* among clients).

After several creative presentations we jointly decided that True Brunette would be best introduced by a celebrity presenter who was known for beautiful brown hair. A series of research projects and group sessions winnowed the possible list down to the eventual winner—Raquel Welch.

Through an odd set of circumstances Miss Welch's agent at the time was a man named Marty Bregman, whose office was about two blocks from mine in the Western Publishing Company building. This produced rather odd phone calls:

"Mr. Bregman's office."

"Is Mr. Bregman in? Mr. Bregman calling."

"Just one moment please."

"Mr. Bregman, Mr. Bregman in on the other line," etc., etc., ad nauseum.

Finally, a deal was struck and we drafted the contract. Unlike any other star talent I had ever dealt with, Raquel acted as her own agent as far as the contract was concerned. To my shock and alarm she dropped by my office one day with a marked-up copy of the proposed contract (she refused to deal with anyone but the president of the agency—they tell me that this is a common ploy by "stars" in Hollywood). I couldn't believe my eyes. She had taken a standard "star talent" contract and made changes and addendums on each and every page. Most were inconsequential but some were doozies:

She had to have her own Winnebago dressing room stocked with specified (by her) foods and drinks (her own special designer water). The mobile home had to have an operating toilet, the underneath of which had to be sandbagged and insulated so no one could ever hear her flushing!

While we expected to provide the obligatory limo to pick her up and return her to her home, she specified that it had to be available all day long exclusively for her use. (This was a pain in the neck as it is customary to utilize the limo during a shoot to fetch and carry props, costumes, etc.)

In addition to normal artistic control "which will not be unreasonably withheld," she demanded total artistic control of the scenes in which she appeared and approval of the "final cut."

After a log and protracted negotiation session we finally signed the contract and proceeded out to Hollywood to shoot the commercial. Thankfully, I didn't have to attend the shoot but I still got several frantic phone calls from Raquel when "the lighting wasn't right," "the costume makes me look fat," and "the director (Hal Tulchin) is a shit!"

At the same time that the shoot ended I decided to take some time off, so my wife and I flew out to Palm Springs to see my mother and stepfather. In the middle of the visit I got yet another call from Raquel demanding my presence the next day at an editing studio on Sunset where the commercial was being assembled. I really had no choice if I wanted to ever see the film on the air so I agreed.

I left Palm Springs early and drove the two hours to Beverly Hills. At the studio I found Raquel and her two children, a boy and a girl, ages eight and nine, I believe. Thence followed the most bizarre experience of my advertising career. After she had rejected the "director's cut," she demanded to see every single take and after each one would say to her children, "How do you think the lady looks in this one?" (Always "the lady," never "Mommy.") As you can imagine, there were hours of takes but she was unrelenting. Endlessly she ran take after take, commenting on the "lady." I was somewhere between catatonic and hysterical. I could have been on the tennis court at the Racquet Club.

Finally she and her children agreed and assembled their idea of what the commercial should look like. I thought it was pretty bad or at least not as good as the one the professionals had put together.

It was time for her coup de grace. "I know how you agency and studio people work," she said.

In my stupefied state I had no idea what she was driving at.

"In order to keep you from changing 'our' commercial, I want a final print produced and I will sign the leader," she stated.

Naturally, I agreed and she haughtily signed the filmstrip. Naturally, as soon as she left the studio, I had the editor remove it from her cut and glue it to ours. At all subsequent viewings she smugly took credit for her version of the commercial.

As a codicil, both the product and commercial bombed and I never did get a substantial piece of Clairol business.

Bill Bernbach

I ran into the legendary Bill Bernbach at a Clairol sales meeting in Puerto Rico. He had just arrived at the hotel and was hot, tired, and exasperated.

"Where's Norman?" he asked.

"He's down at his house at the Ocean Reef Club," I answered.

"Wonderful ... David (Ogilvy) is at his place in the South of France, Fax (Cone) is skiing, and I'm at a damn sales meeting."

"Let's have a drink and cool off," I suggested.

We went to an outdoor bar and ordered a libation.

"This has been a really bad day," he said. "Not only was my Eastern flight packed and late, but I had the damnedest thing happen this morning before I left the office. There was this copywriter that our people were hot to hire so they asked me talk to her and sort of give her a pep talk. Which I did. I spent about an hour with her telling her all about the agency and our creative philosophy.

"At the end of the interview I figured I'd ask for the order so I said, 'Well, after all you've heard what do you think?'

"She looked me square in the eye and said, 'Oh, I'm definitely going to take the job. I've wanted to work at Doyle, Dane all my life.'"

Sic Transit Gloria.

The Perils of Travel

As any professional traveler knows, traveling for business is no picnic. Oh, your friends who work for banks and never go any further than the "home" office for a briefing are impressed when you "jet to the coast," or "run off to Paris for a presentation." They never see the delayed and cancelled flights, the uncomfortable seats, and the ever-present jet lag; not to mention the terrible strain it puts on one's family life.

The above was brought home to me one night as I sat in the bar at the TWA Ambassador's Club at JFK waiting for my "indefinitely delayed" flight to London.

There were only two customers there and the other fellow, an attractive but obviously worried young man, was talking to the bartender.

"Do you think she'll ever forgive me?" he asked.

"Yeah, sure," replied the bartender as he polished his glassware.

"No, seriously, don't hold back, give it to me straight. Do you really think she will?" the young man went on.

"Yeah, I really do. It may take a while but I'm sure she will forgive you," the barkeep said.

"You're just trying to make me feel good. She'll never forgive or forget," the unhappy customer said as he downed the remainder of what was obviously neither his first nor second drink.

"Look, buddy, we've been going over this for the last half hour and I'm not going to change my mind; in time she will definitely forgive you. Now, you'd better get the hell out of here. They just called your plane to Frankfurt."

At this, the sad passenger pulled out his wallet, put a twenty on the bar and said, "Well, thanks, from your mouth to God's ear." And rushed out of the club.

I couldn't contain my curiosity. "What in the world was that all about?" I asked.

"Well, you've just seen the guy that won the schmuck of the year award," the bartender said.

"How come?" I asked.

"The guy's just come in from Chicago, see, and they got a huge snowstorm out there so he asks his wife to drive him to the airport 'cause he doesn't trust the limo companies. He's got to make the New York flight to hook up with his connection to Frankfurt. Naturally, he drives and they take their two little kids and their dog along for the ride.

"Well you see, the traffic is really backed up with the heavy snow and all, and he barely gets to the terminal on time. So, quick he kisses the wife and kids good-bye, jumps out of the car, grabs his suitcase from the trunk, and runs like hell to make his plane. Which he does by the skin of his teeth.

"The plane takes off and as he's sipping his first drink, he reaches in his pocket and, guess what, the idiot's got the friggin' car keys. His old lady is sitting in front of the TWA terminal at O'Hare in her car, in the middle of a snowstorm with two little kids and a dog, but no keys.

"He called home when he got here but there was no answer. That's why he doesn't think she'll forgive him."

"And you really think she will?" I asked, not knowing whether to laugh or cry.

"Nah, he's screwed," he said, "but he seemed like such a nice guy I hated to piss in his shoes."

For what it's worth I agreed with the bartender.

The Lifestyle Change

In the spring of 1973 I decided to really take charge of my life and get into shape. I quit smoking (cold turkey) and stopped drinking at the same time. I also cut way back on the fifteen or twenty cups of coffee I was drinking every day.

Naturally, I felt better from the beginning. I stopped coughing. I slept better. I felt great when I woke up. I had made a major turnaround in my life. I thought things were going along beautifully.

One day after about three weeks into my new regimen I got a phone call from Bill Watchman, the division manager of the Colgate toilet goods division, inviting me to lunch. This was a little unusual but I didn't think anything of it as Bill and I had been friends for years. He had been the Colgate marketing manager in Europe when I was president of NCK Europe and we had worked and traveled extensively together. He told me he had made a reservation at Christ Cella's, a wonderful "chophouse" off of Third Avenue.

I showed up at the appointed time and was shown to his table. After we had exchanged pleasantries for a few minutes he got into the reason for the lunch.

"The reason I invited you to lunch today was to fire NCK off all the toilet goods division business," he said.

I was shocked. Our brands were doing well and there had been no prior indication of trouble.

"I can't believe it," I said. "What's the reason?"

"You're the reason," he answered.

"Me?"

"Yes, you. You've always been a tough son of a bitch, but since you quit smoking and drinking you've become insufferable. None of our people even want to go to a meeting if you're going to be there. They know you'll beat the crap out of them."

I was shocked but held my tongue.

"So here's the deal," Bill went on. "You can have one of these right now," pointing to his Stoli on the rocks, "or one of these," holding out his pack of Larks, "or you're fired. We're not going to put up with the 'new' Wally Bregman any longer."

To an agency man this was no dilemma. I merely took the proffered cigarette, lit it up, and ordered my own Stoli.

Thus ended my "makeover."

Charles Revson

For whatever reason, Norman, Craig & Kummel always attracted eponymous companies as clients. Perhaps it was because Norman related to these self-made men who, in many instances, shared his own modest background and possessed the same burning desire for success and recognition. On our roster over the years were Shulton (George Schultz), Plough Inc. (Abe Plough), Ronson (Louis Aronson), and Chanel (Coco Chanel and later the Wertheimers).

Perhaps the most famous and complex relationship was between the agency and Charles Revson. Charles was, of course, the legendary founder of the Revlon Cosmetics Company, the sponsor of the "Sixty-four Thousand Dollar Question" quiz show and the man who single-handedly ruled and dictated women's cosmetic styles for over thirty years. He was also, like many of his ilk, a bit of a tyrant who treated the agency and its principals as just another set of servants with whom he often dealt harshly.

According to Norman it was not uncommon to have a copy presentation run through the lunch hour. This problem didn't faze Charles. At precisely twelve o'clock he had his ritual lunch, a well-done hamburger, a sliced tomato, and a Coke, served to him at his desk that sat on a raised platform looking down on the agency supplicants. As the meeting continued, Charles would eat his lunch, much to the consternation of the starving agency. Sometimes the meetings would last till mid-afternoon or later but Charles apparently never recognized the other participants' need for nutrition.

Another of his less endearing habits was to call Norman at all hours of the night with new ideas and inspirations. Apparently Charles was an insomniac whose considerable waking hours were devoted to his company and the cosmetics business. Frequently Norman's phone would ring at two or three in the morning and he would hear, "Hey, kiddie (Charles called everybody "kiddie"), I've got a great idea. I'm sending the limo around to get you." Norman would get up and get dressed to be chauffeured to Charles' apartment for yet another predawn meeting. ("The client agency relationship is best described as that of master and slave" –Anonymous.)

233

Charles had a son named Peter who during his adolescent years was somewhat of an educational problem.[24] At the time NCK became involved Peter had been "asked to leave" several prep schools on the East Coast and was giving Charles fits. At one of his late night soirees with Norman he said, "Hey, kiddie, didn't your partner David go to one of those fancy-pantsy, waspy prep schools?"[25]

Norman had no choice but to answer honestly, "Yes, Charles, I believe he did."

B. David Kaplan had indeed gone to a fancy prep school. He had been born in France the son of famous radiologists who were themselves students of Marie Curie. When his family moved to the United States he was educated at the Taft School, a small and exclusive boys-only facility founded by the brother of President William Howard Taft and situated on two hundred rolling acres in Watertown, Connecticut. Kaplan went on to Yale, graduated in the class of 1942, and served with distinction in the OSS. He made two combat jumps into occupied France where his flawless French made him invaluable.

David Kaplan was, if anything, the "anti-Norman." He was a small rotund balding man, meticulous about his appearance; slow to anger, soft spoken and above all a very private person. Norman knew that getting David involved with Charles' wild kid was not going to go down well with his reticent partner.

"What did you have in mind, Charles?" Norman asked, knowing full well what was coming.

"Well, I figured David and I could go up to his school and see if we can get my kid into it." Charles responded predictably.

Thus ensued a number of acrimonious conversations between Norman and Kaplan but the next weekend, David's protests notwithstanding, he and Charles motored up to Watertown for a

---

[24] Peter Revson would eventually become a world-class Grand Prix racing driver and a member of the legendary McLaren Formula 1 Racing Team. In his career he was twice fifth highest-ranking driver and amassed 61 Grand Prix points. He died tragically at age thirty-five in a practice accident in Kyalami, South Africa.

[25] B. David Kaplan was the "silent partner" of NCK. The agency had in fact been founded by Norman, Eugene Kummel, and Kaplan. Norman in a fit of paranoia had thought that "Norman, Kaplan and Kummel" sounded "too Jewish" so he had drafted Walter Craig, a TV producer, to be a "founder" and put him on the letterhead even though Kaplan and not Craig had put up the money.

meeting with Taft's headmaster. It did not go well. Charles, naturally, showed absolutely no deference toward the educator or the institution and as they strolled the beautifully groomed campus he persisted in expectorating on the grounds.

Finally, after a thorough tour of the classrooms, the gym, the library and the dormitories, the three men arrived back at Charles' huge Cadillac limousine where the chauffeur stood stiffly beside the open door.

Charles looked the headmaster in the eye and said, "OK, kiddie, how much?"

Kaplan was horrified and the other man stunned.

"I beg your pardon," croaked the headmaster.

"Look, pal," replied Charles, "it's been my experience that if you want to get the best table you've got to tip the headwaiter. How much?"

There is no record of how this conversation ended; however, David Kaplan told me that a) Peter Revson was admitted to Taft and graduated with some difficulty, and b) the tuition paid by the Revsons was the highest in the history of the Taft School.

A few years later in the fallout from the scandal attached to "The Sixty-four Thousand Dollar Question" NCK lost the Revlon account despite having been responsible for some of the company's most memorable campaigns.

Norman's Genius

Of the many things for which Norman B. Norman was not given proper credit, perhaps the most egregious was his ability to instinctively identify a potentially successful new product. The best example of this knack occurred one fall day in 1972. Norman called me into his office and said, "I think it would be a good idea if you, Tom (Myers, my executive V.P.), Ed (Roncarelli, manager of Canada and the Caribbean), and I bought a house together at the Ocean Reef Club."

I'd never heard of the place but after Norman described all the amenities of the club, it sounded like a good idea to me. It sounded even better when he explained that the company would loan us the money to buy the house.

The next week Norman, Tom, and I flew down to Miami. On the plane Norman took a bottle of pink fluid out of his attaché case and showing it to us said, "I have another reason for going down to Miami. See this stuff, Gail (his wife) buys it at Dwayne-Reed. She swears by it and believes it actually removes wrinkles. I haven't been able to find a thing out about the company except its offices are in Miami near the airport. Let's stop by on the way down to Key Largo."

After we landed and picked up our rental car, we checked the map and drove to a run-down industrial strip by the railroad tracks consisting of a number of small manufacturing operations. Each had an office in the front, shop floors behind the offices, and a loading dock in the back.

As we drove up to our "target" I mentioned to Norman that this didn't look like much. He agreed. It didn't.

We walked in and met the general manager of the company. As it turned out he was also in charge of manufacturing, distribution, sales, and advertising. His sole employees were a number of Cuban refugees who were busily mixing the pink fluid in large vats, pouring it into glass bottles, and packing the bottles into cases of twelve, twenty-four, and forty-eight.

We sat down with him and he told us his story.

The company was South African and the product was a huge success in his homeland. The management decided to branch out into the United States and had sent him over with some of the product's "secret ingredient" and a few hundred thousand dollars. He had set up the "plant" but he was very discouraged. While the product had met with some success, he was having trouble getting and holding distributors because he didn't have any money for advertising and promotion. No one wanted to handle his product "on a shoestring." He was getting ready to fold his tent and go back to South Africa.

Norman was intrigued. "Look, if I can find someone who wants to buy the U.S. and European rights to the product, do you think the parent company would be interested?"

The despondent Afrikaner thought, then replied, "Yes, they very well might be."

Norman got him to give us a couple cases of "twenty-fours," some product material, copies of the little advertising they were doing, and miscellaneous other company literature.

After we returned from our visit to the Ocean Reef Club (we did buy a house), Norman was a man on a mission. He contacted, in descending order of billings, all of our cosmetics and toiletries clients and set up meetings to present his new product acquisition idea.

In short order, Colgate-Palmolive, Chesebrough-Ponds, Plough Incorporated, and Shulton turned us down cold. We only had one more arrow left in our quiver—Richardson-Vick.

Norman was brilliant as he presented the product, its strategy, the market opportunity, and the huge sales potential available once the venerable Vick sales force was selling the product.

I could see that he was making headway. Finally they asked the key question. "How much do you think it will take to buy the company, or should we do a royalty deal?"

Norman was ready and intransigent. "You absolutely don't want to do a royalty deal on this. You guys have no idea how big this product is going to be. Just offer them more than they ever expect to make here and we'll—you'll— own the whole damn thing free and clear for everywhere but South Africa."

After a few more meetings John McLaughlin, the Vick Consumer Product Division general manager, acquiesced and took the proposal to the Richardson-Vick board. The chairman, Smith Richardson, and the board agreed with his proposal, and the pink wrinkle removal product was purchased for four million dollars.

Norman B. Norman (and his wife) had single-handedly discovered and brought Oil of Olay into the mainstream of consumer marketing.

As our only reward, NCK was given the Olay advertising assignment. Norman personally oversaw the continuation of the brand's low-key black-and-white print campaign—"Does your husband look younger than you?" He also fought mightily and successfully against the Vick MBAs who wanted to "modernize" Olay's funky pink and black art nouveau packaging. Soon, with the help of the distribution attained by the Vick sales force, Olay revenue was on an equal footing with Vick's powerhouse brands, Formula 44 and Nyquil.

A few years later Olay had annual sales in excess of one hundred million dollars and was sold along with the other Vick OTC (over-the-counter) brands to Procter & Gamble, who, I am sure, today consider it one of the gems in its diadem.

All of the above, because Norman listened to his wife and was tenacious and stubborn enough to go after the sale even though he was turned down at almost every step along the way.

Norman B. Norman

In the fifties, sixties, and seventies the advertising agency business certainly had its share of remarkable characters. In the days when most of the agencies were eponymous these characters loomed large on the scene and by the strength of their personalities dominated the industry. I'm speaking of Ted Bates, Leo Burnett, Fax Cone, Bill Bernbach, Bill Benton, and Chester Bowles, Marion Harper, and, of course, Jerry Della Famina.

But of this illustrious group no one man more clearly embodied everything that was both good and bad about agency leadership than Norman B. Norman.

Born Norman Bernstein on the Lower East Side of New York, Norman scrapped his way out of his environment, attended CCNY, served as an officer in the Navy during WWII, and emerged from his military service miraculously transformed into Norman B. Norman, advertising man. His early days were spent at the William H. Weintraub agency servicing the Schenley spirits account (famous for the line for Ancient Age— "If you can find a better bourbon, buy it").

Subsequently, in a move that unfortunately defined his career, he and two partners took the Schenley account and several others "across the street" and opened up their own agency. The Weintraub agency disappeared shortly thereafter. Norman was a vicious competitor and never looked back.

He was athletic (tennis and sailing), rapier thin, at least six feet four, with a prodigious nose, prematurely gray hair worn in the shortest of crew cuts, and an impeccable dresser who always sported a bow tie and a healthy tan. In short, you couldn't miss him. The best description I ever heard of him was authored by one of our creative people:

"Norman looks like a cross between a sick parrot and a Jewish Abraham Lincoln."

Like many brilliant men, he suffered fools badly and it was this trait that was probably responsible for his failure to receive the recognition he so justly deserved. In the early days of his career he worked on accounts that were dominated by the founder/owner; hence the agency principals were accustomed to "dealing with the boss." It was this practice that was Norman's greatest strength—and his greatest weakness. On accounts like Schenley, Plough, Spidell, and Revlon he was fantastic as a personal salesman to "the boss." But as the industry changed and more and more companies installed the brand manager system, patterned after P&G, Norman became increasingly frustrated. He often remarked, unfortunately within earshot of his subjects, "I'm not going to waste my time with these children." Well, these "children" grew up and became bosses themselves, and they never forgot their hatred for Norman.

He was also extremely quick, incisive, and impatient with anyone who didn't see things his way. The combination of his charm (he was a great salesman and extremely captivating when he wanted to be) and his frequent intolerance resulted in an extremely high turnover rate at his company.

I suppose some amateur psychiatrists who knew him were right when they attributed his paranoia and insecurity to his childhood background, which, of course, caused him to overcompensate in adulthood.

Whatever the reasons, Norman inevitably hurt and destroyed the ones he loved the most, with the singular exception of his wife, Gail. Over time all of the great talent he was able to recruit were fired or quit. He also drove his original partners, Gene Kummel and David Kaplan, out of the business at the time of the agency's greatest success.

All of this was unnecessary, but as Art Hohmann said to me after we lost the American Tobacco account and, instead of being furious, Norman consoled me, "Norman is the best friend you can ever have in adversity and your worst enemy in success."

In my case, after I had run NCK's European operation for four years and the New York agency for three, I was made Worldwide President. No one else had ever had this title and responsibility; it was the beginning of the end of our relationship. My fate was sealed the day that David Foster, CEO of our biggest account, Colgate-Palmolive, said to Norman, "I don't know why you keep coming to these meetings, Wally and I can handle whatever has to be done." I left for Gallo shortly thereafter and after several failed merger attempts the agency disappeared.

Norman retired to the Ocean Reef Club on North Key Largo, where in better days he had shared a vacation house with me and two other NCK officers. He spent his remaining years sailing, playing tennis, and investing in and managing the Club's shopping center.

He died in 1991 without any acknowledgment, recognition, or appreciation from the industry he had so deeply loved and influenced. In the end, his contributions to advertising and marketing were monumental but his own personal devils prevented him from achieving the status he deserved.

I heard about his passing from a fellow NCK alumnus and was appalled that the "Bible" of our industry had ignored his death.

I wrote the following letter:

December 4, 1991

Mr. Fred Danzig
Advertising Age
220 E. 42nd Street
New York, NY
10017-5806

Dear Fred,
Last week with little fanfare or recognition, the advertising agency lost one of its pioneers and legends.

Norman B. Norman passed away.

Perhaps as much or more than anyone else Norman was the quintessential ad man of the 50's, 60's and 70's.

Brilliant, charming, irascible, exciting, emotional, flamboyant, mercurial, quixotic, sometimes incomprehensible and always difficult, Norman was above all an industry icon and a man who truly believed in advertising and the agency business.

Many people in and out of the industry remember and venerate the advertising Norman and his agency created without really knowing the source.

Who can forget?
"Fire and Ice" for Revlon—"Do You Kiss With Your Eyes Closed?"

"Let Hertz Put You in the Driver's Seat" for Hertz Rent-a-Car
"I Dreamt ..." for Maidenform
"The White Tornado", "The White Knight" and "The House of Ajax" for Colgate-Palmolive

241

> *"Does Your Husband Look Younger than You?" for Oil of Olay*
> *"The Big Bottle" series for Chanel and the Catherine Deneauve television*
> *"The Elevator Commercial" for Silva-Thins*

"Home is the Sailor" for Old Spice with what must be one of the most memorable theme songs of all time.

If Norman had only been responsible for the creative output of his agency, it certainly would have been enough to qualify him as a true industry giant, but Norman did far more than that.

In the area of programming Norman, Craig & Kummel created and aired the "$64,000 Question" for Revlon, one of the most famous and later infamous television series in the history of that industry.

When it was hardly popular, Norman broke the "glass ceiling" for women in the agency business and superstars like Kay Daly, Solita Arbib, Kitty D'Alessio, Ariel Allen and legions more were given the opportunity to grow and prosper in an environment of equal opportunity.

NCK's enormously successful expansion internationally in the 60's resulted from Norman's strategy (developed along with David Kaplan and Gene Kummel) to initially purchase minority interests in key European agencies and convert to a majority on a fixed and mutually profitable basis. This program allowed the NCK to become the fourth largest network in Europe in less than five years (behind JWT, McCann and Y&R) with a minimum of investment and zero chance of failure.

The resulting partnership, NCK Europe, was in the forefront of what Norman preached and is now known as "Global Marketing" for its U.S. and European clients: Colgate, Hertz, Chanel, Aspro-Nicholas, International Wool Secretariat and many others.

Norman also understood how to make money in the agency business and unsuccessfully railed against the networks' control of programming. Again long before his time, he spun off the broadcasting and syndication arm of NCK into a separate entity, CPM, and produced and sold syndicated shows to clients and non-clients alike: the "Sports Challenge" for Old Spice being only one of many.

Lastly, Norman's active imagination and interest in marketing and brand building was never limited to advertising alone.

For Colgate, he and his agency created a whole new category of products in the laundry detergent field. When "door bell ringing" (a research technique perfected by him whereby agency and client alike went out into "the field" and literally rang doorbells to talk to consumer and see them "in vivo") revealed that a new detergent worked as well in cold water as warm, "Cold Power" was born.

But perhaps the most remarkable example of Norman's eclectic talent and perception took place when his wife Gail showed him a new and efficacious skin cream she had found in an upper Manhattan drug store. Not one to ignore a possible new product, Norman traced it to a small mixing facility near the Miami Airport.

On our first visit we met with the manager who had been sent over from South Africa to found the U.S. company with the formula and $500,000. He was mixing and blending in Florida and selling via brokers and small space print ads in women's magazines.

Norman's insight was again better than 20/20 and after prolonged negotiations was given the right to broker the brand to one of his clients.

After turndowns by Colgate, Chesebrough-Ponds, and Revlon, he was finally successful in persuading Richardson-Vick to pay, I think $4,000,000, for the pink cream in the ugly bottle called "Oil of Olay". The rest, as they say, is history.

I'm sure the many veterans and alumni of NCK could tell many more stories of Norman's successes and excesses, (they used to say that the NCK alumni club could meet in Yankee Stadium), but with it all, Norman was something you don't see around much anymore - a true zealot and intuitive marketeer.

Marketing, the agency business and I are better for having experienced Norman's genius.

Best Regards,

*Walter W. Bregman
President NCK Europe 1966-70
President NCK U.S. 1970-74*

*cc: Rance Crain - Advertising Age
         Sid Bernstein - Advertising Age*

PART IV: THE GALLO YEARS

In December of 1973 it became clear to me that my days at NCK were numbered. A merger I had engineered with Tatham-Laird in Chicago had failed due to Norman's unreasonable (in my opinion) requirements. Besides, I was sick of the agency business, commuting, and having to be at the beck and call of clients. In short I wanted to change my work and lifestyle.

Nothing could have been more different than the job I took and the place to which I moved. In March of 1974 after an extended vacation with my family in Australia and New Zealand (for the first time in years I started and finished a vacation), I joined the E&J Gallo Winery as Vice President of Advertising and moved my family from suburban Westport, Connecticut, to a peach ranch in Modesto, California.

I was subsequently promoted to Vice President of Advertising and Marketing; was involved in the United Farm Workers boycott of Gallo, and became what was referred to by many as the only Jewish member of the Gallo family.

Five years later in March of 1979, I left Gallo to move back to Westport and, at the request of my old friend Joel Smilow, become president of International Playtex.

Joining Gallo

In early 1974 after returning from Australia and New Zealand, I got down to serious job hunting.

While I had several calls I refused to talk to agencies. I decided to avoid the "frying pan into the fire" syndrome and concentrated on talking to the client side.

I had several interesting and bizarre interviews, not the least of which was with Jan Wenner, the owner of Rolling Stone. He was looking for a publisher and thought I could bring the magazine legitimacy and thus attract national advertisers. When I told him he would be unlikely to succeed as long as the staff smoked pot at work and sniffed cocaine in the lavatory, he dropped me from consideration. He felt my conditions of servitude would irreversibly change the "culture" of the publication.

While I was in San Francisco, my friend Pete Conway from P&G convinced me to take an interview with the Gallo Winery (he had recently joined them in the sales department) even though their reputation as an impossible place to work had preceded them. They had been a Burnett client while I was there and the horror stories were legion.

My visit to Modesto was quite the opposite of what I had expected. Ernest Gallo was charming and pleasant. I spent a couple of hours with him and Albion Fenderson, his consigliere, and ended up at the Gallo house for dinner. The next day I again visited with Ernest in his office.

"Wally," he said, "we really want you to join us as Vice President of Advertising. We have never hired anyone into this company as a VP but I think you deserve it."

"Thank you," I said, "I am honored. Naturally, I have to talk to my wife but I have to tell you we really love what we've seen of Modesto."

"Well then, it's settled then. When can you join us?" Ernest asked.

I was dumbfounded. "Mr. Gallo," I said, "we haven't discussed salary yet."

"Oh, I thought you wanted to join us because you liked the company and the job, not just for money," he said without emotion.

"Yes, of course, but I have to have some idea of what my salary will be," I replied.

"Well, I won't do it that way, but I'll tell you what, you write down on a piece of paper what you want and give it to me."

At this point, the meeting was taking on an Alice in Wonderland cast, but I complied.

He glanced at my submission and said, "This looks OK, when can you start?"

I actually joined the winery on the fifteenth of March, Ernest's birthday as it turned out. I still had no idea of what my salary was until I received my first check at the end of April (exempt employees were paid monthly). As soon as I opened the envelope I got out my calculator to figure the monthly rate out of the six-week total. I did it several times because the annual figure turned out to be twenty percent higher than the number I had written down on my scrap of paper. I learned an important lesson: "Never try and outguess Ernest Gallo; it can't be done."

* * *

Until my family joined me I was on a per diem expense account. Each week I would fill out my expense forms and submit them for payment. Because of travel and other unusual expenses the totals varied widely from week to week.

My newly assigned secretary, Melinda McCann, was a lovely young girl with great skills but a little unsophisticated. She had spent her entire life in Modesto. One of her duties was opening my mail and sorting it. One day she opened one of my expense checks, which included a couple of trips from New York to Modesto.

"Here's a really big check from the winery," she said. "What's it for?"

I saw an opportunity to pull her leg. "Well," I said, "Ernest isn't sure he wants to hire me full time so he put me on a weekly basis. Each Friday he decides how well I did during the week and sends me a check. I guess I did pretty well last week."

The next week I got another large check and Melinda said, "Wow, you had another good week. This one is even bigger than the last one." She had taken the bait!

Naturally, by the third week the accounting department had caught up with the really big items and was only reimbursing me for normal day-to-day expenses.

Melinda walked in with the mail and looked very glum. "This check isn't very big," she said.

"Well," I said, "I guess I didn't have a very good week," and let my voice trail off in disappointment. Melinda was ashen.

The following week, the mail arrived while Melinda was away from her desk; I pocketed the expense check. A little later when Melinda came in with the mail, she looked very unhappy.

"Where's my salary check?" I asked.

"I don't know," she said. "This is all there was."

"Quick, call the mailroom and see if there is any undelivered mail," I ordered.

She left my office and quickly returned. Now she really looked awful. "They say that they have delivered everything."

"Well," I said with finality, "I guess that's it. Ernest has obviously decided my services are no longer needed." At this point I opened my desk drawers and began to pack items into my attaché case.

I had gone too far. Melinda burst into tears and rushed out of the office. I had to get one of the other secretaries to go into the ladies room and explain that I was only pulling her leg and that I wasn't leaving.

She worked for me for the next five years, but I don't think she ever completely forgave me.

The Gallo Casting Session

My first introduction to the wonders of the Gallo creative process occurred about two weeks after I joined the company. I was sitting in on a run of the mill casting session. The agency, Y&R, came up from L.A. with casting tapes and what was called a "scorecard."

The procedure at Gallo was for Ernest and the "committee," some eight or ten of us, to sit in the boardroom and watch endless casting tapes of actors and actresses reading lines for a commercial; then each aspirant would stare full front, smile; turn sideways and smile. Ernest firmly held that people in commercials should be pleasant and should smile all the time. We would then "score" them on the sheets provided by the agency.

In this particular meeting, as they had previously cast the male part they were now in the process of casting the actress. As is the standard practice when one actor has been cast, the agency had the women hopefuls all read with the selected male actor so we could see how they looked and sounded together. The account man passed out the scorecards, put on the tape, and we settled down for what was clearly going to be a rather long session.

After the first four women had performed, and there were some ten or eleven to go, Ernest said, "Stop the tape!" Someone did; the lights came on, and he said, "Where did that actor come from? He's terrible! How did we ever get him?"

The producer for the production house that was to do the commercial, a knowledgeable professional but totally ignorant of the vagaries of the Gallo system, spoke right up and said, "But, Mr. Gallo, we cast him with you last week, and you loved him."

Ernest waited a moment, stared at him over his rimless spectacles, and said very softly, "What's your point?"

There was a deadly silence. The producer looked around the room for support from the agency personnel, all of whom found something in their notes, or on the wall, or out the window to stare at. He gulped a couple of times and said, "Absolutely nothing, nothing at all."

That was the end of the meeting. The next week the entire commercial was recast. It was in this meeting I learned a corollary to a lesson I had known for a long time: "A fact is an opinion held by the client, and it is particularly important when the opinion is held by Ernest Gallo."

The Gallo Music Presentation

Ernest Gallo prided himself on his attention to detail and his personal involvement in all aspects of marketing, sales, and advertising. "Solve the little problems first and you won't have any big ones" was one of his favorite sayings.

On one occasion, I sat in the packaging conference room for over an hour while we addressed the earthshaking question of whether the shutters on the barn on the Boone's Farm Strawberry Hill label should be opened or not. No ancient debates on the issue of angels on the head of a pin were more arcane. The analogy is quite apt too because the shutters in question were about the size of the proverbial pinhead.

Another memorable encounter involved the Los Angeles office of Young and Rubicam, which was in Modesto for a pre-production meeting prior to the actual shoot in Hollywood. The idea was to present final casting, set sketches, costuming and background music.

As the agency people knew that Ernest was going to attend the meeting, they went to meticulous ends to make sure every detail was covered. Because of their preparation everything went perfectly until they got to the music portion.

Again, they had every detail covered. Even though music was at best an incidental part of the overall commercial, they knew that one overlooked item had doomed their efforts in the past and they were taking no chances.

They had presented a "scorecard" listing all the instrument combinations and melodies they had auditioned; each corresponded to a "take" they prepared to play on their portable Narga tape recorder.

"Now first we have the piano, saxophone, and drum playing version number one," the account man started out.

"Next is version number two by a violin, cello, and bass," he went on. "Now the harp, xylophone, and drum playing version three, followed by the first theme substituting a harpsichord for the piano."

He droned on like that for at least a half an hour while the audience supposedly kept score and wrote down their observations. Early on, I had concluded that it didn't make that much difference in the first place and was thinking about my backhand.

Finally, the endless music came to a conclusion and the breathless agency turned to Ernest for the decision upon which the whole future of the commercial could rest.

"Well, Mr. Gallo, which one do you prefer?" asked the nervous agency man.

"Son, I only know two songs, "The Star Spangled Banner" and "God Bless America," and so far I haven't heard either one of them. You fellows decide, I've got work to do," and he was out of the conference room in a flash.

Once again, I learned that it was impossible to anticipate what E.G. might say or do. It was best to just go with the flow.

Ernest Gallo and the Swimming Pool

During the energy crisis in the winter of 1976, Ernest decided he needed to get more exercise. The way he selected to get his exercise was to swim each morning in his pool. The pool was rather unusual in that it was serpentine shaped and wound through the extensive property in his backyard.

Because Ernest was quite socially conscious, he decided that it would be inappropriate for him to heat his pool. He solicited ideas from many people in our engineering department and whoever else had an idea. The winning one was to fill the pool with ping-pong balls, which would keep the heat in but would allow him to swim with relative ease.

Having solved this problem, he approached Fritz Earl, the owner of the Modesto Swim and Racket Club, to give him lessons. Unfortunately for Fritz, the only time Ernst was available was 6:00 A.M., just before he went to work. And hardly anyone said no to Mr. Gallo!

The lessons were set. Despite the ping-pong balls, Ernest slipped into a wet suit. In the first lesson he told Fritz that his legs got tired so he wanted to wear fins. That was OK.

During the second he said he had decided that the breathing was too much trouble and he wanted to use a snorkel mask. Again OK.

At the third lesson, he explained that he had hurt his left shoulder at some point and the swimming was aggravating it so he had decided to only use one arm.

Right about then the security department (our union disagreements with the United Farm Workers necessitated heightened security) informed Mr. Gallo that they would be more comfortable if one of their people walked along with him while he swam.

"That's perfect," he said. "I've been having trouble following the winding of the pool. He can make himself useful by carrying a golf club and keeping me in the lane by dragging it in front of me."

And so it happened that every morning at six o'clock a wetsuit clad man in a snorkel mask jumped into a swimming pool filled with ping-pong balls and, accompanied by an uniformed guard with a golf club, swam one armed from one end of the winding pool to the other.

Within a few months he got bored and gave up his unusual exercise regimen. I'm sure Fritz and the guard were delighted.

Redd Foxx in Modesto

Not many people realize that the Gallo Winery produces as many cases of wine without the Gallo name (it's called a DBA—"doing business as") as with the Gallo name. In the 1970's, we had many successful brands such as Boone's Farm Strawberry Hill, Spanada, Carlo Rossi, Tyrolia, Madria Madria Sangria, Pizzano, Nighttrain, Thunderbird, and the venerable Ripple.

Probably no one single person made a greater contribution to the sales of Ripple than the legendary nightclub entertainer, Redd Foxx. In almost every routine that he performed, Redd always included a few lines about Ripple. He once said that at his wedding ceremony they served a new drink called Champipple. Within days our distributors told us that they were getting large orders for cases of Andre champagne and pear Ripple. Foxx may have thought it up as a joke, and it was, but it made cash registers ring in African-American communities all over the country.

Naturally, we were heavily indebted to Foxx for his support of Ripple even though he did it in jest. In an attempt to further our relationship with him, I visited him in his Los Angeles office and asked if he would record some radio commercials for Ripple. As it turned out, he wasn't interested but said that he would continue to "make fun" for our benefit.

In passing, he said that he was going to be giving a free concert in Modesto within a month. It seemed than one of the black charities in the area had contacted him and he had agreed to give a free performance.

When I reported my conversation to Ernest Gallo, he suggested that when Foxx was in Modesto he would like to have him out to the house for lunch or dinner. I tried to dissuade him from this idea as I knew of Foxx's reputation for, as they say, "working blue" in his nightclub routine. I didn't think that the Gallos and their friends would be either understanding or appreciative. In typical Ernest Gallo fashion, however, he was not to be denied. He gave me specific orders to invite Foxx to his house on the day of the concert.

In due course, I found out when the concert was to be held and phoned Redd in Los Angeles. I naturally assumed he would turn down the invitation and was shocked and dismayed when he accepted with pleasure. He told me that he was borrowing Frank Sinatra's airplane to fly from Las Vegas to Modesto in the afternoon and would return to Las Vegas in time to do his midnight show at the Sands. From a logistical standpoint, the best arrangement was for us to send a limo to pick him up at the Modesto airport, take him to the hotel where he would relax and change, and then bring him to the Gallos' house for a late lunch. He could then go back to the hotel and rest before the performance.

As the Saturday lunch approached I was in an absolute state of panic. Ernest had invited his brother Julio and his wife as well as several other senior members of management and their wives. I could only imagine the impact Foxx's language would have on these "squares."

And so it happened that a dozen or so of Modesto's leading citizens were assembled at the Gallo home when Redd Foxx drove up in what we jocularly referred to as the "Grapemobile" (a maroon Cadillac limousine that belonged to the winery).

He cut quite a figure with his shaved head, tall erect figure, open-necked white sport shirt and black slacks. As it turned out, my fears were totally unfounded. Redd was the sole of discretion and was incredibly polite and attentive to all the guests and particularly Amelia Gallo, on whose right he was seated. Like all Italian and Jewish women of a certain age, Mrs. Gallo could not stand to see someone fail to eat everything on their plate. Redd had to explain to her several times that he hardly ever ate very much before a performance and I'm not sure she was convinced.

At one point, Amelia asked him whom he was going to vote for in the upcoming election. Without missing a beat he said, "George Wallace."

"But," Amelia said, "why would a black man like you vote for him?"

"It's really quite simple," Redd answered. "I think America ought to have a president who's already been shot, it cuts down the odds!"

In due course, the luncheon ended. I was hugely relieved that all had gone off as well as it had. Just before the limo was to take him back to the hotel, Redd turned to the assembled group and said, "By the way I have reserved special seats for all of you at my show tonight and I would be very disappointed if you weren't there."

The alarm bells started to go off in my head but no amount of persuasion on my part could convince Ernest and the other guests to stay home.

When we arrived at the outdoor stadium where the performance was to take place we found that the entire front row of seats was closed off with white tape and a posted sign stating "Reserved for the E&J Gallo Winery." Shortly thereafter the stadium began to fill and soon there wasn't a seat remaining. There also were no other white faces in the audience except for the members of our party.

When Redd appeared on the stage I had a premonition that my luck had run out, and sure enough it had. It turned out that he had no specially prepared material for this event. In fact, what he presented was his normal, very dirty, nightclub routine. As I recall it started out, "Good evening ladies and gentlemen, let's talk about fucking," and went downhill from there.

Ernest and Julio and the rest of the men had great problems both keeping a straight face and also trying to avoid explaining Foxx's jokes to their wives. The other problem was that because of the combination of our location and skin color, there was no way anyone could leave the performance without creating quite a disturbance.

Everyone sat through the show to the end but it was never discussed afterwards.

This may not have been the most embarrassing moment of my life but it was certainly right up there.

The Apple Orchard

Perhaps the most successful alcoholic beverages ever launched were Boone's Farm Apple and Strawberry Hill wines from E&J Gallo. Introduced in the late sixties, at its height Boone's Farm sold over fourteen million cases in one year. With twelve .750 liter bottles to the case, this means that enough Boone's Farm was sold to provide every man, woman and child in the United States with one bottle. As hardly anyone over twenty-two ever drank the stuff, you can imagine the per capita consumption of those under twenty-two.

By way of example, a liquor store a quarter mile away from the University of Michigan Stadium would typically sell in excess of 500 cases before each game (that's 6,000 bottles!). During the game a phenomenon known as the green wave would occur whereby the bottles would start at the lower field seats and be passed progressively upwards to the top of the stadium. With the sun reflecting on the stands, voila "the Green Wave."

The success of Boone's Farm has been attributed to the anti-establishment attitude of the sixties generation. Rejecting their parents' urban, cultural, and political attitudes, these young people embraced the fruity sweet, fairly high proof, bucolic little wine made by the Boone's Farm Winery of Modesto, California. (What they would have thought if they had known that Boone's Farm was really a DBA for Gallo is open to question.)

My own theory is more simplistic. Boone's Farm went great with pot!

All my informal conversations with consumers conjured up the sight of a lava-lamp-lit college dorm room with long-haired barefooted kids scattered all over the shag rug or sitting in bean bag chairs passing the roach clip one way and the Boone's Farm the other. Multiply this by hundreds of thousands and you've got a hit on your hands.

Whatever the reason, Boone's Farm was an incredible success, so much so that by the late sixties, the winery had a serious problem. It had virtually cornered the market on apples and was risking demand outstripping supply (regardless of their name, all Boone's Farm products were actually apple-based wines).

Ernest and Julio had to find a solution. After scouring the apple-growing areas of Oregon, Washington, and Northern California their agents found a perfect opportunity, a several hundred acre abandoned apple orchard in a fairly inaccessible Northern California location. With the Gallo resources an access road could be built and the Gallo trucks could haul the apples to the winery for crushing. Julio flew into the location in the company helicopter and pronounced the farm perfect for our needs once the road was built.

Problem solved.

The next step was to buy it. The owner was holding a sealed bid blind auction on Monday of the next week. On Thursday the brothers conferred and decided on a bid of 1.5 million dollars.

The next morning Julio called Ernest and said, "I've been thinking. We really need those apples and we'll feel like damn fools if we get outbid."

"You're right," Ernest replied. "Let's go to 2 million."

That afternoon Ernest called Julio and with the same logic talked him into upping the bid to 2.5 million dollars. Over the weekend they conferred twice and argued themselves up to $3,123,456.78 on the premise that they didn't want to lose out to an even money bid.

As Ernest told me the story: "And you know what happened?" he asked.

"No," I replied.

"We got the property."

"That's great," I said. "And what was the next highest bid?"

"That's the point," he laughed. "There weren't any other bids, my brother and I were bidding against ourselves all week."

But as usual, the Gallos got the last laugh. When the road was finally pushed through to the property and the underbrush cleared away, it was found that non-planted acreage was totally covered in gravel.

Ernest concluded with his patented sly smile, "After we sold off the gravel, we got the apples for next to nothing!"

As their competitors learned to their sorrow: Don't bet against the Gallo brothers.

Ernest and Sam

At one point in the mid-seventies, Ernest Gallo was contacted by Sam Bromfman of Seagram's who professed to want to visit the winery "while he was on the West Coast." Ernest suspected that this was a thinly disguised device to begin conversations with the Gallo brothers about a potential takeover, but he invited him anyway.

After an all day tour broken up by the ritual lunch at a local restaurant (Gallo had no executive dining room), Mr. Sam invited Ernest to accompany him and his key assistant back to New York on the Seagram's plane so they could continue their conversations.

According to Ernest, as soon as the plane was airborne Sam began his pitch to combine the companies. He talked of the synergy between the two distributor organizations (in truth, Gallo and Seagram, as the leaders in their respective categories, did share the top distributors in many markets). He also talked of the combined strength of their marketing organizations as well as the financial clout the newly merged company would have.

At this point, Ernest (who I'm sure had absolutely no interest in the prospect) asked how Sam planned to put the "deal" together.

"Well," Sam said, "we'd do some sort of an exchange of stock on a basis established by our market price and an independent bank's valuation of your stock." (Gallo was, of course, private).

"That's interesting," Ernest said, leading him on.

At this point, Sam's assistant jumped to his feet and whispered something in his ear. The venerable liquor executive went ashen.

Ernest later told me, "The young fellow had just figured out that because we are a closely held family company, no matter how they value our stock, instead of them controlling us we would end up owning them." (Ironically, this is exactly what happened when Bristol-Myers took over Clairol.)

Ernest went on, "This conversation took place before we got to Denver and we spent the rest of the flight to New York either making small talk or in silence. The subject of a merger never came up again."

The New York Store Check

I would guess that I probably have made over two hundred "store checks" in my client and agency career. There is no better way to find out what really is going on in the market place. By actually looking at the shelves and checking prices, promotions, competitive products, and movement, one can get a pretty fair idea of the success or failure of a brand's sales and marketing efforts.

Over the years I have "checked" everything from peanut butter/spread (Jif) and light duty liquids (Joy) to tampons (Playtex) and pantyhose (Round-the-Clock), plus many others.

Perhaps the most bizarre "store checking" experiences in my career, however, were the ones I had while accompanying Ernest Gallo. In the first place, Ernest was paranoid that the distributor would take him for a "tour" when he went into the market and thus see only what the locals wanted him to see. He also feared that because many of us at headquarters had friends in the field, we would tip off someone we were coming and they in turn would "tune up" the market.

The way this problem was solved was that Ernest would tell us that we were going out in the field but not where we were going. The only one besides Ernest who did know was his loyal secretary of many years, Ouida (pronounced "Weeda"). She would make all the necessary hotel and airline reservations. We would only be told "hot weather"—Miami, Dallas, Houston, or "cold weather"—New York, Washington, Chicago, Buffalo. When we arrived at the airport, Ernest passed out the tickets and we got on the plane, totally unable to warn anyone if we wanted to.

That evening Ouida would phone the distributorship and say the magic words that sent a chill up and down their spines, "Mr. Gallo and his group will be in your offices tomorrow morning." Clearly, by the time she called, it was too late to "tune up" anything. The fat was in the fire.

Upon arrival, Ernest would greet the local distributor and Gallo people, ask for a brief report on the various brands in which he was interested, divide the group up by cars between the visitors and the locals, and then cheerily say, "Well, time's a-wasting, let's hit the road. We'll meet for lunch at Trattoria XYZ" (always the best Italian restaurant in town).

When he got in the front seat of the car in which he was riding, Ernest would pull a map out of his pocket and say to the driver "Left" or "Right" and then personally give directions for the rest of the day to the stores he wanted to see rather than the stores the local people wanted him to see.

The most memorable of these trips was one we took to New York in the dead of winter. We had just introduced a companion brand to Thunderbird (a nineteen percent fortified wine: "What's the word? Thunderbird"). The new product was named Night Train (also nineteen percent: "Gets you where you want to go—fast") and was designed to compete with the market leader MD 20/20 (known on the mean streets as "Mad Dog"). Our potential customers were downscale blacks. As a result, our store visits were confined to the very poorest and most dangerous sections of Brooklyn, the Bronx, and Manhattan.

When we met first thing in the morning with Marty and David Taub, our father and son distributor team, they told us we absolutely had to be off the street by 3:30. As it didn't get dark till 5:00 or so, I naively asked, "Why so early?"

"Because," Marty said, deadly serious, "that's when school gets out and you don't want to be on the street then."

We the broke up into individual cars: Marty, Ernest, his son, Joey, and Ken Burch, the sales V.P. rode in one and David, George Frank, the eastern regional manager, and I in another. Because it was winter we were all wearing dark overcoats, hats, and gloves; all together we looked like a hit squad from the local "family." The big black Buicks we were riding in only contributed to the impression.

About mid-morning, we pulled up to a "bulletproof" (so called because the storeowner sat behind thick glass and dispensed the bottles he sold via an equally thick glass turntable on which the customer put his money and the owner put the merchandise. At no time was the merchant physically exposed to danger).

This particular store was about ten feet wide and twenty feet long with product on all sides. At the end sat the owner behind his glass with a huge German shepherd at his side—you can't be too careful. He was short, grizzled, and bald, in need of a shave, and chewed on a stub of an unlighted cigar. His tattered flannel shirt, scarf, miller mitts, and dungarees only contributed to the total picture of an archetypical Bronx liquor retailer.

Because of the size of the store, our group filled every available space. For some reason the first people to the counter were from my car, David Taub, George Frank, and me, followed by Ken Burch. As we all were pretty good size, I'm sure the storeowner suspected the worst. You could see fear in his eyes. What the hell were all these big white guys doing in his store at eleven o'clock in the morning? We were either from the ABC (Alcoholic Beverage Commission) or the mob.

When I said, "We're with Gallo," he almost pissed in his pants. He obviously was thinking of the other Gallo family.

After I explained we were from the Gallo Winery he really unloaded.

"You sons of bitches, I hate you bastards, you push all this shit on me that I don't need, you give me crappy terms, you won't take anything back that I can't sell, you say you're going to run advertising and then you don't..." On and on. As he warmed to his subject his voice got louder and shriller. I suspect it was part real anger and part relief that we weren't there to kneecap him.

"If that son of a bitch Ernest Gallo was here himself, I'd give him an earful. He sends you pricks around to do his bidding and then he sits back in California and counts his money. I'd sure like to give him a piece of my mind—the little bastard."

At that point I felt a shoving at my back and Ernest pushed his way past me to stand directly in front of the little storeowner.

"Hello," he said in calm, low voice, "I'm Ernest Gallo. What do you want to say to me?"

Far from backing down, the little man said, "Listen, buddy, don't bullshit me. You ain't Ernest Gallo. I got enough trouble with these other Gallo bastards without you pulling my chain."

At this point Ernest calmly pulled out his wallet and showed his driver's license.

The deathly silence that followed was finally broken by the store owner's desperate reply.

"Sure, I knew it all along," he replied just short of hysterical. "I spotted you as soon as you came in. I just thought I'd give you a few laughs. You can ask anyone, I'm a great practical joker. I'm always pulling gags like this. Ask the guys at my lodge. Ask anyone."

Yeah, right!

Ernest got a great laugh out of it and told the story for years.

As we were leaving, I turned to Marty Taub and said, "What a life, to be stuck in that crappy store all the time and for what?"

"For what?" he said. "This place is a goddamn goldmine. That old bastard lives in a mansion in Great Neck (Long Island); has put three kids through college and graduate school and has a house in Key Biscayne. He sells to three huge projects on either side of the store and across the street. He sells more T-bird and Night Train on a weekend than most stores do in a month. He's our number one account in the Bronx."

Looks are deceiving!

Walter W. Bregman

Ernest Gallo's Favorite Story

One of the stories Ernest Gallo loved to tell most often was one my mother told him. The two became friends when my mother and stepfather visited our family in Modesto.

It seems that my mother, who lived in Rancho Mirage/Palm Springs, was very active in the area's most "in" charity, the Eisenhower Hospital. Not only did she participate in fundraisers but she volunteered at the hospital as well. One of her fellow charity workers and volunteers was the wife of Walter H. Annenberg, the former Ambassador to the Court of St. James, founder of *TV Guide,* and multi- multimillionaire. He was famous for many things—diplomacy, philanthropy—but in Palm Springs he was known for walking off the first tee at Tamarisk Country Club after a delay of his tee time and declaring he "would build his own course so he wouldn't have to wait." He did.

The Annenbergs also had a world-famous collection of sculpture that resided on their spacious back lawn. Mrs. Annenberg decided to have an exclusive charity party for the hospital and allow the "public" to view the family sculpture collection. Naturally, my mother and stepfather were invited.

As one would expect, the party was tres chic: valet parking, white-gloved servants pouring champagne, lavish hors d'oeuvres, and a string quartet playing on the lawn.

While my mother was receiving her glass of champagne, the bottle ran dry. The server unwrapped the linen napkin covering it to retrieve another; to her surprise my mother saw that the champagne was Gallo!

Later she happened to be standing next to her friend, Mrs. Annenberg, and said, "You know that champagne you're serving is just wonderful. Is it French?" I don't think she anticipated the response.

"Don't be silly, Gerry, it's Gallo. Walter and I love it and it's really cheap, too."

Even multi- multimillionaires love a bargain.

You can see why Ernest loved to tell the story.

Mario Andretti

It was Ernest Gallo's policy to personally meet any celebrity who was to endorse one of the winery's products. So it was that we invited the world-famous racing driver, Mario Andretti, to visit the winery and have lunch at Ernest's house.

The vermouth brand group had somehow decided that Andretti would be a perfect spokesperson for the product. Looking backwards, I can't, for the life of me, reconstruct their reasoning. At any rate, Andretti had been contacted and agreed to represent Gallo Vermouth. He was to pose for a life-size floorstand that would be used to encourage large displays of vermouth.

When the racing schedule moved out to the West Coast for the Long Beach Grand Prix, Andretti was invited to fly up to Modesto, tour the winery, and have a meal with the Gallos. Naturally, as Vice President for Advertising and Marketing, I was invited.

Amelia Gallo, Ernest's wife, was particularly enthusiastic about this lunch as she was fiercely proud of her Italian heritage and excited by all Italian Americans who became famous and successful. In the case of Andretti, I'm not quite sure she knew exactly why he was famous but it was enough that he was famous.

The lunch was held out of doors on the Gallos' patio overlooking the family's private vineyard. Mario arrived from his tour and was introduced to one and all. He was quite dapper, loquacious, and surprisingly short. As usual, the guest of honor was seated to Amelia's right and the rest of us arranged around the table.

As the servants served the prosciutto and melon, Amelia said, "Tell me Mr. Andretti, what is it you really do for a living?"

Somewhat taken aback, Mario said, "Well, I race cars."

"Yes, I know, but you can't make much money doing that," Amelia said. "What else do you do?"

"That's really all I do, it's a full-time job," Andretti replied. The rest of us tried to figure out how to extricate him from this conversation. We didn't succeed.

"Isn't it awfully dangerous? Driving around so fast with all those other people, you could get hurt or killed, you know."

"Yes, it is sort of dangerous but I enjoy it and I'm very good at it."

"Well, you may be but you have to think of your family," Amelia said very seriously. "I'd suggest that you look for some other safer line of work. You're not getting any younger, you know." The rest of us tried to suppress our laughter. At this we did succeed.

"Thank you for your concern, Mrs. Gallo. I'll think over what you've said," Mario said, hoping to end it there.

But Amelia had one final shot.

"By the way Mr. Andretti, does your mother know you're doing all these dangerous things?"

The Flight from L.A.

Creative meetings at Gallo were always traumatic experiences, even for the seasoned and experienced creative people who had weathered the storm. For those who had never been exposed to the "committee," it could be a rather harrowing experience.

When we had a crisis on a particular creative assignment, as was his wont, Ernest usually suggested that Y&R call in a "New York creative group," who were selected for such special occasions and generally plucked from the ranks of those who had yet to experience the Gallo system.

On one occasion, an account man and creative person were flown in, landed in San Francisco, spent the evening there, drove the ninety miles in the blistering heat to Modesto, and then faced the infamous "committee." The meeting was extremely difficult, and the creative man's best works were destroyed in one fell swoop. And so, dejected, hot, tired, and psychically destroyed, he and his account man drove back to San Francisco to catch the plane back to New York.

All the way in the car, the creative man said, "I can't wait to get to the Admirals Club to get two or three martinis into me, and I'm going to drink all the way back on the plane."

The traffic was tied up on the San Mateo Bridge to the airport, and they barely made the plane, not having a chance to stop off at the Admirals Club. In fact, they were so late that they weren't even able to get seats together in first class. As it happened, the account man was seated on the aisle in front of the creative man.

Undaunted, the creative man continued mumbling, "As soon as we get into the air, I am going to start drinking martinis, and I'm not going to stop until we get to New York."

When the seat belt sign was turned off, the stewardess came down the aisle to take drink orders. She, of course, came to the account man first who said to her, "Don't look around, but directly behind me is my patient. My name is Dr. Schwartz, and I am paid by the eccentric millionaire who is sitting behind me—don't look around! Don't look at him!—to protect him from the one single thing which can kill him, and that is alcohol.

"Under no circumstances can he ever be allowed to have a drink, so please, Miss..." And then he looked at her name placard, and said,

"A-ha, Miss Bennington!" and wrote it down on a piece of paper. "I am holding you responsible for this man's health, so under no circumstances should he ever be allowed to have a drink, no matter what he says. Now, he is a very tricky fellow and very clever. He will tell you that I am not a doctor; he will tell you that he works for an advertising agency; he's used that story before. He may even tell you that I work for an advertising agency too, as ridiculous as it may seem, and that under some peculiar, sadistic streak, I am trying to prevent him from drinking; but do not be fooled. He is very tricky and very clever, but under no circumstances can he ever be allowed to have alcohol or he will die on your airplane; and you, Miss Bennington, will be responsible."

Naturally, the stewardess was terrified and said, "Thank you so much, Doctor, and what would you like?" Whereupon the account man ordered a double vodka martini on the rocks.

She then went to the next row, leaned over and asked the woman near the window what she would like. She ordered a drink. Then the stewardess tried to brush past the creative director. He grabbed her sleeve and said, "Please, miss, please! I've been dying for a drink all day. I've got to have two double martinis!"

She replied, "Oh, no, I'm sorry, sir. We're not allowed to serve you."

"What do you mean?" screamed the creative man.

"Well, you see, your doctor told us all about your sad condition."

"What condition?" he cried his voice in a high octave.

"I'd just as soon not talk about it," she went on. "But Dr. Schwartz has told me all about it, and I am very sorry, but we're not allowed to serve you."

"What do you mean 'doctor'? he said. "He's no doctor!"

"Oh, yes," she said. "He told us you might say that."

"You're crazy!" he screamed. "He's not a doctor. He works for an advertising agency just like me."

"Yes," she replied patiently, "he said you might say that, too; but we understand. We're awfully sorry but we simply can't serve you under the circumstances." And she walked away.

For the next six hours, no matter what the creative man said, he was not allowed to have a drink.

It is unknown whether he ever spoke to the account man since that memorable flight.

Madria-Ofilia

One of the early campaigns I worked on for Gallo was a new sangria type product called Madria-Madria Sangria. The agency, again Y&R, had worked up a very interesting campaign that played on the Spanish heritage of sangria and, particularly, on Madria-Madria. They wrote an excellent commercial using a woman presenter who talked about the glories of Madria-Madria and explained that her family had made the product and how it had all of the Spanish heritage, and so on and so on. Very effective.

The problem was the networks wouldn't clear the commercial because the "Spanish" girl was clearly giving the impression that she, in fact, was part of the Spanish family that made the product. Of course, the closest that this product had come to Spain was the picture on the label; it was made by Gallo in Modesto, California.

We were sitting in a copy meeting with Ernest one day discussing the problem and trying to figure out how to solve it, when he said, "Just a minute. What if we had a girl who could say her husband, her father-in-law, and her uncle made the wine, and had a Spanish accent and was beautiful? And would work for nothing."

I thought to myself, he's obviously fantasizing. There is no such person. But, at this point, I knew the man better than I had earlier so I said, "That would be fantastic. Where will we ever find such a person?"

He said, "We already have her. It's my daughter-in-law, Ofilia, Joey's wife.[26] At this juncture, I had never met Ofilia and did not know her. It turns out that she was truly beautiful, was born in Nicaragua, spoke fluent Spanish, and, of course, spoke English with a distinct Spanish accent.

And thus a star was born. Ofilia Gallo continued to make these commercials for some two years in various iterations; and in every commercial, she said the memorable line, "My husband and his 'huncle' who make de wine, put all of the flavor of true Spanish sangria into it."

---

[26] Ernest had two sons, David the older and Joe the younger. David died in the late 1990's of a heart attack and Joe is now one of the triumvirate of executives that runs the winery.

The impression to the consumer was, of course, that here was a Spanish lady whose Spanish family made the sangria. Only if you looked closely at the bottle would you see that it was Madria-Madria Sangria, Modesto, California (a Gallo DBA—"doing business as").

In one of our later commercials, we decided to do an impromptu shooting of Ofilia just talking to the camera dressed in her Spanish costume. And so, with Hal Tulchin again directing, we turned the cameras on her. (We set up one medium shot and one close-up and taped both at the same time. In this way, we could later intercut from camera A to camera B and eliminate whatever we didn't want to use without the final result becoming jerky.)

The plan was that Hal would sit in front of the camera but out of the shot and chat with Ofilia, asking her various questions to which she would reply. I was in the control booth and would feed questions to Hal through his earphones.

Everything went swimmingly as he asked her about the wine and its heritage, the taste, the color, the rich deep aroma; and finally I said, "Why don't you ask her why she makes these commercials."

So he asked, "Ofilia, why do you make these commercials?"

And she replied without blinking, "I make these commercials because my father-in-law made me."

We then wrote what was perhaps one of the most memorable lines from this series when I said, "Ask her to tell you why she wants people to buy the wine."

So he said, "Ofilia, why do you want the audience to buy Madria-Madria?"

She looked at him with her beautiful and ingenuous look and said, "If you buy lots of Madria-Madria, then I won't have to make any more of these stupid commercials."

That line ran in the commercial and received the highest recall score we ever achieved in the Madria series.

Carlo Rossi

In 1973 one of the "sick" brands at Gallo was Red Mountain. The product was a "jug" wine that came in three flavors: Burgundy, Chablis, and Rose. It had been originally conceived as a sort of "fun" brand that would appeal to college kids and act as a transition between the fruit-flavored Boone's Farm and Gallo's mainstream product, Hearty Burgundy. For a while the strategy worked and Red Mountain prospered, but now sales had fallen off and the brand had lost support in many markets and was threatened with extinction.

As V.P. for Advertising and Marketing, I had the responsibility of finding a way to save Red Mountain by giving it a new personality and sales proposition. The agency and I had struggled for weeks with this tough problem and come up with little to show for our efforts. One morning as I was shaving and listening to KCBS radio in San Francisco I heard the gravelly voice of one of their regular commentators, Joe Carcione—The Green Grocer. Each day he would come on the radio and tell his audience what fruits and vegetables were in season and what were the best buys in produce.

Lightning bolt!

Here was what we had been looking for—a distinctive personality with down-to-earth ties to wholesome agricultural products who would fit in perfectly with our no-nonsense wines. Not only that but as an added bonus Carcione was well-known in KCBS's large clear channel broadcasting area. I phoned the agency and told them to prepare some scripts and storyboards that we could present to Ernest and the committee.

A week later after I had reviewed the agency's work in L.A., they brought it down to Modesto for our big meeting with Ernest. As usual I very quickly set the stage by explaining the dire straights Red Mountain was in and the new strategic direction we recommended and then turned it over to the agency to present the creative.

Throughout the presentation, Ernest sat quietly and never made a remark. At the end, as was his custom, he turned to the lowest ranking person present and asked his or her opinion. He then went around the room working his way up the pecking order, soliciting comments without revealing his thoughts. By this method, he could get honest observations. It was virtually impossible to second-guess Ernest and play "Emperor's Clothes."

Finally, after everyone had spoken, Ernest turned to me and said, "Wally, I think you and the agency are really on to something with this new direction." I let out a pent-up breath. "But why in the world use an old gumba like Carcione? He's going to cost a fortune and we don't need him."

I was aghast. "But Ernest," I replied, "Carcione is the whole campaign. His voice, his look, it's the thing that ties everything together."

I should have known better. Ernest fixed me with a gaze that basically said, "Do you think I got where I am by being stupid?" and went on, "We've got someone right here in the building that can do a better job than Carcione and he'll work cheap." He then turned to his son David and said, "Call downstairs and get Uncle Charlie up here."

A few minutes later a balding, sixty-plus-year-old man joined the meeting. It was the first time I ever set eyes on Charlie (Carlo) Rossi even though I had, at this point, been with the winery for two years. Ernest introduced him to the assembled throng with, "This is Amelia's cousin Charlie Rossi[27] who works in the promotion distribution department. I think he would be perfect for our Red Mountain campaign."

The moment Charlie opened his mouth I knew Ernest was right (again). Charlie had a wonderful raspy, down-to-earth, non-dialectic voice that was both honest and memorable. On top of that he had a twinkle in his eye that was both mischievous and captivating.[28]

Charlie," Ernest said, "I want you to do some Red Mountain commercials for these fellas. OK?"

"Whatever you say, Ernest, but I'm no actor and I probably won't be able to remember my lines," said the great voice.

---

[27] Charlie Rossi was a cousin of Amelia Gallo, who was the daughter of Joe Franzia, founder of the Franzia winery. Rossi had worked for Franzia but had been employed by Gallo for many years. He was "Uncle Charlie" to Ernest's sons David and Joe.

[28] Charlie was certainly mischievous. In his youth he was one of the first licensed pilots in California but lost his license forever when he was caught dropping rocks from his plane on an open car driven by the companion of a girlfriend who had spurned him.

"Don't worry," I said. "I've got a great director who will make the whole thing quite painless." And so Hal Tulchin and I were once again united on a major production project.

A few weeks later my assistant Dan Solomon, who had been assigned to be Charlie's "keeper," and Tulchin went over to Charlie's house to go over the commercial scripts and tape some "for instance" tracks. In order not to make Charlie nervous, the technique Hal employed was to switch the tape recorder on to record, leave it on, and then work with Charlie on his lines. The plan was to go into a sound studio afterwards and edit together a workable "scratch track" that we would play for Ernest and the committee to get the go ahead for full-scale TV production.

I remember when Hal and Dan brought the raw track over to my office. They were grinning like the proverbial cat that ate the canary.

"I think we really have something here," Hal said and proceeded to play the thirty minutes of line readings.

I thought they were OK but not great. I didn't see what they were so excited about.

"Listen to the end," Dan said.

Hal was talking, "OK Charlie, we're almost done now. How do you like making commercials for Red Mountain?"

Charlie responded with the line that would soon become the cornerstone of one of the most successful jug wine advertising campaigns in history: "It's OK, but frankly I'd rather drink the wine than talk about it."

Bingo!

Some of the most experienced copywriters and marketing people we could find had been struggling for months to come up with a down-to-earth line that encapsulated our strategy for Red Mountain and this guy, lately of the promotion shipping department, ad-libbed it without even thinking.

Well, as they say, the rest is history. The Carlo Rossi campaign was so successful that in two years we did a total brand/label transition: first—Red Mountain by Carlo Rossi, second—Carlo Rossi's Red Mountain, and finally—Carlo Rossi Wine, with a likeness of Charlie on the label.

We totally redefined the brand to reflect the warm, human, unsophisticated personality of Charlie Rossi and every commercial ended with Charlie looking full face into the camera, winking, and saying. "I'd rather drink the wine than talk about it."

The campaign ran in many iterations for over four years. At its height, Carlo Rossi was the largest volume table wine Gallo sold, even exceeding the corporate mainstays: Hearty Burgundy, Chablis Blanc, and Rose. It is marketed to this very day.

Charlie became a minor celebrity and made appearances at trade shows, sales meetings, and store openings. His old workmates in the promotional shipping department worked overtime answering requests for thousands of autographed pictures of the "famous winemaker Carlo Rossi."

But Charlie never changed. He was always unsophisticated, warm, and generous. In this case "what you saw was what you got"—no more and certainly no less.

Peter Ustinov at the Fairmont

When Julio Gallo developed our first varietal wines (wines named for the grape from which they are made) and the first with a cork finish, it became clear to me that we had to have a major personality to introduce and present them.

After a long and arduous struggle, we were finally able to convince Ernest to use Peter Ustinov as our star talent presenter. Ernest had never heard of Ustinov and his "outrageous fee" of $100,000 grated on him. Nonetheless, he agreed to use Ustinov if "all of you other fellows really want him," and provided Ustinov would come to the winery, visit with Ernest, drink the wine, and actually learn to love and understand the wines the way Ernest did.

The latter was not an issue as, unbeknownst to Ernest, in my negotiations with Ustinov, his caveat to do the commercials was that he had to come to California, taste the wines, and truly believe in the wines' quality. Ustinov was actually an amateur winemaker himself and owned a small vineyard near Geneva.

In fact, Ustinov was not all that keen on doing commercials in the first place. Up until then he had never done commercial television in the United States. In our conversations he referenced his only commercial experience: "Lawrence (Olivier) did Polaroid commercials in the United States but naturally refused to do them in England, and so I did his part in the United Kingdom, but I have not done any commercials in the U.S." With the background of this somewhat sophistic logic and delicate negotiations, we prepared for the important meeting and wine tasting. I felt like Eisenhower at D-day as I worked out every detail of the plan.

It was arranged that Peter and his wife, Hélène, would fly from their home in Switzerland to San Francisco, be picked up at the airport and whisked to the Fairmont where they would be ensconced in the presidential suite, replete with Gallo champagne, fruit, and flowers. After a good night's sleep, I along with my boss, Albion Fenderson, would pick Peter up at eight o'clock in the "Grapemobile" and drive him to Modesto. Once there, he would receive a full tour of the winery, along with a complete indoctrination on the varietals, and participate in a tasting with Ernest and Julio.

Meanwhile, the "Grapemobile" would return to the Fairmont. Hélène, having done some shopping in the "city," would be picked up and brought to Ernest's house where we would all meet for dinner. Like all great plans this one was brilliant in its simplicity!

From the beginning things fell totally apart. First of all, the plane from Zurich suffered a mechanical problem and landed in New York instead of San Francisco. Because the delay was billed as "to be determined," Peter and Hélène somehow ended up on a private jet owned by a young Hollywood star and admirer of Peter's.

In itself, this would have been fine except that they didn't bother to tell anyone at the airline where they were going. Shortly after they boarded the private jet, the TWA plane took off and landed at SFO about two hours late. My brand manager, who was detailed to meet the plane and who spoke fluent French for Hélène's sake (Daniel DeMarangne from Mauritius), had been waiting at the San Francisco airport for the plane to arrive.

He also had been calling me at my home in Modesto every hour to give me a report (and, incidentally, waking me up). Finally, at two o'clock in the morning he called in a panic to say that the plane had landed but without the Ustinovs. Further, he didn't know what to do as the airline had them listed on the plane out of Zurich but had them debarking in New York.

"Go to the Fairmont and wait," I instructed him in my sleep-deprived state. "They've got to show up sooner or later."

The next thing I knew Daniel called me at six o'clock in the morning to inform me that, in fact, the Ustinovs had shown up at the Fairmont around four o'clock in the morning. Apparently they had taken a cab from the San Francisco Airport and arrived with absolutely no American money. As all they had were British Pounds and Swiss Francs, they had had to borrow dollars from the desk clerk to pay the cab driver.

I thanked Daniel and told him not to worry and to go home and get some sleep. Two hours later, Al Fenderson and I boarded the "Grapemobile" but, in deference to the Ustinovs' late arrival, delayed our appearance until approximately ten o'clock. Once in the Fairmont's sumptuous lobby, I called Peter on the house phone and announced myself. I was slightly nervous. I had talked to Peter many times during our negotiation process, but had never met him in person.

276

I said, "Good morning, Peter, it's Wally Bregman, and I'm down in the lobby. I am very sorry you had such a distressing flight."

"No problem," he answered, "I'll be down in a moment."

As we stood in the center of the lobby (made famous in the television series "Hotel") and waited for Peter, I realized he had no money. Turning to Al Fenderson I asked, "Do you have any spare cash?"

"Oh yes," he said, "I always carry a hundred dollar bill as 'mad money,'" and gave it to me.

Soon Peter appeared at the top of the mezzanine steps leading down to the lobby, all imposing 250 pounds worth, wavy salt and pepper hair, Armani blazer and slacks, and a patterned ascot at the neck.

As the great man walked down the wide staircase and before he had a chance to say anything other than hello, I held out the hundred dollar bill and said, "Oh, Peter, I realize Hélène has no American money and she wanted to do some shopping. Here's a hundred dollars. You can pay me back when you get a chance."

Without missing a beat, he turned to me with a withering look and, addressing the entire lobby, said in a stentorian accent reeking of corn pone and black-eyed peas. "Just a minute, boy, I'm a U.S. Senator. You can't just stand here in the lobby and hand me money. If you want to hand me money, son, you're going to have to come up to the room; and, by the way, a hundred ain't enough!"

There I stood transfixed with a hundred dollar bill dangling from my fingers as an eerie silence came over the lobby jammed with hundreds of conventioneers wearing "Hello, My Name Is" badges. They all stared up at us. Peter then took the money and continued in his normal voice as if nothing had happened, "Oh, thanks very much, Wally. I appreciate it. I'll leave the money at the concierge's desk for Hélène and we can be on our way."

This was my introduction to Ustinov's magnificent humor and only the first of many times he put me on, broke me up, and always amused his audience with his seemingly unlimited range of ad lib voices and personalities.

Ernest and Amelia Gallo never did understand or properly appreciate him.

The Varietal Shoot

As a direct result of his meeting, tasting, and dining with Ernest Gallo, Peter Ustinov was cast as our presenter for the Gallo Varietals. With the help of our wonderful and semi-insane director, Hal Tulchin, with whom I had worked many times (see Alice Faye, Madria-Ofilia), we proceeded to write a pool of commercials in which Peter talked about the new varietals and his "close friends, Ernest and Julio Gallo."

Because of Peter's prominence, cachet, and sophistication, it immediately became clear to all involved that to be effective our commercials would have to surround him with beauty and dignity. We needed one of the great sets of all time. To produce it our set designer invaded every antique shop in West L.A. and Beverly Hills. He and his assistants toured up and down Robertson Boulevard picking up a Louis XIV chair here, a Tiffany lamp there, a Chesterfield sofa here, and so on. Finally, we had assembled four beautiful rooms of furniture, replete with flocked wallpaper, crystal chandeliers, verdant greenery, an Empire dining room with twelve chairs, a huge world globe, a magnificent tantalus, and, of course, a wonderful little Georgian table on which to place the stars of the show, the varietal wines of Ernest and Julio Gallo.

Peter, while he had never performed in U.S. commercials before, turned out to be the consummate professional and adapted to taped commercial television immediately. He was absolutely superb in his timing and retention of lines. So perfect was his delivery and so complete was his immediate mastery of the medium that, unlike with normal commercials, Tulchin elected to shoot all of Peter's efforts in one "master" shot. In other words, all of Peter's actions and words were continuously filmed from the beginning to the end of the commercial. Later we picked up close-ups shots and beauty shots of the bottle and edited them into the final production.

On one particularly memorable day, when we were in our third day of shooting, I was sitting in the tape truck some distance away from the enormous soundstage upon which we had constructed our "four-room house." Peter was doing a sixty-second commercial, the video of which required him to appear in the dining room and, while holding an elegant wine goblet, walk through an archway into the middle of the living room. He ended up in front of a small table that held the varietals and from there delivered his pitch on the product. We had laid track across the floor and the camera was trucked backwards to keep Peter in frame throughout his walk.

His lines as he walked went something like, "Being a bit of a winemaker myself, I was naturally delighted when my good friends Ernest and Julio Gallo asked me to try their fine new Barbera wine…." At this point Peter would be standing in front of the small table, having passed through the dining room, under the arch, and into the living room. He would then look directly into the camera and go through the product pitch.

He'd done about five takes, and in each one some technical glitch had occurred. At this point, I was staring at the monitor without much interest, being pretty well bored with the whole proceedings. As I glanced up at take six, Peter passed through the arch into the living room on the line, "I was naturally delighted when my good friends…," suddenly from behind him and on camera left appeared a beautiful young lady in a raincoat.

As the unknowing Ustinov continued his walk and his lines, she proceeded to wave and vamp to the camera. She then removed her raincoat, under which she was stark naked, and draped herself across the Chesterfield couch just behind Peter. Naturally, I was apoplectic. I ripped off my earphones and ran across the 500 yards from the production truck to the sound stage.

Peter was, of course, totally unaware of what was going on behind him and continued to read his lines. Just prior to the end of the commercial, the girl again waved at the camera, picked up her raincoat, put it on, and walked back through the archway from which she had appeared. Tulchin, who had set up the whole performance, yelled, "Cut!"

Peter, completely oblivious, asked, "How was that, Hal?"

Tulchin said, "It's almost there but I've still got some problems, Peter. We're getting a little light kick (reflection) off the glass when you raise it at the end. How about you come over here and look at the monitor with me? Perhaps we can figure out what the move is to solve the flaring."

At this point I ran onto the stage, somewhere between anger and convulsions. Tulchin put his fingers to his lips, and I knew, having worked with him for the last ten years on at least fifty different shoots, to go along with the gag. Peter stood at the monitor, and Hal said into his mike, "Hello, in the truck, can you roll the last take and feed it to the floor?"

On came the commercial. Sure enough, as Peter walked through the door, behind him, in full view, was the script girl who at Tulchin's request had taken off her clothes, put on the raincoat, and then sauntered on to the stage.

Peter instantly knew he was being put on and reacted not at all; he just stared intently at the playback monitor while everyone else on the floor was biting their lips and bursting at the seams. But no one said a word, we just watched the great man for a cue.

He turned to Hal and conversationally said, "OK, Hal, I think I've got it now. Let's go for another take."

Tulchin himself, not to be one-upped, said, OK, Peter, let's do it." And to the AD (assistant director) said, "Quiet 'em down and let's go for take seven."

Naturally I stayed on the stage, wanting to see how this little scenario played out. Peter stood quietly as the makeup lady powdered him down and adjusted his hair with her ubiquitous rattail comb. The crew rolled the camera back on its rails and the microphone boom man repositioned his equipment over the archway. Peter took his spot out of sight in the dining room and awaited his cue to start his walk.

The technical director said, "Speed," indicating that the tape was rolling.

The soundman said, "Sound rolling."

The AD held up the slate and said, "Very quiet everyone, Gallo Ustinov Barbera take seven" and clacked the little wooden arms together.

Tulchin waited a few seconds and said, "Action."

Right on cue, the great Ustinov appeared and delivered his lines: "Being a bit of a winemaker myself, I was naturally delighted when my good friends...." The only difference was that when he appeared he was facing backwards and he performed the entire commercial while walking backwards through the archway and the living room. At no time did his eyes ever leave the Chesterfield couch. But alas no script girl!

To my certain knowledge this tape was never shown in Modesto or anywhere else, and Ernest and the family never knew of its existence. Further, I don't know where the master of this tape is. Hal Tulchin said he "burned it" (erased it) but I'm not sure.

I learned a big lesson from this experience. Don't ever try and get the last laugh on Peter Ustinov—it's impossible!

The Beverly Hills Hotel

My family had had a long relationship with the Beverly Hills Hotel. Not only did I stay there whenever I was on the "Coast" for a shoot, but my mother and father, who had retired to Palm Springs, frequently rented a casita during the summer months when it was uncomfortably warm in the desert.

As a result, I was considered what the British call a "CIP" (commercially important person) whenever I stayed there.

One evening in the mid 1970's, I flew down from Modesto to L.A. in the evening. Early the next morning I planned to interview several prospective employees at the hotel and then go over to Y&R for a series of creative presentations. All in all I had a full day planned.

I turned over my rental car to the doorman, who always impressed me by remembering my name, and strolled into the lobby. One must understand that in the best of times the Beverly Hills' reservation system was a shambles. The assistant manager, Ramon, with whom I had dealt for at least fifteen years, took on the look of a deer in the headlights whenever I approached the desk.

"Mr. Bregman, you're here," he would always gasp, as if seeing me was a profound shock from which he was unlikely to recover.

This night things seemed to be more chaotic than usual. There was a line at the desk and the attitude of the standees made me distinctly nervous. When I was next in line I heard the following exchange between Ramon and a nervous young couple.

"I'm terribly sorry but we don't have a single room available in the house tonight."

"That's impossible. This is our honeymoon and we've had a reservation for months," the young groom gasped. The bride was close to tears.

"I understand, sir," Ramon said. "But you see several people extended their stay unexpectedly (CIP's no doubt) and there is nothing we can do."

Now the bride was in tears, "But what are we going to do? This is our honeymoon!" she sobbed.

"Don't worry," answered Ramon. "We will have you accommodated at the Holiday Inn on Sunset at our expense."

Big deal. The Holiday Inn on Sunset (and Route 405!) was a round, incredibly ugly, noisy traveling salesman's hotel. Not the place to spend a honeymoon, I thought. Or for that matter to interview prospective employees. I was livid and ready to do battle before I got to the desk.

"Mr. Bregman, you're here," said the ever-alert Ramon.

"That's right," I said grimly and waited to get the "several people extended their stay unexpectedly" routine.

As usual, Ramon fumbled through all the papers on the desk seemingly looking for my reservation. Finally he looked up and said. "Mr. Bregman, there seems to be a small problem."

Here it comes, I thought, I going to kill this son of a bitch. There is no way I can contact the guys that are going to show up here tomorrow and I'm not going to interview them at that crummy Holiday Inn.

"We're really heavily booked, so we can't give you your regular room." he said. The BH prided itself in those days on giving "regulars" the same room every time, if possible. My regular room was number 100 at the end of the hall on the first floor, in the opposite direction from the Polo Lounge but close to the pool.

"Just so I have a room, I don't care," I said with great relief.

"Oh, you have a room all right, and at your usual rate," he said in a rather arch way and winked. I had never seen him wink and didn't have the foggiest idea what this was all about.

After I had registered he called a bellboy to take me to my room. All I had was an attaché case and an overnight bag but it was the house rules.

"Take Mr. Bregman to number 702," Ramon said.

Now I was really confused. I had stayed in the Beverly Hills Hotel maybe fifty or sixty times and *never* heard of the seventh floor. Sure enough, however, the bellboy ushered me into the elevator and there was a number 7 button. When we got off, I was in for another shock. The elevator was in a small alcove that opened onto a long north-south hallway. As we turned down the right hallway toward 702, I saw a man sitting in a chair in the middle of the left hallway wearing sunglasses and a hearing aid. Odd.

I followed the bellman down the seemingly endless corridor that, unlike all the other hotel corridors I'd been in, contained not a single door. Finally we got to the end and there was a single ornate door on the left side with the number 702 on it.

When we entered, I almost fainted. This was the biggest goddamn suite I'd ever seen. It had a coffee table that a helicopter could have landed on; three conversation areas with couches; a complete bar, the front of which was tufted leather; an ornate partners' desk and chairs; a kitchenette; and a phone with four lines. The bedroom had a canopied king-size bed, makeup table, chaise lounge, and huge TV. The bathroom and dressing area were the size of my first apartment and contained gold fixtures (real or fake—I never found out) and two toilets and bidets.

The patio ran along the entire east side of the hotel and was accessed from both the living room and the bedroom. It must have had ten loungers and three tables with chairs and umbrellas.

After the bellman left I wandered around in a stupor and then called everybody I knew in L.A.

Party time! Naturally no one was in. I did call my wife, Robbie, and then decided to go down to the Polo Lounge and see if I knew anybody. I had to show this place to someone!

When I left the room, I had a good couple of minutes to look at the fellow sitting in the middle of the northern hallway. It took me that long to walk to the elevator. Ever the friendly type, I said, "Hi, how're you doing?" I probably said it a little loudly, him wearing a hearing aid and all.

He had been watching me all during my long walk. "OK."

Talkative guy, I thought. Then I looked closer at him and realized he had a holster under his coat. Hard of hearing, my ass. This guy was some kind of a cop or secret service.

"How long are you going to be here?" I asked. He'd sure put a damper on my plans to have a big party.

He gestured with his thumb toward what I guessed to be number 701 and said, "As long as she's here," and made it clear with his body language and expression that our little *tête-à-tête* was at an end.

After a couple of drinks in the Polo Lounge and a fruitless search for a familiar face, my curiosity got the best of me. I decided to track down Ramon and find out just what was going on.

After he finished sending yet another unhappy couple to the crappy Holiday Inn, I asked, "Ramon, what's going on? How the hell did I get that fabulous suite?"

"Well", he said, "we were in a bit of a pickle. You see, the Shahrini of Iran is staying here in number 700 with her sister while the Shah is being treated for cancer at the UCLA Medical Center."[29]

A-ha, I thought, that's who "she" is.

"And", he continued in a hushed tone, "the Secret Service said we could only rent number 702 to someone that the management could absolutely vouch for. Well, because of your mother and father and all, we figured we could vouch for you and two hundred dollars (my rate) is better than nothing."

And so it happened that the son of a Jewish scrap iron broker from Chicago became the "suitemate" of the wife of the Shah of Iran.

---

[29] In 1979 the religious opposition, lead by Ayatollah Ruhollah Khomeini, drove the Shah into exile. Khomeini sought the capture of the Shah, and when it was learned that he had been admitted into the United States for medical treatment, Iran's response was the start of the hostage crisis at the U.S. embassy in Tehran. After dismissal from the hospital the Shah fled to Panama, then Egypt. He died on July 27, 1980, at age 60.

Famous Sons - II

One day after I had been at Gallo for three years I received a rare phone call from Julio Gallo. Because I was in advertising and marketing I spent almost all my time with Ernest Gallo. Those in production, bottling, growing, and purchasing spent almost all their time with Julio Gallo. The company was quite literally divided by the loading dock. Julio was responsible for almost everything *before* the wine got to the loading dock and Ernest controlled everything *after* the wine got to the loading back.

In the Gallo manner, Julio got right to the point. "Wally, I'd like you to do me a favor."

At Gallo, as at most companies, when one of the people whose "name is on the door" asks you to do them a favor you have two possible answers: "Yes sir" or "I'll have my office cleaned out by five o'clock." Because I liked Modesto and I liked my job, I chose the former.

"Certainly, Julio. What can I do for you?"

"Well, its this way," he replied. "I'm the program chairman for the Rotary this year and I was wondering if you'd give a presentation to us at one of our meetings. My idea is to have you take us through one of our commercials and explain to the boys exactly how they are made."

"Sure, no problem. I'll be glad to do it for you."

He went on to give me the date and time. I thought it would be a good idea to take them through a single commercial. I'd start at the beginning with the strategy, then the script, the storyboards, the rough cuts, and finally the finished commercial.

As I was going through my preparation, I realized that the audience would not be familiar with the argot of the business and therefore it would probably be helpful if I put together a little vocabulary sheet for them. Most of the words I included were those of television production (ECU—extreme close-up, truck—move camera along the subject, two shot—two people in the shot, MOS—without sound, etc.).

The presentation went off extremely well, if I do say so myself. The audience, the Rotary of Modesto, was typical of the Central Valley. Most of them either made a living from agriculture or from the infrastructure that supported the city of Modesto. While they were extremely well off they were not particularly sophisticated. As a result, they were fascinated with the "peek into showbiz" I gave them.

One gentleman, who was the owner of the local stationery store, was particularly effusive in his praise of my material. Specifically, he thanked me for providing the film production vocabulary list.

"This is just great," he said. "I'm going use it at Christmas when my son comes home for a visit."

"How's that?"

"Well," he replied, "I'm George Lucas Sr. and whenever my son, Georgie, comes home and tells us what he's doing, my wife and I are at a total loss. Now we'll study your list and understand what the hell he's talking about."

Yes, that grateful man was the father of one of the most famous filmmakers in history, George Lucas Jr. He had just completed *American Graffiti*. A year later, I was invited to the premiere of *Star Wars*, which took place at the Modesto movie theater, and I had the privilege of telling this story to the famous son.

Like John Crichton, (see Famous Sons—I), George Sr. told me later that he had asked a friend of "young Georgie" to try and talk him out of going to USC film school and take up something practical like accounting.

Fortunately for all the book readers and filmgoers, the world was robbed of a doctor and an accountant.

Boycott Personalities

In 1977, Ernest Gallo asked me to take over the odious job of defending Gallo from the attacks being made by the United Farm Workers. Basically, Gallo was caught in the middle between the UFW and the Teamsters (talk about the devil and the deep blue sea) in a jurisdictional dispute over the Gallo farm workers.

What the world never knew, and it was my job to tell it, was that there were only 385 Gallo farm workers in total, even at peak harvest time. Most everyone suspected that because we were the largest winery in the world we had tens of thousands of workers. What they didn't know was that Gallo bought almost all of its grapes from contracted vineyards and owned only about a couple hundred experimental acres attached to our winery in Livingston, CA. Further, Gallo was, as are all companies, restrained from dictating union affiliations to its suppliers.

The above notwithstanding, Cesar Chavez and his union directed the full force of its venom and public relations effort against the E&J Gallo Winery. We believed they used this tactic because Ernest and Julio Gallo were real people and thus could be subject to successful personal attacks, as opposed to anonymous public corporations like United Vintners and Almaden. As will be discussed in other chapters, it was my job to blunt their efforts whenever possible and provide the public with the "truth" as we knew it.

I—Jesse Jackson

As the boycotts worsened and the UFW continued its attacks, Cesar Chavez cast his net in ever widening circles and sought support from other special interest organizations not affiliated with agriculture or the Hispanic cause.

One such group was Jesse Jackson's political pressure group, PUSH, which had successfully boycotted Coca-Cola and several other major corporations over supposed racial insensitivity. We were informed that Chavez had been introduced to Jackson (probably by Eunice Shriver) and that Jackson was considering injecting PUSH into the middle of the Gallo boycott. Clearly, such an action would have been a disaster for us. We derived enormous revenue from the black community (this was before "African American" became the accepted identity) and a boycott against Ripple, Thunderbird, Night Train, Boone's Farm, and Gallo White Port would have crippled us.

"What are we going to do about this PUSH thing?" Ernest asked me in one of our daily meetings.

"The only thing I can think of is to try and reason with Reverend Jackson," I replied. "I'll try and get him on the phone and see if he'll let me come and talk to him in Chicago." We had learned that the only way we had a chance was to get face-to-face with our adversaries.

Later that day I called the PUSH office and, after I had identified myself to a secretary, was told that the reverend would call me back when he had a chance.

The next day my phone rang and I answered (I had learned at the Leo Burnett Company to always answer my own phone and continued to so for my entire business career).

"Walter Bregman."

"Mr. Bregman, this is Reverend Jackson. I understand you want to talk to me about the Gallo boycott."

"Yes, sir, that's right. I want to come out to Chicago and meet with you before you and PUSH decide to take sides in what is a very complicated matter," I replied.

"Well, I'll tell you, Mr. Bregman. I don't want to even talk to you about anything until you can answer three questions about your company. When I have this information and if I think it is acceptable, then and only then will I agree to meet with you," he said in his deep, serious voice.

He followed up by listing the three questions which I suspect were *de rigueur* for any company wanting to "do business" with PUSH:

1. What percentage of your employees is black? What percentage of your executives is black? What is the highest position held by a black person in your company?

2. How much has your company contributed to black charities over the last five years, in total and by year?

3. What percentage of your advertising budget is directed toward black media? Specifically, how much have you spent and where over the last five years?

"I'll have your answers to you within a day or so," I responded. "In the meantime, can I have your assurance that you won't take a public stance till you have my answers?" I had learned by sad experience to always try to "ice" my opponent until I could get a meeting.

Surprisingly, Jackson agreed.

My next steps were clear. I had to get the answers. Numbers one and three were a snap. All our distributors had large black sales forces to service the black community. Gallo itself employed a number of black sales executives and I had a black brand manager on my personal staff. I was sure that our employment percentages were better than almost any company and would pass muster.

Number three was also a slam-dunk. We used all the ethnic magazines, newspapers, and especially radio stations to sell our products. We created special advertising using black talent and a black-owned advertising agency. As it turned out, Gallo had been one of the top five advertisers in black media for years.

Number two was a bitch. Ernest and Julio were absolutely unbending in their desire for anonymity, particularly where their charitable contributions were concerned. It was rumored that most of the medical facilities, parks, and public amenities in Modesto existed because of the largess provided by the Gallo family, but you couldn't prove it. Not a single sign, plaque, statue, or other means of attribution existed. There was no Gallo Hospital or Gallo Pool or Gallo anything. Not even the winery had a sign. And I had to get Ernest to throw open his books.

I figured I'd try an end run to start with so I approached Jon Shastid, a trusted member of the Gallo inner circle and the company's CFO. His reply to my query was direct.

"You must be out of your mind, Ernest will never divulge that information. He'd fire me if I told you." So much for the indirect approach.

Next I approached Ernest directly and got it straight from the horse's mouth. "My brother and I consider what we give to charity our business and no one else's. Tell that to Jackson."

Yeah, right! "Ernest says to stuff it" didn't seem appropriate. I had to come up with a way to convince Ernest. Like all great ideas it was quite simple. I merely totaled up all the cases of product we forecasted to sell to the black community and subtracted seventy-five percent (I figured three out of four black consumers would follow Jackson.) I sent the new numbers into Ernest's office in a memo entitled "Revised Case Sales Estimate for Ethnic Beverages" and waited for his call.

"Wally, what do you mean by the new downward revision in ethnic sales? This is a disaster!" he exclaimed.

"Well, Ernest, if I can't convince Reverend Jackson to stay out of the boycott, what you see is what will happen. And I have to give him his answers, and soon, if I'm to have any chance."

Silence…more silence.

"OK, tell Jon what you need and I'll tell him to give it to you, but don't tell anyone else, and I mean anyone," he said quietly.

The next day I had what I needed. For years the Gallo brothers had been contributing big, big amounts to the United Negro College Fund, the NAACP, and several local and Northern California AME churches. There was no question that what they gave was way above and beyond anything Jackson could have expected.

I had my answers typed up and faxed them to the PUSH headquarters in Chicago. The next day, I was invited to a meeting with Reverend Jackson in Chicago.

The meeting was an anticlimax. Jackson greeted me warmly and informed me that he had checked on all my answers (I suspected he would).

"They're all correct and basically acceptable," he said. "However, we'd like to see more of our people employed at your headquarters in Modesto. Please pass that on to Mr. Gallo." (Nothing's ever perfect.)

"As to the boycott, our executive council" (was there really one?) "has decided that our best interests will not be served by getting involved at this point. PUSH will take no formal position either way." I tried not to show my jubilation.

He went on, "One more thing, did you know that because of the Gallo brothers' consistent support of the NAACP, Coretta King invited them to walk in Martin's funeral procession?"

Wonders never cease; Ernest was either too modest, self-effacing or absentminded to bother to tell me.

To the end of the boycott, PUSH never became involved.

II—Ted Kennedy

The first time I met Ted Kennedy we were both candidates for the Harvard football team. We had been invited back to "early practice" (the candidates assembled in Cambridge around the middle of August for three weeks of "two-a-days" before the rest of the undergraduates returned). He was semi-famous, but not because of his family connection; there were far more famous sons and brothers on campus than Teddy. He was famous because his roommate, Bill Frate, had taken a Spanish exam for him two years previously. They had both been caught and were "asked" to take a two-year leave of absence. They had now returned from military service and were candidates for Lloyd Jordan's Crimson; Frate a tackle and Teddy an end.

291

Walter W. Bregman

We were all housed in the IAB (Indoor Athletic Building) and slept on two-high bunk beds set up on the gym floor. To foster team spirit and closeness by positions we were assigned bunks by position; hence, as ends, Teddy and I not only played together, we slept together. Both of us tried to make up for lack of natural ability with enthusiasm, and to some degree we were successful.

Somehow we survived the cut. Ted did clip me one day in practice, which put me in Stillman Infirmary for four days with bruised and bleeding kidneys. No hard feelings. After all we both belonged to the "jock" Pi Eta Club (as had his deceased brother Joe, and older brothers Jack and Bobby).

After graduation (he finished with us in 1955 but took his original class of 1953 for the record) I only saw him at occasional football games where members of the Varsity Club were all seated together or at après game parties at the "Club." That is, until 1977.

At another of our UFW strategy meetings, Ernest informed me that our Washington lawyer and lobbyist had called with the chilling news that Senator Ted Kennedy was about to endorse the Gallo boycott and give his unqualified support to Cesar Chavez and the UFW. This was not exactly a shock; after all, his brother Bobby had paraded with Chavez during his presidential campaign and the Shrivers had supplied the labor leader with their private jet. Nonetheless, to have this enormously powerful liberal politician support a commercial boycott would have been much worse than PUSH.

"Abe (our Washington lawyer) doubts if we can do anything. It has gone too far. He is supposed to announce at the end of the week. I think we're stuck," Ernest said with dejection.

"Not necessarily," I responded. "I went to school with Ted and played football with him. Maybe I can talk some sense into him if I can get an appointment." I knew this was a long shot but "never up never in." I'd give it a shot. Ernest looked at me with a combination of shock and admiration.

I returned to my office and told my secretary, Melinda, to get Senator Kennedy's phone number from Abe and get his appointments secretary on the line for me. I certainly couldn't trust this delicate conversation to Melinda.

Soon she buzzed me and informed me that she had the senator's personal secretary on the line.

"Good morning, my name is Wally Bregman, I'm a college friend of the Senator's. I wonder if you could get a message to him for me. Tell him that I know he is about to take a position on the Gallo boycott and that I am working for Gallo (no point obfuscating). I would greatly appreciate talking to him about the situation before he makes his final decision.

"Also, tell him that I am in California at present but that I can be in Washington tomorrow morning and that I need only a half an hour of his time. I will meet him any day, anywhere, and anytime that is convenient for him." I hoped the latter point would work; after all, to turn me down would mean a totally closed mind.

To everyone's surprise, I got a call back in an hour proposing a meeting at 3:00 P.M. the following day. I grabbed the overnight bag I always kept in the office, had Melinda tell George Frank, our eastern sales manager, and Abe Buchman, Gallo's lawyer/lobbyist, to meet me in Washington. I picked up my "truth kit" (a set of materials specifically designed to refute the litany of charges the UFW normally made against Gallo) and took the "Grapemobile" to the San Francisco Airport.

In Washington the next day, the three of us taxied to the Russell Senate Office Building and soon found the sumptuous offices of the Senior Senator from Massachusetts. Even by Washington standards it was impressive. An aide showed us into the waiting room. The atmosphere was electric; intense young "staffers" bustled back and forth with the "I'm preserving the American way of life" look on their shiny faces, phones rang incessantly, doors opened and shut. So this is what it's like at the leading edge of the sword of freedom, I thought.

Finally we were called into the Senator's office. It was huge, as high as it was wide. There sat my pal Ted. He was also huge, almost as wide as he was high.

"Hi, Wally," he said with that peculiar Bostonian accent that semi-emphasizes the "Wally." "How're you doing and what the hell are you doing at Gallo?" My stock soared with our team. His staff looked at each other a little nervously. Obviously this particular supplicant had some clout with the boss.

He introduced us to his staffers, specifically his AA (administrative assistant) for agriculture. He was a tall, thin, spectacled, twenty-something who looked like the closest he had ever been to farming was watching *Grapes of Wrath* at a Georgetown art cinema and discussing its social implications over a double latte.

Ted came from behind his desk (he *was* enormous—300 pounds at least) and we all sat down in his conversation area around a large coffee table.

"OK, Ari (have you ever heard of a Democratic staffer named Butch or Bud?). Tell them why we are going to support the UFW boycott," Ted said.

The kid then proceeded to dredge up the standard list of charges against Gallo:

1. "You employ "children and here are the pictures." I pointed out that the picture he exhibited was taken in the Imperial Valley, three hundred miles from any vineyards; the crop was tomatoes and the short-handled hoe constantly referred to by Chavez was never used in the cultivation of grapes.

2. "Thousands of migrant farm workers are oppressed by Gallo and work in unspeakable conditions." I admitted to some abuses in California but not by us. I explained and demonstrated with pictures that we only employed 385 farm workers in total (raised eyebrows from Ted); about 200 full time and the rest at harvest time. The regulars lived in brick homes (show the pictures), the migrants in dormitories and small houses (more pictures—more raised eyebrows).

3. "Gallo is trying to break the UFW and go nonunion." This guy was such an idiot I almost felt sorry for him. I explained that Ernest and Julio had invited the UFW onto the Gallo property years ago and that Julio's son Bob had served on the union's health plan board. The current situation was the result of the UFW's attempt to keep the Teamsters out of agriculture and we were caught in the middle. At the mention of the Teamsters, Ted really became engaged. I had a feeling that the briefing papers had omitted their mention and that, ever the practical politician, he had quickly calculated that there were more Teamsters in Massachusetts than Mexican farm workers.

After a few more softly hit fly balls, which I effortlessly caught and fired back into the infield, Ari lamely concluded his presentation.

Ted looked around at his chastened AA and said, "You know, this is a lot more complicated than I first thought. We sure don't seem to have all the answers. (At this point, Ari was probably thinking of going back law school.) I don't see how I possibly can take a position on this issue. Let's just pass on any endorsement."

Victory!

Ted looked at me, glanced at the "floor call" board with colored lights over his desk and said, "I've got to go vote in a few minutes, but perhaps we can chat for a while till then." This was the signal for his guys and mine to leave.

After they left I said, "Jesus Christ, Ted, you're as big as a goddamn house. You look like you swallowed a basketball." No shrinking violet me.

"Yeah, I know," he replied, "I try but there are all these parties and receptions every damn night. Drinks and food all the time. But you ought to see Culver. (John Culver was the star fullback on our Harvard team from 1952-54, a Rhodes scholar, and now the junior Senator from Iowa).[30] He's even heavier than I am."

We continued to chat about people we knew until the red light lit up and a buzzer went off indicating an imminent floor vote.

"I've got to run—Foreign Appropriations bill vote—it was great seeing you, having a chance to catch up," he said, pulling on his jacket and walking me out.

I had the feeling that he had really relished those few minutes when a couple of ex-jocks could just BS without any political implications.

Our political positions are now infinitely far apart but I'll never forget his honest and open-minded approach to the Gallo boycott.

---

[30] After his graduation from law school, Culver worked as a Legislative Assistant to Kennedy. He then returned to his home state of Iowa and in 1964 was elected to the United States House of Representatives (D-Iowa, 2nd District). In 1974, Sen. Culver was elected to the United States Senate.

The Freezing Nuns

During the height of the UFW boycott against Gallo, our normal business proceedings were constantly being interrupted for one type of emergency or another. In the middle of December 1977 the "committee" had been convened for one of its regular advertising/marketing sessions.

The "committee" consisted of Ernest Gallo, his two sons, Joey and David, Albion Fenderson, the most senior employee and consigliere of the family, Mike Boyd, our research director, and me. Typically, the agency and brand people would also be present sitting around an enormous oblong table—Ernest in the center and the rest of us arrayed on either side of him.

On this particular day we were well into our meeting when the sales vice president, Ken Burch, interrupted the meeting with an urgent problem.

"Ernest, I'm terribly sorry to interrupt but we have a real disaster brewing in Minneapolis," he said.

The agency presentation was stopped in full flight when Ernest said, "What seems to be the problem, Kenny?"

"It's the damn UFW again. They've got a bunch of nuns out blockading our distributor. They're lying down in the snow in the driveway so the trucks can't get out and this is the busiest delivery day of the holiday season. If we can't get the trucks out we'll lose a ton of business and customers. Not only that, they've called all the TV and radio stations; if we try to have the nuns removed we'll be the feature story on the six o'clock news. What shall I tell the distributor to do?" He was really stressed.

Ernest removed his rimless glasses, thought for a moment and said quietly, "Call back and ask them what the temperature is and what it's been for the last few days."

All of us were stunned. I figured it had something to do with the freezing point of nuns, but hadn't a clue as to how the information would help solve the problem. Ken left and the shaken agency began their presentation all over again. At about the same point in the presentation as before, Ken reappeared.

"Do you have an answer?" Ernest asked.

"Yes, it's fifteen degrees now and it hasn't been above twenty for a couple of weeks."

Wonderful, I thought, and wrote the lead for the news: "Frozen nuns forcibly removed from Gallo distributor—boycotted trucks roll." A true PR nightmare. I could see Dan Rather taking a live feed from Minneapolis.

"OK," Ernest said, "no problem. I know that distributorship very well. Tell them to get some bolt cutters and cut a big opening in the back fence on the backside of the building. Then quietly take the trucks out one at a time across the open field to the road that runs along the fence. The field should be hard frozen and they can easily drive over it. After they're gone tell the news people we don't want to hurt the nuns so we're canceling deliveries. That shouldn't be much of a story and besides we'll already be making deliveries."

The rest of us sat stunned by the simple brilliance of his plan and the ease with which he came up with it. He then said *sotto voce,* "Why do I have to solve all the problems around here? Now let's get back to the agency presentation."

His hands were where they always were, firmly on the tiller, and he loved it.

Stop the Presses!

My assistant during the Gallo-United Farm Workers confrontation was Dan Solomon, a tall, thin, thirty-five-year-old whose boyish good looks and demeanor disguised a keen command of agriculture public relations and a razor sharp wit. For over two years we battled shoulder to shoulder against the "forces of evil" (the UFW) and the campaign of disinformation they waged relentlessly against us.

We had a saying that was more truth than fiction: "The support the UFW received increased proportionately to its distance from Modesto." In other words, the UFW's "leading phalanx of the legions" was heavily populated by eastern liberals who wouldn't know a grape vine from a rose bush (see Ted Kennedy).

Further, we found that not only geography but also religious persuasion and ethnic background played a huge part in UFW support. Setting aside the Hispanic community's idolization of Cesar Chavez, the next most supportive groups were the liberal Jewish and Catholic factions.

Taking the above into account, my ever-flexible and adroit assistant was usually able get an appointment with his chameleon-like demeanor. As in:

"Hello, Father Flaherty, this is Danny Sullivan and I'd like to talk to you about the United Farm Workers." Note there was no mention of Gallo.

Or,

"Hello, Rabbi Ginsberg, this is Daniel Solomon and I'd like to talk to you about the United Farm Workers."

He almost always got us an appointment.

The biggest problem we faced was an age old one. An attack usually is given page one prominence while the response is buried between the used car ads and the obituaries. The broadcast media were even worse. While almost any claim, however outrageous, could always make the six o'clock news," any response on our part was usually greeted by waves of apathy.

All of the above was, of course, compounded by the fact that most of the working press had liberal leanings in the first place and were prepared to think the worst of us.

With increasing frustration, Dan and I traveled to various "hot spots" and attempted to explain the facts as we knew them and to defuse the emotions churned up by the UFW propaganda machine. As they say, "We couldn't get arrested." No one wanted to talk to us and if they did our material rarely appeared in print or on the air. We were in a desperate situation. We knew that if we were allowed to honestly discuss the accusations leveled against Gallo we could usually win people over, but no one in the media wanted to listen.

One day, Dan stopped by my office with a mischievous smile on his face. "Boss, I think I really earned my pay today," he said. "I just figured out how to get us in print and on TV every time we visit a local market."

"Well, if it involves me going in drag or flashing the reporters, forget it," I replied, figuring he was pulling my chain.

"No, no, it's nothing like that. Like all great solutions it is the essence of simplicity," he said smiling. "The problem is that when we come into town no one will come out to the airport to interview us or attend our press conferences when we invite them, right?"

"Right, except the *4H Journal*, *The Inland Waterways Guide*, the public access TV stations, and a few college papers," I replied with disdain.

"Why?"

"'Cause they don't consider what we have to say newsworthy and they don't want to hear it in the first place," I said.

"Right," he said with a sly smile. "So what we have to do is present our story in an atmosphere so newsworthy they can't avoid covering us."

"Oh, is that all. Gee, I wish I'd thought of that," I said with a hint of irritation.

"Hear me out," he said. "What we do is this. The next time we go to a market, like day after tomorrow in St. Louis (a heavily Catholic city) I'll have my secretary call the Modesto UFW office and tell them that while she works for Gallo, she is secretly a UFW sympathizer.

"She'll tell them that she has access to our travel schedule and thought they'd want to know that you and I are arriving at the airport at such and such time on such and such a flight. Then I'll call the local media and tell them that we have heard that there may be trouble at the airport because the UFW is planning on protesting our arrival.

Finally, I'll book a room at the airport or a nearby motel where we can have a press conference to reply to the demonstration.

"The whole thing will be orchestrated so that we arrive around three in the afternoon. We'll finish our conference by five so the TV people can make the six o'clock news and the press guys can easily make their morning edition deadlines. *And,* and this is the beauty part, by the time we finish our press conference and the "one on ones" it will be too late to get any reply from the UFW. Is that brilliant or what?" he finished smiling.

I was blown away. Dan was a genius. It couldn't miss and it didn't.

For the best part of a year we employed what we called "the tactic" and it never failed. Dan's secretary called the UFW; Dan called the media; we showed up and the UFW was always at the airport with huge signs and banners. The press shot pictures and video of the protest.

I would feign shock and anger and say something like, "I am disappointed that the UFW chose to disrupt our peaceful visit to (fill in the city's name). Obviously, they don't want me to talk to the press, but after their shocking behavior, I feel compelled to reply…" On to the press conference.

The funny thing is that the UFW never caught on. They considered Dan's secretary one of their most important information sources and frequently thanked her profusely for her "loyalty."

And we got miles of press coverage!

During the recent presidential campaign I often wondered if both parties had not adopted the "tactic."

The Ethnic Market

One of the less noble aspects of the E&J Gallo Winery in the 1960's and 1970's was the reliance it put on sales of what were euphemistically known as "ethnic products." Such products included Thunderbird, Night Train (see New York Store Check), Ripple (see Redd Foxx), and White Port; all were targeted at the black community. We also sold a strange but highly profitable peppermint flavored brand called Twister that was sold exclusively on Indian reservations in Arizona.

All of these products were so-called "fortified" wines. This meant that the basic wine product had been fortified by additional alcohol, raising its proof to thirty-eight percent. On the surface, this may not sound like much but if one were to chug-a-lug a couple fifths of any of these beverages it produced serious intoxication. The Gallo products, as well as those of our competitors, all sold for around a dollar and a quarter a fifth; they were therefore the drink of choice on every skid row in America.

As one can imagine, these products were enormously profitable to the wineries, the distributors, and the retailers and hence competition was fierce. Gallo's number one competitor was MD 20/20, a product of the Mogen David winery, and Red Dog, a brand from Manechevitz. Ironically, two Jewish companies and one Italian one fought fiercely for the few pennies indigent blacks could scrape together to get a load on.

From a marketing standpoint, the "ethnic" brands presented a serious problem. Our target audience clearly wasn't susceptible to normal media. TV was out of the question as was magazine and even outdoor. TV ownership and literacy were not high among our core consumers. Further, the BATF regulations were extremely stringent in terms of what could and couldn't be done at the point of sale. And yet the battle went on.

One of the problems we faced was estimating our share of market. The retailers were usually too busy or too remote (they generally operated out of "bullet proof" stores) so we were left to our own devices. In Chicago, the biggest Thunderbird market, our distributor, Buddy Romano, had an infallible method of developing relative market share. After we visited a key store he would walk around back in the alley (all Chicago stores on the South Side had alleys) and look at the broken glass. All Gallo products were sold in our patented "favor-guard" green bottles while the competition's were sold in clear bottles. Buddy was an expert at calculating our "share of broken glass" and extrapolating to case movement. He was never wrong!

Thunderbird like its competitors came in many sizes all the way down to twentieths. We even had fortieths that were similar to the little bottles sold and given away on airlines. In the stores they sold for as little as twenty-five cents each.

I remember being in one store when a poor old black man sidled up to the counter with some change clutched in his hand and said, "How much for one of those Little Birds."

The clerk looked him squarely in the eye and said, "How much you got?"

The customer opened his hand to display a bunch of pennies and nickels. About twenty cents.

"That's enough," the clerk said and handed over a T-bird sampler.

Sampler was, of course, a misnomer as the BATF specifically prohibited broadscale sampling. Nonetheless, one of the enterprising salesmen at Romano Brothers solved the problem in a most ingenious way.

First he would load up the trunk of his car with the little fortieth bottles of Thunderbird (96 to a case). Then he would pull up in front of one of the super high volume ethnic stores, walk inside, and announce to the store manager in a loud voice, "God damn it! I've got the trunk full of "Little Birds" and the friggin' latch is broken. Anybody could just go in there and take the damn things while I'm in here talking to you and I'd be screwed."

Surprise, surprise—when the brilliant marketing salesman came out of the store twenty minutes later all of his "Little Birds" had flown the coop. Another victory for the Gallo sales force and Yankee ingenuity!

On one foray into the ethnic market of Chicago I decided to take our research director, Mike Boyd, on his first Night Train store check. We rented our car at O'Hare and proceeded down the freeway to the South Side. It was an area I was very familiar with. I had lived at 51st and Hyde Park during the war and my father had been raised on Stony Island Avenue. Both areas had now fallen on hard times and while not exactly ghettos were far from what Mike had expected. I chose a big store on Cottage Grove Avenue as our first stop.

This particular store was somewhat unusual in that it had both an "off-sale" license (the normal liquor store license) as well as an "on-sale" license (meaning it could sell drinks on the premises like a bar). It wasn't the Polo Lounge. The drinks it sold on premise were ten-cent shots of T-bird and MD 20/20 in a paper cup like you get at the dentist's.

When we entered the store we had to step over a man who was sleeping in the doorway. It didn't particularly impress me but Mike was affected.

While I was talking to the store manager about the Night Train movement, Mike became more and more distressed and obviously wanted to say something. Finally I completed my interview and said, "What is it, Mike? Did you want to ask a question?"

"No" he said. "I just wanted to tell this gentleman that there is a guy passed out across the threshold of the front door."

"Oh, no problem," the store manager said. "That's Charlie, he lives there."

Not the finest moment for the wine industry.

PART V: THE PLAYTEX YEARS

In the fall of 1978, my wife and I went back east for a Harvard-Yale game in Cambridge. After the game we drove south to Westport and visited with our friends the Smilows. Joel was an old friend from P&G and NCK days and was President and Chairman of International Playtex. In the course of our visit he explained that he wanted to vacate the job of president and thought I would make a wonderful replacement. I was stunned but intrigued.

It was clear that as long as my name ended in a consonant instead of a vowel I couldn't rise further at Gallo. The idea of running Playtex and moving back to Westport was enticing. Also, Joel was moving the company to Stamford, Connecticut, which was a short drive from Westport.

After much soul searching and lengthy conversations with Ernest and Joel, I resigned from Gallo and joined IPI (International Playtex Inc.) in March of 1979, where I remained until February 1985.

During my years at Playtex, in addition to the "Bra/Girdle Division" (renamed "Intimate Apparel"), our "Family Products Division" sold Playtex Tampons (a billion a year), Playtex Baby Nursers, and Playtex Gloves. We acquired Round-the-Clock Hosiery, Danskin, Almay Cosmetics, Jhirmack Shampoos and Conditioners, and were assigned Halston Perfumes and Couturier Clothing and Max Factor Cosmetics when our parent company, Esmark, acquired Norton Simon Inc. To one degree or another all of our products were sold both domestically and internationally

In total our worldwide sales exceeded three billion dollars and we employed over 40,000 people.

Sales Training at Bullock's

In the U.S. Marine Corps everyone is first and foremost a rifleman. At Playtex everyone was first and foremost a salesman. Regardless of where any new employee ultimately worked in the company, it was required that they first take sales training and work in the field for at least a month.

When I was recruited out of Gallo to become president of Playtex, it was made clear to me by the man I was succeeding, Joel Smilow, that my first official duties were to take sales training and sell in the field. He did not even want me to come into the company headquarters until after I had my sales training, correctly believing that once I got into my office I would never get out.

And so it happened that I went to Denver for two weeks to work with a trainer on the intricacies of Playtex selling. There was no question but that the strength of Playtex was in its sales force and the selling techniques they employed. Time and space does not permit a full discussion of their selling program; suffice it to say that the Playtex salesman was trained to produce an order for the buyer and not to leave the store till the sale was made.

The main device used by Playtex was for the sales person to "count the stock on hand," subtract that amount from the previous month's opening inventory and then fill back to plan. As a way of staying ahead of demand the salesperson doubled each item sold until he or she found the section overstocked at which point they would go back to a one-for-one replacement. In a very real sense a good Playtex salesperson had absolute control of the section.

Reading the above makes it all sound rather easy but in actual fact it was far from that. The problem was that an average Playtex section could have approximately 300 SKU's (stock keeping units). If you had four or five bra lines, three girdles, and two or three panties, you had a ton of product that had to be counted and kept segregated. Remember, each bra came in at least four cup sizes and five or six back sizes. Adding to the confusion, were the three standard colors of white, beige, and black. One single brand of bra such as 18-Hour could therefore have close to 75 different SKUs.

The salesman was charged with counting each and every one of the different items using what we in the field called the bed sheet (it was a huge piece of paper on which was printed every single Playtex SKU). He would mark down via a stroke count how many of each item was present in the Playtex section. It was a tedious, time-consuming, and extremely boring exercise that had to be done accurately or the whole system collapsed.

In addition to the above, the salesman also had to count the "back stock" (the product that was kept in the store's storeroom) and add that to his inventory. He would then exchange soiled or torn packages and generally straighten up the display. At the end, he would go to the store employees' cafeteria were he would work out the order to be presented to the buyer.

After I had "graduated" from sales training, I was assigned to the Southern California region and specifically the Los Angeles district.

One of the best Playtex accounts in the area was the famous Bullock's Wilshire. Because of its location and history, it had a very large middle-aged to elderly population and one that was fiercely loyal to Playtex and the bra department's fitters and buyers.

I entered the store with the district manager, who proceeded to introduce me to the buyer simply as, "This is Wally Bregman, one of our new salesmen. He'll be working your section this morning."

The buyer was a lovely matronly woman about sixty years old wearing a dark dress and sensible shoes. She was everyone's idea of what a foundation garment buyer would look like. She told me to get on with my work and that if I had any questions I should just ask her or one of her assistants.

I walked over to the display and almost fainted. I had never seen such a large Playtex display in my life; it had to have close to 1,000 SKUs in it. I told the district manager that I'd need most of the morning and probably part of the afternoon. He agreed to come back around three o'clock.

I pulled out my "bed sheet" and went to work. It was an unbelievable challenge and one that I was not entirely up to. Try as I might, I kept getting confused and having to go back and recount.

Finally I finished but I was sure that I had made quite a few mistakes and that my proposed order would at best be an approximation of what a truly qualified salesman would have produced.

I took it to the buyer and, in a most motherly fashion, she signed off without question. At about this time the district manager showed up. The buyer asked to talk to him privately.

After a while, he came out and appeared about to strangle with laughter. I asked him what it was all about and he choked out, "She said you were the worst counter she had ever seen and never wants you back in her section again. She also said we'd be doing you a favor if we told you that you had absolutely no future at Playtex."

After my return to headquarters, this story became standard fare whenever I was introduced at an intimate apparel division sales meeting.

She sure was right about my counting.

Nancy the Model

One of my duties as President of International Playtex was to spend one day a month at our research and development facility in Paramus, New Jersey. Normally, I would arrive in the morning and sit through six or seven hours of intensive product viewing.

During the course of an average day it was not unusual to inspect a dozen bras, girdles, and other intimate apparel items. Naturally, most of these garments were viewed and discussed *in vivo* (on a live model) rather than loose and unworn.

Despite the disbelief of my non-industry friends, the R&D sessions were very serious and businesslike. Somehow my buddies in banking and real estate always thought they were somewhere between a stag party and Carnaval in Rio.

The models we used were actually Paramus housewives who augmented their family income by modeling our garments. They provided us with "normal" figures on which to view our products.

One day after an intensive morning of product review (I believe it was the 18-Hour bra collection), I went downstairs to the company cafeteria for a bite to eat. As was my custom, I avoided having lunch with the brand people from Stamford (our headquarters) but rather selected my lunch and joined a table of R&D employees I didn't know.

As I sat down, I introduced myself to the other people already at the table. "Hi, my name is Wally Bregman, I am the president of Playtex. I thought it would be nice to get to know some of you."

Two of the three people at the table proceeded to introduce themselves to me but the third, a rather attractive young, brunette, looked at me in astonishment and said, "Mr. Bregman, don't you recognize me, I'm Nancy, the model you've been looking at all morning."

In total embarrassment I've blurted out, "I'm sorry Nancy, I've just never seen you with your clothes on before."

Believe it or not!

The Missing Tux Pants

One of my closest friends, Bob Schechinger, was the marketing director of the DuPont Fiber Division, headquartered in the Empire State Building.

One night in February during "Market Week," he was scheduled to make a major speech to all of the retail industry's luminaries in the Waldorf Hotel ballroom. The speech was to be proceeded by a black tie dinner to which wives and guests were invited.

As Bob had to take the train into New York early in the morning, he asked his wife, Dotty, to bring his tuxedo in with her on the train from Westport. Around six, after Dotty had checked in and before Bob arrived, she decided to hang out the tux to eliminate any wrinkles developed on the trip into New York.

When she opened the cleaner's wrapper she was horrified to find that there were no pants with the jacket. Apparently, because of the satin stripe on the seam, the pants had slipped off the hanger in the closet at home.

Bob had worn a brown suit to the office!

The dinner and speech were in less than an hour and all the stores were closed. In a panic she ran out in the hall and found a waiter. She asked him if there was anywhere she could get a pair of tuxedo pants at this hour. He replied in the negative.

Then she had a brainstorm.

"What time do you get off work?" she asked

"In a half an hour," he replied

"How'd you like to rent your pants for fifty dollars?" she shot back.

And the rest is history. Up until now, no one but the Schechingers and the waiter were any the wiser.

The Corporate Plane

At Playtex, one of the advantages of being a part of Don Kelley's conglomerate, the Esmark Corporation, was the opportunity to occasionally utilize the corporate "air force" and fly in a company plane from one location to another.

On one occasion, we had a Playtex Board Meeting in Stamford, and some of our Esmark board members had flown out on a "baby Lear" to Westchester. As Kelley and his entourage were remaining on the East Coast to meet with some Wall Street types, and I had a meeting with Sears Roebuck the next day, the plane was available to fly me back to Chicago.

I was driven out to the Westchester Airport and entered the private lounge at Butler Aviation. The Esmark captain and co-pilot greeted me effusively and took my small overnight bag. As I was the only passenger, I ensconced myself in the huge, soft leather seat and proceeded to enjoy all the comforts of the executive aircraft. I poured myself a drink and had a few snacks. In short, I took full advantage of the sybaritic comforts of executive travel.

The flight was perfect. We landed on time and the Esmark limousine pulled up to the air-stair door. I told them to wait a second as I had a phone call to make. I went into the FBO (the fixed-base operation where corporate jets land), made my call, and then got into the waiting car. The limousine whisked me to the Whitehall Hotel whereupon the driver handed me my attaché case and said, "Will that be all, Mr. Bregman?"

I said, "Well, where is my suitcase?"

"What suitcase?" he asked.

Apparently at Westchester, the pilot thought that the co-pilot had loaded my bag and vice versa. As a result, it was sitting in Butler Aviation when the pilot called back. Fortunately, he was able to have it loaded on the next corporate jet flying to Chicago (*Reader's Digest*). It was retrieved at Midway and was at my hotel in four hours.

This was one for the *Guinness Book of Records*—I must be the only person ever to have flown as the only passenger on a corporate jet and lost his luggage.

The Big Glove Sale

I was always a "hands-on" manager, so it was only natural that after I joined Playtex I would want to attend various trade association meetings along with our sales people. By so doing, I not only got a chance to meet our customers but also to see our sales management people in action.

One such meeting was conducted in San Diego at the Town and Country Convention Center. It was a meeting of the Mass Merchandise Retailer's Association, and its location also afforded me an opportunity to visit the Price Club (a new concept of membership mass merchandising, now merged with Cosco).

The MMRA show was importantly a "booth" show meaning that not only were lectures and seminars available but also every "vendor" had a booth which customers would visit to discuss new products, promotions, problems, opportunities, or just to stay in contact with the company.

The Playtex booth was dedicated to and manned by the Family Products Division. In the early eighties, we had not yet developed any substantial business for our intimate apparel products in mass merchandisers. Hence, our displays and merchandising were devoted to tampons (our biggest product), baby nursers, and gloves. We had four people at the show: the sales VP, the West Coast regional manager, the San Diego district manager, and me. The plan was that someone had to be at the booth at all times while the others kept appointments with customers in our suite at the hotel.

On the afternoon of the last day of the convention, things were very slow at the booth so I told the others to go out and check some stores and grab a bite of lunch. I would man the booth alone. I felt pretty confident in my ability to handle things as I knew the product line and I had a complete set of "show special" price lists.

After about a half hour of total inaction, I was about to close up shop when a rather elderly gentleman walked up and said, "You with Playtex?"

"I thought this a rather dumb question but answered politely,"Yes sir, I am; as a matter of fact I am the president of Playtex." In retrospect, sort of a self-important answer.

"Good," he said, "then you should be able to give me a couple prices."

"I'm sure I can. What are you interested in?"

"Well, I'm thinking of buying some gloves."

"Wonderful. We have a terrific show special on Playtex Living Gloves by the gross either mixed colors or any specific color." Then I thought I'd push him a little. "And there is an additional discount for five and ten gross." This guy'll be lucky to pony up for a mixed dozen, I thought.

"That's not exactly what I had in mind, young fellow. How about giving me your best price on a carload?"

I was sure I misunderstood him, "You mean a truckload?" This still would have been a huge order.

"No, you heard me right. I want a price on a railcar of Living Gloves," he said.

To humor him, I frantically searched our price lists, but I knew in advance that there was no way we had a price for his order. We'd never, ever sold this many gloves. You have to understand that a box of Living Gloves measured about ten inches long, five inches wide and an inch and a half thick. Imagine how many of these little beauties could fit in a rail car!

He knew what was coming. "I'll have to get back to you on this one," I said. "Can you come back in about an hour and a half and I'll have a price for you?"

"Fine," he said. "I'll be back at two o'clock and it better be a great price. Forget those discounts you have for small orders." And he departed for someone else's booth and I figured that was the last I'd ever see of him.

When the sales VP came back he was as confused as I was as to how to figure a price so we called our manufacturing headquarters in Dover, Delaware. Someone in the traffic department was able to figure the cube of the railcar and thus come up with the quantity of gloves that would fit in one, after allowing for headroom and other arcane elements of packing and shipping. With this information plus our known product costs it was not much of a problem to develop the first ever "carload" price. I was convinced it was a fool's errand and we'd never see the nut again, but sure enough he showed up as advertised.

Thence followed the most intense bargaining session in which I'd ever participated. In the middle of my discussions, the sales VP returned to the booth and frantically signaled me. "Do you know whom you're bargaining with?" he asked in awe.

"No, I told you, some nut who's pulling my chain."

"I don't think so," he said. "That's Sam Walton."

WHAM!

I had heard he loved to go around and "hondel" with vendors but I had never seen him before. This deal was for real.

In the end we concluded our negotiations and it was all I could do to keep from selling the gloves to him at cost. I got the order signed and later framed. It probably still resides somewhere in the sales department of Playtex as not only the first carload order for Living Gloves but also an order signed by the retailing legend himself.

Later in the day I was visiting other booths when I saw an ex-Playtex guy I knew working the GE booth. I started to tell him my story when he interrupted me.

"Don't tell me about him, I just sold him a railcar of 75-watt bulbs."

Sometimes salesmen have all the fun.

Halston and Max Factor

In 1984, Don Kelley, CEO of Esmark (Playtex's parent company), bought the Norton Simon Companies. The group included Samsonite, Avis, Wesson Foods, Halston Fashions, and Max Factor.

For my sins, I was given responsibility for both Halston and Max Factor. Two companies with operating philosophies more different from Playtex probably didn't exist on the planet. Both were in the "fashion" business while the motto of Playtex was "function not fashion." Further, the operating heads of the two acquired companies had huge egos and expense accounts to match—both of which it was my job to rein in. At Halston, the founder Halston (aka Roy Frowich) had a monthly bill for orchids well into five figures while across the continent at Max Factor, Linda Wachner's expense account for limos and entertainment looked like the national debt of Sri Lanka.

My dealings with Halston were surreal. He was tanned, elegant, rakishly thin, wore his hair combed straight back, and was always attired entirely in black. He would receive me in his huge office/showroom in the W.R. Grace building with its two-story high-mirrored doors and ever-present orchids. From behind his enormous desk he would peer at me in mock surprise and condescension and say, "Hello, Bregman, what is your problem this time?" I guess he figured if I called him Halston, he could call me Bregman.

What always followed was a series of arguments about expenses, lack of proper controls, a failing business plan, and, most often, his lack of interest in the J.C. Penney "Halston Collection" which the previous CEO of Norton Simon (David J. Mahoney) had negotiated. Frequently, we would seem to be getting around to some resolution when he would excuse himself, return five minutes later, and be completely impossible. To my mind he had undergone a complete personality reversal. There were also traces of white down the front of his black cashmere turtleneck.

In my straitlaced, naïve world, I had no hint that he was sniffing a controlled substance during his "time outs" and that it was the cause of his mood swings.

Over time his habit became worse, he lost all interest in the company, his designs were considered "out," and we struggled on without him. As he had sold the rights to his name, I took pleasure in the thought that his next company, if any, would have to be called "Fashions by Frowich."

Meanwhile, on the West Coast another fire was merrily burning out of control. Max Factor was hemorrhaging money and the president, Linda Wachner, was continuing on in her profligate ways. Today the world has read a great deal about her management style, which can best be described as unusual. In my own meetings with her, her language would make a longshoreman blush, and the way she treated subordinates would never win any prizes at the Harvard Business School.

One incident probably best encapsulates the lady's *modus operandi*. After we obtained Max Factor we found that the previous management had contracted to build a huge manufacturing facility in North Carolina, one that far exceeded the company's needs. To solve this problem I decided to combine production of Max Factor with two other of our companies, Almay (hypoallergenic cosmetics), and Jhirmack (hair care products).

To facilitate a smooth transition and set up a reasonable timetable, I asked our VP of toiletries manufacturing, Walt Laidlow, to fly out to Hollywood and meet with Linda. As is the case with most of the best production guys, this fellow was a true "good old boy," a tried and true son of the Deep South; slow moving, soft talking, gentlemanly to fault, and relatively unsophisticated. I am sure he had never been to the "Coast" and certainly never encountered anyone like our Linda.

The result was a disaster. I got the details in his phone call from LAX.

"Wally," he said in great excitement, "I just had the Goddamnest experience of my life."

"What happened?" I asked, fully prepared for the worst.

"Well, I got to the Max Factor office for my appointment at nine o'clock, a little early so I wouldn't be late. I ended up cooling my heels for two hours in the damn reception room. Then I finally get ushered in to see the great lady and guess what?"

I didn't answer the rhetorical question because I had a general idea of what was coming next.

"There she is lying back in her chair with her bare feet up on the desk. She's got cotton between her toes and some fag is painting her nails. Her face is covered with some gook and she's got fucking

315

cucumbers on her eyes. And she greets me with, 'What the hell do you want?'

"I explained about the production transition schedule and damned if we didn't have the whole meeting with her having her feet diddled with and me trying to show her the pert charts through the Goddamn cucumbers. And her using language I never ever heard from a woman before. Man, I never want to see her again."

And he never did see her again. Within three weeks it became clear that her style was a total mismatch with Playtex and I had the not unpleasant duty of telling her that her services were no longer required.

She has gone on to become both rich and (in)famous, listed as one of the highest paid women in business.

I wonder if she still wears cucumbers to business meetings.

Harry Walker

When I joined Playtex, I found a very successful company with excellent sales and profit numbers. However, as I learned on sales training (see Bullock's) the company was not well-liked by it own customers. The fact was we weren't just disliked we were despised.

The reason was simple. While we didn't provide the trade with the margin they got from our competitors they had to stock us anyway. They had to stock us because unlike all other foundation garment companies, Playtex didn't rely on trade incentives and store display to move goods ("push") but rather spent heavily on national television advertising for sales ("pull").

With a "pull" brand the trade really had no choice but to stock us. Customers actually would come into a store looking for one of our products and walk out if they couldn't get it. Obviously, this loss of control infuriated the trade and created an overly aggressive, arrogant sales force.

Compounding my problem was the fact that Playtex future growth had to come from more fashion oriented products that would inevitably be more in the "push" area than the "pull."

What to do? I reasoned that the first thing we should do was to get to know our customers from the top down. Heretofore, there had been little contact at the presidential level and I feared we were suffering because of it. I decided that the best way to jump-start our campaign would be to have a major dinner during "Market Week" when all the CEO's of all retail chains were in New York for their own trade meetings. I also decided that considering the way they felt about us, the only way we would ever get these top executives to a Playtex dinner was to offer them something of enormous value.

It had to be a top speaker. I was stumped. I didn't have the foggiest idea of how to line up a headliner. I called my ad agencies but they didn't know either. It happened, however, that the next day I was reading *Fortune Magazine* and they had a small article about the unknown super agent to political stars. His name was Harry Walker. It also mentioned that President Gerald Ford was going to be represented by him.

Bingo!

I buzzed my secretary and told her to look up the Walker Agency and get Mr. Harry Walker on the line. Two minutes later she buzzed back, "Mr. Walker is on the line."

"Mr. Walker, my name is Walter Bregman and I am president of International Playtex. I understand you represent President Ford."

"Yes, I do, when do you want him?" the voice at the other end said. I was stunned. Ford was to leave office on January 20 and I could book his first speech as a private citizen.

"The second week in February would be perfect," I managed to say.

"Just a minute." I could hear him rustling through the pages of a book. "How about Tuesday night?' he asked.

This couldn't be happening, but it was. "That would be fine with us," I said.

"OK then," he said. "It'll cost you $20,000 plus transportation from Palm Springs for him. The Secret Service pays their own way and, in this case, you'll get a good deal because he has to be in Ft. Lauderdale the next day so you get him to New York and I'll have the Florida guys pay for the travel from New York to their affair."

I was taking notes and trying to keep up with his rapid-fire delivery. "Oh, and a couple of other things. No receiving lines. He likes to circulate buts hates formal lines and you'll have to book the Presidential Suite at the Waldorf Towers for him to change in. It's the only place the Secret Service will approve. He won't be staying overnight. He'll fly down to Florida after your event. Give me your address and I'll send you a contract— $5,000 on signing, and $15,000 after the speech," he concluded.

It was that simple. Five minutes ago I had no idea what I was going to do and now I had the former President of the United States speaking at my dinner.

We quickly booked the Tavern on the Green for the event, made up a guest list of the CEO's of all our top customers (the invitation was non-transferable), and sent them out. The response was unbelievable. Hardly anyone turned us down. We had the presidents of Wal-Mart, J.C. Penney, Sears, Federated Stores, Allied, Marshall Fields, Neiman-Marcus, and many others. You name them, we had them. *Woman's Wear Daily* called our party "the event of market week."

Just before the event, I explained the details to Joel Smilow. He had an idea.

"As long as we're paying for it and Ford isn't using it after the dinner, why don't we stay in the Presidential Suite with our wives?" Why hadn't I thought of that?

The party was a smash. President Ford was wonderful. He posed for pictures with all of our guests. We later sent prints to them in a Tiffany frame. Before his talk we cleared the room of all the press and he was able to speak "off the cuff" and take questions without fear of attribution. He got a standing ovation and Playtex shone in reflected glory.

That night Joan and Joel Smilow and Robbie and Wally Bregman slept in the Presidential Suite at the Waldorf complete with the Presidential seal in the carpet and marvelous antiques (Lincoln's desk, Roosevelt's chairs, etc.). It wasn't the Lincoln bedroom but then again we didn't have to make a major contribution to the party.

For the next four years we continued to give the "Playtex Chief Executives Dinner" although we moved it to the Helmsley Palace. I also continued to deal with Harry Walker, always by phone. I never met him or was in his office. Through him we booked Al Haig, Henry Kissinger, Walter Cronkite, and Howard Baker. And every dinner was a great success.

Press reports indicate that Harry is still going strong and now represents Bill Clinton. It is unconfirmed as to whether he is also representing Monica Lewinsky. But it wouldn't surprise me.

Henry Kissinger

Perhaps our most successful "Playtex CEO Dinner" was the one at which Henry Kissinger spoke. As would be expected, the great man was timely, articulate, funny, and spellbinding. He walked up to the podium without a note and spoke and took questions for an hour. I had the impression that he could have gone on all night and the audience would have loved it.

After this performance, it occurred to me that our European subsidiaries could also profit by "shining in reflected glory." I quickly called Harry Walker and booked Kissinger for dinner speeches in London and Paris. Our English and French country managers were delighted and immediately sent invitations to their most important clients. As revered and respected as Kissinger was in the United States at that time, his fame in Europe was greater by many magnitudes.

All the plans were made and we flew to London for the first dinner to be held in the grand dining room at Claridge's (nothing but the best for International Playtex). I was disappointed that Nancy Kissinger did not make the trip but figured that would give me more time with the great man.

On the night of the event the room at Claridge's was elegantly appointed when our invited guests arrived in evening clothes. After a lengthy cocktail hour the guests and hosts were ushered to their assigned tables. At each place was an autographed copy of Kissinger's latest book, *Years of Upheaval,* a huge volume of at least seven hundred pages.

Following a wonderful dinner and a selection of the finest wines, the cigars and brandy were passed around and I rose to introduce our honored guest.

"My lords, ladies, and gentlemen,"[31] I said, "it is indeed a great pleasure for me and International Playtex to host such a distinguished gathering and to introduce our speaker for the evening. As you may not know, my relationship with Dr. Kissinger goes back almost thirty years to the time when I was an undergraduate at Harvard College and

---

[31] One of our guests was the chairman of Marks & Spenser, who had been awarded an OBE (Order of the British Empire) and was addressed as "Sir."

Dr. Kissinger was a teaching fellow in the government department. As a matter of fact, it was so long ago, it was before he had an accent." This was followed by an uproarious laugh from Kissinger and then titters from the audience. Sometimes American humor escapes the Brits.

Kissinger stood to thunderous applause and began his talk.

"Thank you, Volly. (I won't attempt the rest of the dialect.) It is a great pleasure to talk to the English clients of International Playtex. I hope all of you enjoyed your dinner as much as I did and that you will also enjoy my book, which is a gift to you from International Playtex and me. I sent a copy of this book to my mother and someone asked her if she thought her son was a great writer. She said she didn't know if I was a great writer but she did know that anyone who could read such a huge book had to be a great reader."

He went on for the next hour to charm, entertain, and challenge the audience. It was a smash.

The next day we left for Paris and a repeat performance at the Ritz that evening. It too was an enormous success. That ended our European trip. We were all scheduled to fly back to New York in the morning. Unfortunately, I was awakened early by the concierge, who called to tell me that the French air controllers were on strike (again).

He further said that it was unlikely we could leave in the foreseeable future. I immediately told him to rent a big limousine (la grande voiture) to drive us to Brussels and to book all of us out of there on a Sabina flight. (My years of traveling throughout Europe for NCK made such planning a reflex action.)

Ten minutes later he called back to inform me that all was arranged. The car would depart the hotel at 9:00 A.M. for the three-hour drive to the Brussels airport and we would easily make our two o'clock flight to New York. Perfect.

I was secretly delighted. With all the rushing to London and Paris, I had not had any time alone with Kissinger and was looking forward to three hours together in the back seat of the limo.

My mind was jammed with thought-provoking questions. "Was Nixon really a bad guy or just a victim of bad staff work?" "How did we get into the Vietnam mess?" "How can we win the Cold War?" And so on and so on.

After a quick coffee and croissant we all assembled at the front door where a huge Mercedes 900 awaited. Naturally, I escorted

Kissinger into the back seat and took my place beside him. The others took the facing "jump seats" some distance away.

As we left Paris and proceeded to the superhighway that would take us to Brussels, I turned to Kissinger to begin my private three-hour seminar on American foreign policy in the seventies and eighties. To my horror, my tutor was sound asleep and stayed that way until we pulled into the driveway of the Brussels airport. All I heard from him for three hours was an occasional low guttural snore, naturally in a German accent.

"The best laid schemes o' mice an' men, Gang aft a-gley." – Robert Burns

The Telephone Call

As I have mentioned previously, I learned to always answer my own phone when I was a media research assistant (there was no lower position) at the Leo Burnett Company. For the next thirty-eight years in business I continued with this practice. Leo used to say, "If you can't get rid of someone you don't want to talk to, you probably shouldn't have a phone of your own."

One day the phone rang in my office at Playtex and I answered in my usual fashion, "Walter Bregman."

"Is this the president of Playtex?" said a young, obviously distressed female voice.

"Yes, it is."

"Well, I have a horrible problem and I hope you can help." She sounded close to tears. Wrong. She was in tears.

"What can I do to help?" I said, having no idea where this conversation was leading.

"I'm getting married this Saturday (this was Monday) and I have spent a fortune for my dress and the bridesmaids dresses and now I can't find the Playtex underwire bra I had the dress designed around. I don't know what I am going to do. My wedding is going to be a disaster." It is true that brides-to-be can get a little histrionic.

"Where do you live and what was the style, size, and color of the bra you wanted?" I asked. I also wondered if maybe Leo's idea was really all that great.

She told me she lived somewhere in Alabama and need a style 110, white, underwire, 32B. It is odd how women have no problem telling complete strangers their bra sizes.

I took down her phone number and promised to call her back that day. I next called Don Francisceni,[32] my VP of production and told him my problem. Shortly thereafter, he called back to inform me that we had discontinued that style in the smaller sizes and therefore, the bra wasn't available.

---

[32] Don would go on to become the head of all Hanes brands at Sara Lee, which eventually bought Playtex.

323

"Is there anyplace we might have some?" I asked. "What about among the SLOBS?" SLOBS were a Playtex acronym for "slow moving and obsolete" products.

"Yeah, there could be some there 'cause we just knocked it off a few months ago, but we'd have to have someone go through the warehouse by hand to find them. They're not computerized," he said without enthusiasm.

"Well, call down to Dover (Dover, Delaware, was our manufacturing and distribution headquarters) and get someone on it right away. I need to find some of those bras." I didn't tell him why.

I called the young girl and told her I would do what I could and got her address in case I found the bra.

In about an hour I got a call from Don; they had found a dozen of the bras in some corner of the warehouse. I told him to Fed Ex three of them to the girl in Alabama with a note from me saying: "Have wonderful wedding and a wonderful life."

In a week or so I got a charming letter from her telling me how I had "saved her life" and "that the dress had been a great success."

It's funny, but I have fonder memories of this incident than of the many "big deals" I participated in while at Playtex.

CODICIL

Perhaps the most compelling thing about the years I spent in advertising and marketing was the creativity of the people with whom I worked.

Following is a sample of some of the pithy "one liners" I remember from those days:

- "The thing I like about you Lee is you approach every problem with an open mouth."

  Draper Daniels to Lee Rich

- "Being complimented for coming in second in this new business pitch is like winning a prize for being the world's tallest midget."

  Norman B. Norman, when we didn't get the American Motors account

- "I'm in a terrible hurry, can't you put two men on it?"

  Lee Rich to the barber at the Beverly Hills Hotel when told his haircut would take a half an hour

- "We have quarterly reviews—every hour at a quarter of and a quarter after."

  Albion Fenderson when asked how frequently Ernest Gallo reviewed plans

- "We'll call it 'The Importance of Being Ernest.'"

  Dan Solomon replying as to what the name of the Gallo Winery history would be called

325

- "Well, in that case send up another Bible."

> "Name withheld," when told by a hotel manager that he would have to charge him for a double room if he kept the young lady in his room overnight

- "If this baby goes in they'll have to publish a special issue of *Ad Age*."

> Art Hohmann, boarding a Cincinnati to Chicago flight full of agency personnel

- "That's like treating dandruff on a dog with cancer."

> Bob Hanslip, responding to the suggestion that Salvo Tablet Detergent's problems could be solved by a redesigned package

- "Every time he finds a new orifice into which he can insert his member he gets married."

> Draper Daniels commenting on the fourth marriage of an associate creative director

- "A fact is an opinion held by the client."

> G. Gordon Rothrock, explaining the nuances of account work

- "It's the price tag."

> Arthur Hohmann, in the Polo Lounge when asked what a remarkably pretty young girl on the arm of a much older man had around her ankle

- "They remind me of my grandmother, she was so kind that she always warmed the water before she drowned the kittens."

> Jim Hill, remarking on how the P&G copy section was required to make a positive comment before ripping our proposals apart

- "A cat that sits on a hot stove will never sit on a hot stove again; of course, it will never sit on a cold stove either."

> Jim Hill, explaining the timidity bred by P&G's reliance on empirical evidence

- "I call it the Geppetto syndrome."

> Walter Bregman, explaining the phenomenon that occurs when one visits a foreign subsidiary:
> "Everyone jumps around like mad when you're there but when you leave, the strings go slack."

- "I've fallen on my sword so many times I feel like a Goddamned sieve."

> Marty Snitzer, returning from a confrontational meeting with the Camay brand group

- "It always sounds good if you say it fast enough."

> Walter Bregman, to any subordinate who tries to "slip one by him"

- "The proper management progression in a successful company is: Dreamer (he has the idea), Reamer (he makes it work), and Schemer (he develops the exit strategy)."

> Dr. Mort Feinberg, industrial psychologist and Playtex consultant

- "I've never seen a pro forma that didn't work."

> Don Kelley, Chairman of Esmark, skeptically responding to an acquisition proposal

- "Public relations is like a man in a blue serge suit who pisses in his pants—no one else knows about it but he gets a nice warm feeling."

> Leo Burnett, before his company had a Public Relations Department

- "Every time a hearse goes by it's fifty/fifty odds that we just lost a customer."

> Walter Bregman, describing the problem with Playtex's aging demographics

- "It's a product that little old ladies buy for their mothers at Christmas."

> Norman B. Norman, describing the problem Chanel had with its aging demographics

- "I can get a high Burke score anytime I want. All I have to do is open on a dog walking down the stairs with a sock in his mouth."

> Leo Burnett commenting on how to "beat" the P&G system for evaluating successful TV advertising.

Postscript

In mid-1984, Esmark was sold to Beatrice Foods and everybody's life changed. From Don Kelley's hands off, "just show me the profits" environment we were plunged into Beatrice Chairman Jim Dutt's[33] Byzantine world of court politics and "emperor's clothes."

Joel Smilow resigned in November and on the twenty-eighth of February, as I was about to announce the highest sales and profits in the history of the company, Frank Grezlecki, Smilow's Beatrice-appointed replacement, summoned me out of a staff meeting and fired me.

In July of that year, my wife and I purchased twenty acres of land on St. Croix in the U.S. Virgin Islands and proceeded to renovate a hotel that had been abandoned for ten years.

But that's a story for another book.

Perhaps.

---

[33] After over twenty vice presidents and general managers either quit or were fired, the Beatrice board fired Dutt in September of 1984. Don Kelly bought the company back in a leveraged buy-out and Smilow reacquired Playtex. I was building closets in my resort.

Index

Printed in the United States
724100002B

9 781403 306579